MY BEST MISTAKE

MY
BEST
MISTAKE

Epic Fails and Silver Linings

TERRY O'REILLY

Published by Collins, an imprint of HarperCollins Publishers Ltd

First edition

Ski-Doo is a Trademark of BRP

HarperCollins books may be purchased for educational, business,
or sales promotional use through our Special Markets Department.

HarperCollins Publishers Ltd
Bay Adelaide Centre, East Tower
22 Adelaide Street West, 41st Floor
Toronto, Ontario, Canada
M5H 4E3

www.harpercollins.ca

Library and Archives Canada Cataloguing in Publication

Title: My best mistake : epic fails and silver linings / Terry O'Reilly.
Names: O'Reilly, Terry, 1959- author.
Description: First edition.
Identifiers: Canadiana (print) 20210273151 | Canadiana (ebook) 2021027316X
ISBN 9781443459464 (hardcover) | ISBN 9781443459471 (ebook)
Subjects: LCSH: Success—Anecdotes. | LCSH: Errors—Anecdotes.
LCSH: Life change events—Anecdotes.
Classification: LCC BF637.S8 O73 2021 | DDC 158.1—dc23

Printed and bound in the United States of America
LSC/H 9 8 7 6 5 4 3 2

Dedicated to the worst boss I ever had—
who taught me the best lesson:
how not to do it.

Contents

Introduction | 1

1. *Jaws*: You're Gonna Need a Better Shark | 5
2. Scotty Bowman: The First Cut Is the Deepest | 11
3. Ski-Doo®: How Do You Spell Success? | 22
4. Brian Williams: The Unofficial Spokesperson of the Second Chance Club | 31
5. Billy Joel: They Sit at the Bar and Put Bread in My Jar | 49
6. Steve Madden: The Shoe of Wall Street | 61
7. Swanson's TV Dinners: The Problem with Leftovers | 72
8. Bill Maher: The Problem with Being Politically Incorrect on *Politically Incorrect* | 76
9. The Dixie Chicks: On Getting Dixie-Chicked | 87
10. Seth MacFarlane: The Gate Is Now Closed | 105
11. Steve Jobs: The Second Bite of the Apple | 113
12. Kellogg's Corn Flakes: Supressing Your Desires since 1896 | 143
13. Rob Lowe: Sex, Lies and Videotape | 147
14. The Who: Who Are You? | 162
15. Ellen DeGeneres: When a Door Shuts, a Closet Opens | 171
16. The Incredible Hulk: Fifty Shades of Grey | 186
17. Anthony Carter: Turning Up the Heat in Miami | 192
18. Popsicles: Air Conditioning on a Stick | 197

19. Sam Phillips: Rocket 'n' Roll | 201

20. Kathleen King: Watching the Cookie Crumble | 206

21. Fiberglas Pink: How a Successful Product Dyed | 218

22. Mario Puzo: An Offer Everyone Can Refuse | 224

23. *The Old Farmer's Almanac*: White Day in July | 233

24. Atul Gawande: Planes, Pains and Operating Tables | 237

Afterword: Embrace the Obstacle | 247

Acknowledgements | 251

Sources | 255

MY BEST MISTAKE

Introduction

Back in 2004, I was working with Denny Doherty in a recording studio. He was narrating a 265-episode radio series our company had developed to celebrate the fortieth anniversary of the Beatles landing in North America. As you may know, Denny was one of the founding members of the iconic group the Mamas and the Papas. Born in Halifax, Denny formed his first band at age nineteen, then left Canada in 1964 to seek fame and fortune in the folk scene in New York. As recounted in the Mamas and the Papas' hit song "Creeque Alley," guitarist (and fellow Canuck) Zal Yanovsky and singer Denny would pass the hat after performing numbers in Greenwich Village. Soon, Denny met Cass Elliot, then the two of them joined up with married folk singers Michelle and John Phillips in 1965.

The rest is California dreaming.

Working with Denny was always fun because he had the best stories to tell between takes. He was part of the sixties pop, rock and folk scene and had crossed paths with everyone from Bob Dylan to my cherished Beatles. But I remember one story in particular.

He told me about John finding out he had conducted an affair with Michelle Phillips. To punish Denny before actually confronting him about it, John had him sing a new song titled "I Saw Her Again." The lyrics were about sneaking around to see a woman you shouldn't be seeing. As he made Denny sing it over and over again in the studio, John just glared at Denny through the glass, waiting for him to get the message.

While recording the final vocal, Denny made a mistake. At around the 2:43 mark, he came in at the wrong beat. He sang, "I saw her," then stopped, realized his mistake, waited a second, then continued with the chorus. When he finished the take, he said, "Sorry about that mistake, you can edit it out." But both John and producer Lou Adler said, "No, we won't—we loved it," and kept it in the final mix.

That was interesting to me. It was always my favourite Mamas and Papas song and that little moment from Denny—that tiny mistake—is my favourite moment in the song. I wait for it every time I hear it. When Denny told me that story, we talked about other mistakes in popular songs that turned out to be interesting moments. Like when Sting laughs at the start of "Roxanne" because he tripped on a piano while he made his way to the microphone. Or when Paul McCartney whispers "fucking hell" at the 2:53 mark of "Hey Jude." Or the time Sun Records producer Sam Phillips was recording "Time Has Made a Change" with Jimmy DeBerry when the microphones picked up the shrill sound of a telephone ringing in the outer office—and Phillips left it in the record because the mistake "just felt right."

Sam Phillips chased something he called "perfect imperfection." He felt mistakes in a great thing were infinitely better than perfection in a good thing. Paul Simon once said he was more intrigued by an interesting mistake than a safe move. I'm with

Sam and Simon on that one. Back when I directed commercials, I always chose the take that *felt* best, rarely the perfect one.

The concept of meaningful mistakes that actually made something better was intriguing. My mind raced through all the stories I'd collected over the years, as well as the stories I'd told on my CBC radio show about mistakes that led to multimillion-dollar brands. I was particularly interested in finding two types of stories. First, stories where someone had made a catastrophic decision, only to discover it was the best thing that ever happened to them. Second, stories where people had made a tiny, inadvertent mistake that was just a little left of right but that led to a breakthrough. In the former, the people featured in this book went through an almost violent life change, losing their jobs, their companies and often their credibility—only to discover an even better life on the other shore. In the latter, the people or companies made a mistake that seemed small, almost insignificant—yet it would be the beginning of famous brands or legendary bands or groundbreaking art. In one instance, it saved lives.

Churchill once wrote, "You never can tell whether bad luck may not after all turn out to be good luck . . . when you make some great mistake, it may very easily serve you better than the best-advised decision."

Sir Winston was right.

A raging forest fire often leads to beautiful green growth sprouting up through the ashes.

Jaws

You're Gonna Need a Better Shark

When Steven Spielberg was given the green light to bring Peter Benchley's novel *Jaws* to the big screen, he was just twenty-eight years old. He had made only one movie so far, titled *The Sugarland Express*. Prior to that, he had directed a few television shows like *Night Gallery* and *Columbo* and had done a few made-for-TV movies. One of those TV movies, *Duel*, was the dry run that would eventually land him *Jaws*. It was a story of a man being pursued by a mysterious and menacing eighteen-wheel tanker truck for no apparent reason. When Spielberg put himself up for the directing job for *Jaws*, he told the producers to watch *Duel* because it, too, was a story of someone being hunted by a powerful and mysterious force. *Duel* imparted other lessons to the young director. For instance, it contains a scene where Spielberg is mistakenly reflected in the glass of a phone booth. As he later said in an interview on *Inside the Actors Studio*, when *Duel* was shown in Europe, there were, in fact, eighteen different instances when Spielberg was visible because of the change in aspect ratio for the theatrical release.

5

Live and learn.

When planning *Jaws*, Spielberg rejected the idea of using miniatures and shooting in Hollywood water tanks. With youthful bravado, he insisted on creating a full-scale mechanical shark and shooting in the ocean. He wanted realism. He asked his production designer, Joe Alves, to design a fully operational animatronic shark. He explicitly wanted a full-scale twenty-five-foot beast that could move and swim and attack like a real shark. He wanted the eyes to roll back, the gill slits to breathe and the jaws to work. The request was unprecedented, even by Hollywood standards.

Alves began with sketches of the shark based on Benchley's descriptions in the book. Then he sketched different actions the shark would have to perform in the storyline. Next, Alves drew a schematic cross-section of the shark showing the mechanics and pneumatic hoses required to manipulate the massive creation. When he approached special effects experts with his plan, they all said it couldn't be done. All except for one. His name was Robert Mattey, and he was convinced he could build it. As it turned out, Mattey couldn't build one shark to achieve everything Spielberg wanted, so he had to build three sharks. Each one had a steel skeleton, hydraulics to open and close its mouth and air-powered mechanisms to make the various body parts move. One shark moved left-to-right with its hidden left side exposing the vast array of hoses, wiring and mechanics, one moved right-to-left with an open right side and one fully skinned shark was attached to an adjustable arm on a twelve-ton, sixty-foot-long submersible steel trolley that moved back and forth on rails mounted on the sea floor. To achieve the realistic motion of a shark, the main model would require a barge and fourteen operators to control all the moving parts via a set of three-hundred-foot pneumatic hoses. It also required scuba divers to manipulate the other end of the shark, additional frogmen filming from underwater and a second barge for the camera and crew—all of which floated alongside Quint's hero boat, the *Orca* (named after the only natural enemy of the great white shark). Tests done in a freshwater tank at Universal Studios were tricky but successful. Spielberg was optimistic. He nicknamed the 1.2-ton shark "Bruce," after his lawyer, Bruce Ramer.

But unbeknownst to them all, they had already made a corrosive mistake.

Martha's Vineyard was chosen as the filming location because even twelve miles out to sea, the average depth of the water is only thirty-five feet. When Bruce was first lowered into the ocean off the Vineyard, it sunk straight to the bottom. But that wasn't the biggest issue. Almost immediately, the mechanics inside Bruce started to corrode. Leaks sprang everywhere and soon the pneumatic hoses were compromised. Although an animatronic shark was difficult to work at the best of times, Bruce became increasingly unresponsive. Then the team slowly realized their mistake.

No one had tested Bruce in salt water.

This was an expensive mistake. The three Bruces already had a combined cost close to $250,000, a big bite out of the $3.5 million total production budget. And every day Bruce malfunctioned delayed the shooting schedule and increased overages. As the problems kept mounting, the crew began quietly referring to the film as Flaws. Spielberg was filming a movie about a great white shark that made an appearance on a majority of the script pages. He didn't have years of experience to fall back on, but he knew it would easily take another month to rebuild a saline-proof shark and his budget allowed for only fifty-five principal shooting days.

He had two immediate thoughts: First, he needed a solution and he needed one fast. Second, he feared his career as a filmmaker was over.

But obstacles often generate astonishing waves of creativity. Spielberg, faced with a seemingly insurmountable problem, sat in his hotel room one night and asked himself, How would Hitchcock handle the situation?

Then it came to him: what we can't see is the most frightening thing of all.

So Spielberg began rewriting the script to employ invisible terror. (It's astounding to think that, at this point, Spielberg is on location with no working script and no shark.) He decided to shoot many of the scenes from a shark's-eye view and had his director of photography devise a platform that lowered the camera to water level. Skimming a giant dorsal fin and tail through the water would easily suggest the awe-inspiring length of the shark. And when he added the scene with the yellow barrels, they could imply the speed and power of the terrifying beast.

The pièce de résistance would come in the postproduction stage, compliments of composer John Williams. His simple yet terrifying two-note motif would become the shark: intense in volume and tempo when the shark was approaching, diminishing as the shark swam away. Williams has described it as "grinding away at you, just as a shark would do, instinctual, relentless, unstoppable." It was an astonishing feat of sound and silence, with a heroic French horn countermelody possibly representing the Ahab-like quest of Quint, Hooper and Brody set against the menacing two-note assault (with hints of Stravinsky's *The Rite of Spring* so intricately folded in).

Then—severing stillness.

The only shark in many of the most memorable attack scenes was Williams's two-note masterpiece. Maybe the best example is the opening skinny-dipping scene, when Chrissie is thrashed back and forth in a terrifying attack. The actor wore a harness attached to two different cables run through submerged three-hundred-pound weights. One cable was pulled by eight men on the beach and the other was manned by Spielberg. The very first shark-bite/jerk-down was done by Spielberg and the subsequent sudden moves were the result of back-and-forth pulling from both ends. According to the sound technician on the film, there was a miscalculation when both cables were yanked at the same time. The sudden cross-tension broke some of the actress's ribs. She screamed, and when she did, she went underwater. According to the soundman, she started saying, "Please God. Dear God . . ." The water was rolling in her mouth and the word "God" would come out sporadically. She was in agonizing pain. That moment, that very scream, is the scene that is in the film.

Another toe-curling scene showed two fishermen trying to catch the shark to collect the bounty money, when the dock they are standing on breaks away. Then it slowly turns to surge back toward them as they flail their way to shore. We never see the shark in either scene—no teeth, no fins, no lifeless black eyes—yet the predator is absolutely vivid in our imaginations, all due to Williams's visceral score.

It's hard to believe in hindsight, but the great white shark doesn't make a full appearance in the two-hour film until the one-hour-and-twenty-one-minute mark. And get a load of this: it only had four minutes of actual screen time. Yet moviegoers saw the shark in their minds for two full hours. And probably for quite a few days after they got home. Many of us still see it in our minds forty-six years later whenever we're near the ocean.

Even though it took 159 days to complete filming instead of the original 55 and the budget ballooned 100 percent to $7 million, *Jaws* was the first film in history to break $100 million at the box office. It became the highest-grossing film of all time after just seventy-eight days in theatres. It delivered a domestic gross of $260,798,300 and a worldwide haul of $470,653,000. The movie heralded the arrival of the summer blockbuster. It won three Academy Awards, including one for John Williams's original score. *Jaws* put the young Steven Spielberg on the map. It is on the American Film Institute's list of best films of all time.

And the saltwater mistake is easily forgivable.

Spielberg has said the failure of Bruce the shark contributed at least $175 million to the box office take.

Scotty Bowman

The First Cut Is the Deepest

One night in March 1952, nineteen-year-old Scotty Bowman suffered a fractured skull. It was an injury that would dictate the path of his life. He was playing for the Montreal Canadiens Junior A team in a five-out-of-nine play-off series against the Trois-Rivières Reds at the storied Montreal Forum. Scotty was a smart left-winger who could score goals and that made him a prospect for the Montreal Canadiens. The Junior Canadiens were on their way to trouncing the Reds in the fourth game of the series. With just thirty seconds left in the 5–1 game, Scotty took a pass in a patch of open ice and barrelled toward the Reds' net. Defenceman Jean-Guy Talbot, the Reds' best player, was in hot pursuit. Talbot had already taken four penalties in the game and the lopsided score had made him chippy all night. Just as Scotty got near the net, Talbot brought him down from behind, forcing Scotty to slide feet first into the Reds goaltender. With Scotty pinned underneath the goalie, Talbot raised his stick in frustration and struck Scotty twice in the head, breaking his stick on the second impact.

Scotty was rushed to hospital, where they discovered his skull was fractured. A five-inch gash was closed with fourteen stitches. For the next few months and into the summer, Scotty suffered headaches and blurred vision. When training camp rolled around in the fall, he was feeling better and ready to play again. But the Canadiens organization didn't want him because they felt the risk of further injury was too great. He was shifted to the Montreal Junior Royals, but he wasn't the same player he once was. His confidence was gone and he no longer took chances. Scotty knew what it all meant: He wasn't an NHL hopeful anymore. His playing days were over. Talbot was given a one-year suspension and later wrote Scotty a genuine letter of apology. But unlike Scotty, he remained a hot prospect.

William Scott Bowman was born in 1933 in the working-class neighbourhood of Verdun, located on the southwestern part of the island of Montreal. His father, Jack, a blacksmith, met his mother, Jean, in their homeland of Scotland. When the Canadian National Railway offered free ship passage to Canada for any young men willing to work in the CNR's Canadian railyards, Jack took the offer. Arriving in Montreal in 1929, he started work and, once established, sent for Jean. The two were married two months later. The hardworking couple would eventually have four children: Freda, Scotty, Jack Jr. and, ten years later, Martin. Jack Sr. found an 850-square-foot flat for the family of six to live in. Then his sister Minnie came over from Scotland to live with them. Make that seven.

Most of the flats in the neighbourhood were the same size and layout and the suffocating 850 square feet eventually squeezed everybody outside. Scotty was definitely an outdoors kid. He also did well at school, had a paper route and played sports like basketball and floor hockey. He grew up in the Depression years and his father was one of the lucky ones who managed to hold on to his job. Almost every family found a way to afford a radio and it was on those magical airwaves that Scotty first heard a National Hockey League game, broadcast out of Boston during the 1939–40 season. The Bruins had won the Stanley Cup the year before and were atop the standings that year. Scotty worshipped the team, and his mother bought him a Bruins sweater that he wore with pride in the land of the Habs. Hockey seeped into Scotty's blood and he played pickup hockey anywhere he could find a game. Eventually, he earned positions on organized bantam and midget teams.

Meanwhile, the legendary Sam Pollock, who would later be the general manager of nine Stanley Cup–winning Montreal Canadiens teams, was tasked with running the farm system for the Habs. Long before the NHL had a draft system, the original six clubs had multiple farm teams that would groom a crop of players for the jump up to the pros. Frank Selke Sr. had set up a very fruitful junior farm system for the Canadiens and Pollock and his scouts would hit the road to spot up-and-coming players. One of those scouts spotted Scotty, offering him a position on the newly formed Verdun Canadiens. To entice him to sign, the scout offered Scotty new gloves and pants as well as a precious Forum standing-room pass to watch the Canadiens any time he wished. Scotty was in seventh heaven. He was now the property of the fabled Montreal Canadiens of the National Hockey League. He now had a shot at making the pros. He could now waltz into the Forum to watch any Habs game he wanted, any time. All love of the Bruins drained from his heart.

Then all his dreams came crashing down that night when he caught the pass in the open ice and Jean-Guy Talbot's anger got the better of him. Most NHL teams would offer to help players whose careers were ended due to serious injury and the Canadiens offered to help Scotty with university tuition. With his future now uncertain, Scotty opted to take a college business course while moving behind the bench nights and weekends to coach some bantam and juvenile teams sponsored by the Canadiens' farm system. All the games were outdoors and the season was less than a dozen games, but Scotty was slowly learning to become a game coach.

Meanwhile, Scotty landed a job at the Sherwin-Williams paint company, where he began a two-year training program to become a salesperson. Part of his responsibility was to cross town every day by bus to pick up order sheets at one of the company's warehouses. Scotty knew the Canadiens practised at the Forum most Wednesday and Thursday mornings between ten and eleven thirty, depending on their road schedule, and they were always home to practise on Fridays. So he would eat his lunch on the bus and spend his lunch hour watching the Habs, courtesy of his all-access Forum pass. Scotty would be the only fan in the thirteen thousand seats on those mornings. He would watch all the fabled Canadiens players, like Rocket Richard and Boom Boom Geoffrion, and carefully observe how coach Dick Irvin ran the practices. Scotty had an eye for the details and he would try and bring those insights back to his team. Occasionally, Irvin or one of the players would nod in his direction or say a few words.

When Scotty was asked to coach a Junior B squad that wasn't sponsored by the Canadiens, it was a step up. He took that team to the finals, where they gave a Habs-sponsored team a lot of trouble. Sam Pollock, who was aware of Scotty from his Junior Canadiens playing days, noticed his coaching potential and offered him a job in 1956 as assistant coach and manager of the Junior A Ottawa-Hull Canadiens. Up until that moment, Scotty had never thought he would have a full-time job in hockey. But the twenty-two-year-old jumped at the opportunity to learn under Pollock, who would become his mentor. Scotty left the world of oil and latex behind to begin his full-time hockey career for the princely sum of $4,200 a year.

While Pollock was running the Ottawa-Hull Canadiens, he was also busy scouting players throughout his farm system. That meant he was on the road a lot, leaving Scotty to coach the majority of the games and run the practices. In his first year, the team lost in the finals. In his second year, they won the Memorial Cup. When a head coaching job opened up with the Peterborough Petes, Pollock offered the position to Scotty. He was only twenty-five. The Petes had finished fifth out of seven teams the year before, but under Scotty's watch, they made it to the Memorial Cup finals, losing to the Winnipeg Braves. He would coach in Peterborough for two years before Pollock devised another assignment for him, as the Canadiens' head scout for eastern Canada from 1961 to 1963. But Scotty didn't enjoy scouting. It made him feel too disconnected from the team.

He told Pollock he wanted to coach again, so Pollock sent him to coach the Omaha Knights of the Central Professional Hockey League. Even though the Knights won their games under Scotty, he was bumping against the team owners and the sparks weren't good. They didn't have time or patience for Scotty's detailed coaching methods, things like faceoff drills or changing on the fly. The owners had too many fingers in the day-to-day. As Ken Dryden says, coaches have to manage up and manage down. Scotty wasn't able to manage the upper level of owners yet. So he quit and went back to scouting for Pollock. As a Canadiens scout, he felt connected to the team again and was able to spend more time around Sam Pollock.

And it was while scouting for the Canadiens this time around that Scotty made an embarrassing mistake.

Serge Savard was born in 1946 in the tiny community of Landrienne, Quebec, about 370 miles northwest of Montreal. His father, Laurent, was mayor of the town and also ran a creamery out of their small house. On the walls of their home hung three pictures: one of Pope Pius XII, one of Premier Maurice Duplessis and one of Maurice "Rocket" Richard. Religion, politics and sports, the holy trinity of the Savard household. Young Serge worshipped only one of those pictures. Hockey was the second religion to Québécois Roman Catholics. The Savard family would gather around the radio and listen to Montreal Canadiens games. Serge and every one of his friends dreamed of one day wearing the famous *bleu, blanc, rouge* jersey.

Always big for his age, Savard towered over his schoolmates. At eleven, he was over six feet tall in his skates. A few years later, a Canadiens scout noticed the big kid playing in a school league game. Savard was gangly but the scout saw potential. While Savard had the heft of a defenceman, he played all positions and had good instincts. The scout was impressed and put Savard on the team's list of promising reserves. That year, Savard moved to Montreal to attend boarding school and start playing serious hockey.

This is where Serge Savard crossed paths fatefully with Scotty Bowman.

Cliff Fletcher worked with Scotty as a part-time scout for the Junior Canadiens. (He would eventually go on to a Hall of Fame career in the NHL, including a Stanley Cup as general manager of the Calgary Flames when they defeated the Canadiens in 1989.) Cliff was what was then called a "bird dog," looking to flush potential players out of the small towns around the northern edges of eastern Canada. Each of the original six teams was allowed to sponsor two junior teams to secure up-and-coming players. Frank Selke's Quebec farm system was the best in the league, along with that of the Toronto Maple Leafs, who plucked the best players from Ontario. The Canadiens would also make occasional deals with a handful of teams in the American leagues. It was within this system that Cliff Fletcher and Scotty Bowman trained their eagle eyes for talent.

The Canadiens had a time-tested process. Each year, the team would bring twelve young players to Montreal—always twelve—from small northern towns like Val-d'Or, Rouyn-Noranda and Landrienne, and disperse these players around the Metropolitan Junior B league. Aged fourteen or fifteen, they would be billeted in homes or attend boarding school. Selke and Pollock had patience with young hopefuls, and as Cliff says, their success was based on consistency and continuity. The plan was to let the young players get some experience and mature so that they could maybe move up to the Junior Canadiens, then hopefully make the big hop up to the Habs. Even if a rookie had a bad season, he would be given another year to see if he could turn a corner and improve. More than one great player proved himself in his second Junior B season.

Fifteen-year-old Serge Savard was placed on a team in Rosemont, in the east end of Montreal. But he didn't get any ice time. The owner, Roger Poitras, didn't play any of his young players because he wasn't interested in developing young talent. He was fixated, preoccupied and hell-bent on winning, so he gave all the ice time to his tried-and-true twenty-year-old skaters. As a matter of fact, Poitras told Pollock that Savard would never be an NHL player. Cliff and Scotty didn't agree with that assessment. When it came to deciding on those twelve players, Cliff and Scotty would make a long list, Scotty would decide on the short list and present it to Pollock. Pollock would make the final decision and the boys who didn't make the list were notified when school ended in June. Cliff would then make the arrangements to bring the twelve players to Montreal in the fall, arrange schooling and find lodging. But when Pollock looked at Scotty's twelve recommendations after Savard's first year in Montreal, the first thing he did was scratch Savard off the list, saying, "We're not bringing him back because he didn't play." Pollock understood it wasn't Savard's fault that he polished the pine, but as Pollock said at the time, that's the way it goes sometimes. Cliff and Scotty tried to rally for Savard, but Pollock had made up his mind and that was that.

Then Scotty Bowman and Cliff Fletcher made a big mistake.

Like all his teammates, Serge Savard went home that summer and worked with his father. When September rolled around, Cliff got a call from Savard saying he had just stepped off the bus from his 370-mile trip from Landrienne, returned to the same Montreal boarding house and wanted to arrange his transportation and other expenses. According to Savard, after a long pause on the phone, Cliff mumbled something incomprehensible, then said he would get back to him and hung up. Cliff then grabbed Scotty and said, "Savard's in town."

Scotty replied, "He can't be!"

Cliff said, "Well, he is."

That's the moment head scout Scotty Bowman realized he had forgotten to tell Savard he had been cut from the team.

It was a big problem. Sam Pollock was a demanding boss and far too busy for this kind of embarrassing and annoying snafu. Scotty had no choice but to fess up to the mistake, but he and Cliff decided they would delicately, subtly, try to persuade Pollock to consider something he had never contemplated before—the number thirteen. According to Scotty, he waited for the right moment in their meeting, then said, in a roundabout way, "About Serge Savard, somehow Cliff and I didn't call him." It took a beat for Pollock to understand what Scotty meant by that, but when the penny did drop, he said, "Well, he's not going to stay here now. We've already got our twelve." That's when Cliff Fletcher threw their Hail Mary pass. He said, "You know, Sam, Savard never got a chance last year . . ." Cliff was trying to persuade Pollock to change his mind by coming in through the back door on the problem. In that nanosecond between the ellipsis and the next sound in the room, Scotty offered his boss a tiny olive branch. If they could find a team to take him and play him, could they at least keep Savard until Christmas? Pollock looked at them both and thundered, "Only until Christmas!!"

With that, Cliff and Scotty reached out to Canadiens great Doug Harvey to see if Doug's brother Alf, who coached another Montreal team called the Notre-Dame-de-Grâce Monarchs, would take Savard. That particular team never seemed to get many good players, but Alf Harvey always played everyone on his bench. He happily took the young player from Landrienne. It was challenging for Savard, as he didn't speak English and Alf didn't speak French. But an astonishing thing happened. Finally getting some ice time to prove himself, Savard blossomed. He was a dominant player on the ice, he was leading the team and in one game he notched all four goals. Just before Christmas, he was named to the all-star team. A few days later, Cliff handed him an envelope that contained a handsome sum of money reimbursing all his expenses, including the cost of the bus ticket that had brought him back to Montreal after the summer break. Savard was such a standout, he was soon brought up to the Junior Canadiens. During his three seasons with the team between 1963 and 1967, he was promoted to captain and became the leader, on and off the ice, of a team that included future greats Jacques Lemaire and Carol Vadnais, his close friend.

In 1967, the Canadiens signed Savard to a contract and sent him to the Houston Apollos of the Central League to tune him up for the big league. There, Savard was selected to the second all-star team and was voted Rookie of the Year. That outstanding performance landed him a spot with the Montreal Canadiens at the age of twenty. The team won the Stanley Cup in Savard's first year. In his second season, Savard began to show his dominant playing style. Standing six foot three, 210 pounds, he was an immovable force patrolling the Canadiens' blue line, blocking shots and clearing the zone with very few turnovers. In the playoffs, he collected ten points in fourteen games, helping Montreal win the cup again. His four goals were just one shy of the NHL record for playoff goals by a defenceman in one season and he became the first defenceman ever to win the Conn Smythe Trophy as playoff MVP.

But here's the thing. Cliff and Scotty's mistake was one of the best things to happen to the Montreal Canadiens. To begin with, a Detroit scout was also interested in Savard when the mistake was made. Had Savard known he had been cut, he would most likely have gone on to play for the Red Wings and his career would have taken a very different turn. But because of that mistake, Savard not only played fourteen seasons with the Canadiens, he became an integral force in one of the team's historic eras, one that saw eight Stanley Cups in twelve years, including the fabled 1976–77 season when the Habs lost only eight games all season—coached by none other than Scotty Bowman. Together with Larry Robinson and Guy Lapointe, Savard made up the Big Three defensive squad. He had what Scotty calls a "high hockey IQ" and under Scotty's coaching, they won four straight Stanley Cups together. Savard's spectacular ability to pivot on the ice prompted famed play-by-play sportscaster Danny Gallivan to coin the term "Savardian spin-o-rama!" Because of that original mistake, Savard would eventually become the captain of the mighty Habs. Later, Savard became the general manager of the Montreal Canadiens, and the team won two more cups under his watch. He is ranked one of the top hundred NHL players of all time. In 1986, he was inducted into the Hockey Hall of Fame. He was made an officer of the Order of Canada and a knight of the National Order of Québec.

And because of that mistake Scotty Bowman made back in 1963, Serge Savard's number 18 was retired by the Montreal Canadiens and hoisted to the rafters, where it hangs with those of other legendary players.

Including one very revered face that hung on the wall of his home in Landrienne all those many years ago.

3.

Ski-Doo®

How Do You Spell Success?

Joseph-Armand Bombardier was born on April 16, 1907, in Valcourt, a small town tucked in the Eastern Townships of Quebec. From his earliest days, Bombardier was a tinkerer. He loved to take things apart to see how they worked. At the age of thirteen, he built a miniature locomotive driven by a clock mechanism, painting the train in great detail. Already a budding entrepreneur, he paid a local jeweller for the clock parts by using the money he earned serving mass as an altar boy. Much to the delight of his siblings, he went on to build mobile toy tractors and boats.

Joseph-Armand's curious mind saw opportunities to experiment everywhere. He built a steam engine out of old sewing machine parts and convinced an aunt to let him attach it to her spinning wheel. As the wheel spun faster and faster, Joseph-Armand's joy was surpassed only by his aunt's dismay. Next, he convinced a local veterinarian to give him a broken 12-calibre gun. Joseph-Armand shortened the barrel, modified the firing system, cut and polished the butt, changed the breech and mounted the entire device on metal wheels. He then rolled it over to the veterinarian's house and detonated his mini-cannon with black powder. Joseph-Armand was fourteen years old. The vet was dumbfounded.

Young Joseph-Armand also spent hours happily disassembling and reassembling the family car, much to the dismay of his father, Alfred. To save the car from total bolt-by-bolt dismantlement, Alfred gave Joseph-Armand a junky, irreparable Model T Ford to fiddle with. In no time, he had the car running smoothly, modifying it with novel tweaks.

Sensing his son needed some grounding, Alfred sent him to a seminary in nearby Sherbrooke to study for the priesthood. While there, Joseph-Armand started dreaming of a new mechanical idea. When he came back home for the Christmas holidays, he retreated immediately to his father's garage to turn the dream into a reality. On New Year's Day, Alfred watched in astonishment as Joseph-Armand rolled a strange-looking contraption out onto the snow. It was a sled powered by the old Model T motor and steered using rope reins. But the sled's biggest feature was the giant plane propeller attached at the back. As Joseph-Armand demonstrated his invention to his amazed siblings and cousins, his father was not nearly as impressed by the contraption and ordered it dismantled immediately, worried the exposed propeller would result in serious injury. A very proud fifteen-year-old Joseph-Armand did as he was told. It was a historic moment—albeit lost on Alfred.

His son had just created his first snowmobile.

Heading back to the seminary, Joseph-Armand knew in his heart the priesthood was not his calling. At the age of seventeen, he finally received his father's blessing to pursue his dream of being a mechanic. In the spring of 1924, he landed an apprenticeship in a nearby town. He eventually left for Montreal, where he took night classes in mechanics and electrical engineering.

In 1926, Joseph-Armand, with his round Harry Potter glasses

and dark hair, returned to his hometown, married and started a family. He also built a garage of his own with some financial help from his father and elbow grease from his siblings. His remarkable ability to solve any mechanical problem earned him an admirable reputation throughout the area. Business expanded so rapidly, he was able to repay his father's loan in just three years. As his company ramped up, one persistent issue tugged at his inventive mind: the villages of the Quebec townships were literally marooned by snow every winter, preventing any kind of travel outside the town limits. His snow vehicle idea began to take on an ever-evolving, three-dimensional shape in his mind. A vehicle able to traverse snow would completely transform his community and other communities like it across Quebec. But the notion presented formidable challenges. For starters, car motors made vehicles too heavy to glide over soft snow. The design needed to be light, with traction and a floating suspension that could adapt to various conditions, from hard-packed snow to soft, deep powder.

For the next decade, Joseph-Armand worked on his project. The quest ate up weekends and late nights, not to mention his savings. One early incarnation looked like a plywood bathtub on tracks, the next one looked like a baby buggy on skis and still another looked like a cross between a Model T and a sleigh. Some of the townsfolk laughed and mocked him when he rolled the prototypes out of his garage, only to see them cough, sputter, sink into the snow and fail. Because Ford and Dodge motors were too heavy, he built a lighter, forty-five-kilogram engine, but it kept overheating. In spite of the setbacks, he was patient and persistent.

Malcolm Gladwell says all successful entrepreneurs share one key characteristic. Conventional wisdom says it is a high tolerance for risk. Gladwell disagrees. He says all true entrepreneurs believe they are on to a sure thing. Conforming to Gladwell's rule, Joseph-Armand was utterly convinced a functioning snow vehicle was possible. Undaunted, he inched closer to success with every failure. As the saying goes, the nine-to-five pays the bills, the six-to-twelve builds the empire.

Then came heartbreak.

His two-year-old son, Yvon, died from peritonitis in the winter of 1934. The town was completely snowbound and the family could not get him to the hospital, even though it was only thirty miles away. An unfinished snowmobile sat in his garage. The emotional loss redoubled Joseph-Armand's determination to find a way to overcome the winter isolation suffered by all small northern towns. Driven by tragedy, he diverted his attention from a small two-person sled to a larger model that could transport several people.

The following year, he made a breakthrough.

He developed a wooden cogged gearwheel covered with rubber to pull a track. This sprocket wheel/rubber belt system was so revolutionary, he applied for a patent on December 19, 1936, and was granted one six months later. This breakthrough finally put Joseph-Armand's dream of a snow vehicle within reach. It also allowed his company to leapfrog ahead in the process and build a production plant that functioned year-round, employing many of the townsfolk. The first machine that emerged from the new Bombardier factory was labelled the B7, B for Bombardier and 7 for the number of people it could transport. The B7 was a large, boxy, fully enclosed snow vehicle, running on his innovative track system. When Joseph-Armand spotted a problem of snow buildup around the wheel spokes, it sparked another breakthrough—solid wheels. The first B7s with solid wheels slid out of the plant in 1940. The vehicles forever changed life in small towns. Now the formidable Canadian winters no longer meant isolation.

Not only did Joseph-Armand have a visionary mind, he possessed a shrewd marketing instinct. He fuelled demand for his B7s by driving them on otherwise impassable roads across the province, giving demonstrations in all kinds of snow conditions. One of his most powerful marketing ideas was to roar into town and park right beside the local newspaper office to attract the attention of the editors, guaranteeing that most elusive advertising goal—free publicity. The resulting orders stacked up and his plant had to expand again. A larger L'Auto-Neige Bombardier plant was built in 1941 with the capacity to produce two hundred B7s. In June of that same year, Joseph-Armand introduced an updated model. The B12 was more streamlined and, as the number indicated, it could seat twelve passengers. The B12 was a huge success, but just as production increased it was suddenly halted due to the outbreak of the Second World War.

Bombardier then offered its services to the Department of Munitions and Supply and received an order to develop prototype snowmobiles to transport troops in snowbound military zones. Using the B12 as a foundation, Joseph-Armand developed what he called the B1 and the Canadian Army ordered 130 vehicles that had to be delivered in just four months. It was a tall order for the Valcourt plant, so Bombardier moved production to a vacant facility in Montreal but continued to manufacture the parts in Valcourt in order to keep the village employed. Not long after, the army requested an armoured snow vehicle and Bombardier produced a prototype called the Kaki. Between 1942 and 1946, the company delivered over nineteen hundred military snow vehicles.

When the war effort finally ended, Joseph-Armand returned home to steer the growth of his company. Business boomed once again with the demand for civilian snowmobiles. Once again, the plant couldn't keep up with the orders, so in 1947 L'Auto-Neige Bombardier built an assembly-line plant inspired by Ford. The company also invented many of the tools it needed. Along with personal snowmobiles, demand for the B12 intensified as communities in the north wanted them for a wide range of needs, including the maintenance of hydro and telephone lines, mine prospecting, public transportation, materials haulage, mail delivery, ambulance services and rescue teams, as well as the transport of missionaries to remote communities. By 1947, Bombardier's revenues topped $2.3 million, with a profit of $324,000—more than ten times the company's earnings in 1942. Over twenty-eight hundred B12s were built and delivered. Next came the C18 that seated eighteen adults or twenty-five children, which soon became known as the school snowmobile.

But 1949 brought Bombardier to another crossroad.

The Quebec government decreed all rural roads must be plowed in the winter. Now people were able to drive their cars or pull horse-drawn sleds with relative ease along plowed country roads. Demand for large snow vehicles plummeted by $1 million instantly. But L'Auto-Neige Bombardier was adaptable and Joseph-Armand pivoted to an all-terrain vehicle with an interchangeable system of wheels and skis, allowing it to navigate both snow and asphalt. That innovation led to several successful patents and models, including the very successful Muskeg tractor (still sold around the world today).

The company's increasing demand for quality raw materials led Joseph-Armand to open his first subsidiary to manufacture rubber components. That move, combined with his remarkable ingenuity, resulted in yet another breakthrough—an all-rubber, unbreakable, shape-retaining continuous track, which greatly enhanced the machine's reliability. As the fifties came to an end, L'Auto-Neige Bombardier boasted sales of $3.5 million with a profit of $850,000. The success, the breakthroughs and the patents set the stage for Joseph-Armand's greatest invention.

He had the basic design figured out for what he called a "miniature" snowmobile. With advances in lighter motors and the company's own patented continuous track design, the time was right to develop his lifelong dream. With the war in the rearview mirror, it wasn't just hunters and trappers who were enamoured with the snowmobile; the public now had the money and time to pursue outdoor recreational activities. A prototype for a sporty, light-footed snow machine was built near the end of 1958, and the next April, Joseph-Armand took the first snowmobile all the way to northern Ontario to show it to a friend who was a missionary. The priest and the indigenous people of the village were captivated with it and took turns driving it for three days straight. Joseph-Armand left it with the missionary as a gift. The intense interest in the snowmobile confirmed what he had known since he was a teenager: there was a market for the personal snowmobile.

He headed back home to get mass production underway after some final crucial decisions. He chose the colour yellow to brand the machines because it was the most identifiable colour in the snow. The machines came with one seat, wooden skis and no headlight. Joseph-Armand coined a name for the machines, calling them "Ski-Dogs" because he saw them as a mechanical replacement for dog sleds—then the only viable form of deep winter transportation for hunters and trappers.

The name said it all.

It was perfect.

Then a fortuitous mistake was made.

The first four Ski-Dogs rolled off the L'Auto-Neige Bombardier assembly line in 1959. They contained no logos yet because the branding was still being developed. As part of the launch, a sales brochure was commissioned to detail all the innovations embedded in the new Ski-Dogs. But the brochure contained a critical typo. Instead of the word "Ski-Dog," it was misspelled as "Ski-Doo." The brochures were printed before the single-consonant mistake was caught. Joseph-Armand looked at the error, and instead of being angry, he smiled. He liked the sound of it. "Ski-Doo." It smacked of the slang phrase "to skiddoo"—a form of "skedaddle"—which meant to get away quickly. The memorable name captured the sporty nature of the beast, and moreover, it could be protected with a trademark. In that first year, 225 Ski-Doo snowmobiles were sold. Just four years later, 8,210 were in the hands of happy customers.

When the Ski-Doo snowmobile hit the market, the modern era of snowmobiling was born. While L'Auto-Neige Bombardier would one day have up to a hundred competitors, its yellow machine was so popular that the word "Ski-Doo" became a household name.

Joseph-Armand would enjoy the phenomenal success of his Ski-Doo snowmobile for only a few short years. Even though he had even bigger plans in his inventive mind—including generating hydro power from nearby waterways—he was limited by time and health. Joseph-Armand Bombardier died of cancer in 1964 at the still young age of fifty-six. He had accomplished so much in so few years. A moving letter was left for his children, encouraging them to keep pursuing his work.

They did.

By 1967, 1,700 of the 3,500 residents of Valcourt were employed by his company. Little did Joseph-Armand know the demand for his "miniature" snowmobiles would explode into an industry that was manufacturing over 500,000 units per year by the early seventies. Today, some 600,000 snowmobiles are registered in Canada—one for every sixty Canadians. Quebec alone has over twenty thousand miles of snowmobiling trails. The Bombardier company estimates the world's four major manufacturers together sell about 158,000 units a year.

The Bombardier company would continue to expand well beyond its original Valcourt footprint to have offices and plants around the world, with over sixty thousand employees and annual revenues topping $16 billion. Today, Bombardier is two separate publicly traded companies, one for the aircraft and rail division and Bombardier Recreational Products, or BRP, which is still controlled by the Bombardier family. BRP is a worldwide manufacturer of land and snow machines, as well as Sea-Doo personal watercraft.

Back in 1967, a CBC documentary said that what Henry Ford was to the open road, Joseph-Armand Bombardier was to the backwoods. A fitting tribute for the man who built his first snowmobile at age fifteen and empowered an entire snowmobile industry in 1959 with his first yellow Ski-Dog.

And a tiny typo.

4.

Brian Williams

The Unofficial Spokesman of the Second Chance Club

E ven though he never learned to skate, his downfall began at a hockey game. NBC news anchor and managing editor Brian Williams was attending a game between the New York Rangers and the Montreal Canadiens at Madison Square Garden on January 29, 2015. Williams had brought a special guest with him that night. Sitting to his left was U.S. Army Command Sergeant Major Tim Terpak. Twelve years prior, Terpak had been responsible for Williams's safety in Iraq after what Williams would later describe as a harrowing flight on a Chinook helicopter on March 24, 2003. Although they had kept in touch over the years, this was the first time they had seen each other since the incident. In a surprise moment, no doubt orchestrated by Williams, the cameras turned to Terpak and the arena announcer told the crowd that during the Iraq invasion, U.S. Army Command Sergeant Major Terpak had been responsible for the safety of Brian Williams and his NBC News team after their Chinook helicopter was hit and crippled by enemy fire and that Terpak had been awarded three

Bronze Stars for combat valour. The announcer ended by saying both men were Rangers fans and had reunited for the first time in twelve years for that night's game. The crowd of eighteen thousand gave Terpak a standing ovation. The next evening on the *NBC Nightly News*, Williams made a special point of telling his viewers what had unfolded at the Garden:

> We want to share with you a great moment that took place here in New York last night. The story actually started with a terrible moment a dozen years back during the invasion of Iraq when the helicopter we were travelling in was forced down after being hit by an RPG. Our travelling NBC News team was rescued, surrounded and kept alive by an armoured mechanized platoon from the U.S. Army Third Infantry. Command Sergeant Major Tim Terpak was put in charge of our safety.

It was an uplifting, heartfelt moment on a news program usually dominated by bad news. But it would turn out to be a bad news story for Brian Williams.

NBC posted a video of the story on its Facebook page, praising Terpak and Williams. Viewers left many positive messages of thanks and respect on the page. But there was one curious post from someone named Lance Reynolds. It read, in part, "Sorry dude, I don't remember you being on my aircraft. I do remember you walking up about an hour after we had landed to ask me what had happened."

The military newspaper *Stars and Stripes* picked up on this post. It identified Reynolds as the flight engineer on the Chinook that had been hit by two rocket-propelled grenades (RPGs) and small arms fire. According to Reynolds, the chopper carrying Williams and his NBC camera crew landed roughly an hour later. Importantly, it had encountered no enemy fire. Reynolds said Williams had talked to him briefly about the attack, taken some photographs of the damage and left about ten minutes later. When *Stars and Stripes* spoke to the flight engineer on the chopper carrying the journalists, Sergeant First Class Joseph Miller, he confirmed their helicopter had taken no direct fire.

Back when Brian Williams first reported on the incident, on March 26, 2003, he recounted the incident accurately, saying that when his chopper landed, they learned the Chinook ahead of them had taken fire and was almost blown out of the sky. Two years later, in March 2005, Williams was interviewed on Tim Russert's MSNBC show and again accurately stated that the helicopter in front of them had been hit by an RPG. Two years after that, in March 2007, Williams became the first network news anchor to go back to Iraq after ABC's Bob Woodruff had sustained critical injuries as the result of a roadside bomb. Without quoting Williams directly, the Associated Press reported Williams was travelling with retired general Wayne Downing, who was with him on a previous visit "when Williams' helicopter was forced down by insurgent gunfire." However, after General Downing died in July 2007, Williams wrote in a blog post that an RPG attack hit "the chopper in front of ours. There was small arms fire. A chopper pilot took a bullet through the earlobe. All four choppers dropped their heavy loads and landed quickly and hard on the desert floor."

Soon after, we see the first signs of the story changing. In a television interview after Downing's death, Williams suggested that all the choppers, including his, were fired upon: "When the Chinook helicopters we were travelling in at the start of the Iraq war were fired on and forced down for three days in a stretch of hostile desert in a sandstorm, we were comforted only by the fact that we were flying with the general."

In September 2007, Williams was interviewing four-star general David Petraeus, who was overseeing the war in Iraq at that time. He reiterated his close call, telling Petraeus the chopper he was flying in with General Downing had taken ground fire. In November of that same year, Williams told a student reporter he had experienced many close calls in his career, saying he had "looked down the tube of an RPG that had been fired at us and had hit the chopper in front of ours."

On the very day of the tenth anniversary of the incident in 2013, Brian Williams appeared on David Letterman's show. He told the host that two of the four helicopters were hit by ground fire, "including the one I was in, RPG and AK-47." When Letterman asked what happened the minute everyone realized they'd been hit, Williams said, "We figure out how to land—safely—and we did." That same month, Williams was interviewed by Alec Baldwin on his *Here's the Thing* podcast. He told Baldwin the story of being in a helicopter in Iraq with bullets coming into the airframe. When asked if he thought he was going to die in the moment, Williams replied, "Briefly, sure."

Then came the New York Rangers game in 2015.

The *NBC Nightly News* story.

The posting of the video on Facebook.

And the post from Reynolds.

Brian Williams then responded on Facebook. He said, in part:

To Joseph, Lance, Jonathan, Pate, Michael and all those who have posted: You are absolutely right and I was wrong. In fact, I spent much of the weekend thinking I'd gone crazy.

I feel terrible about making this mistake, especially since I found my OWN WRITING about the incident from back in '08, and I was indeed on the Chinook behind the bird that took the RPG in the tail housing just above the ramp. Because I have no desire to fictionalize my experience (we all saw it happened the first time) and no need to dramatize events as they actually happened, I think the constant viewing of the video showing us inspecting the impact area—and the fog of memory over 12 years—made me conflate the two, and I apologize.

Next, Brian Williams made a very careful and modulated apology on his newscast, saying he had made a mistake in recalling the events of twelve years earlier:

I want to apologize. I said I was travelling in an aircraft that was hit by RPG fire. I was instead in a following aircraft. We all landed after the ground-fire incident and spent two harrowing nights in a sandstorm in the Iraq desert. This was a bungled attempt by me to thank one special veteran and, by extension, our brave military men and women, veterans everywhere, those who have served while I have not. I hope they know they have my greatest respect, and also now—my apology.

Vanity Fair would later call his wording "elliptical" because it circled the trespass but never landed. Williams's inability to explain himself frustrated NBC executives. And it failed to limit the damage to his reputation.

· · · ·

Tom Brokaw, Dan Rather and Peter Jennings all began and left their respective network anchor jobs roughly within a year of each other. Those departures in 2004 and 2005 signalled a huge changing of the guard, because each had held his seat for over twenty years. Brokaw's NBC heir apparent was Brian Williams, who, at the time, was the news anchor for sister cable channel MSNBC. Many may not remember, but MSNBC was launched in 1996 as a partnership between Microsoft and NBC—hence the MS in its name. Microsoft eventually divested itself and ownership reverted fully to NBC. When Brokaw's retirement was announced, NBC stated it would begin raising Brian Williams's profile by giving him overseas assignments as well as having him sit in for Brokaw as often as possible.

It was a full-circle moment. Brokaw had recruited Williams from WCBS-TV in New York back in 1993. The two had met discreetly at the Sherry-Netherland Hotel, where Brokaw asked Williams to consider moving over to NBC News. Brokaw said he was at the age where he needed to start thinking of a successor, and if Williams came to NBC, he would be considered for that role. Williams accepted, and during the next three years, he did stints as a weekend anchor and White House correspondent. In 1996, Williams was elevated to anchor an hour-long news program on the newly created MSNBC. For the next eight years, he was groomed for the big chair. That opportunity finally came on December 2, 2004.

NBC assumed Brokaw's departure would result in a tumble in the ratings and subsequent drop in advertising revenue. But the program held on to its number-one spot throughout the transition, retaining its approximately 10 million nightly viewers. This stability was a tribute to Brian Williams's skill and acute awareness that he was on probation with the audience. He took the baton and ran gracefully with it. His profile continued to rise and took a big jump in 2005 with NBC's on-the-spot reporting during Hurricane Katrina. Williams travelled to New Orleans with his crew and filed live reports from the Superdome as the storm devastated the city and ripped some of the roof off the stadium. His team captured heartbreaking moments as residents tried to escape the storm and evacuees sought shelter. Williams covered the hurricane from many meaningful angles and asked difficult questions of government officials. He also didn't hide his anger at the government's failure to act quickly. For that reporting, NBC News received a prestigious Peabody Award, cited for exemplifying the highest levels of journalistic excellence. *Vanity Fair* said that during the Katrina reporting, Williams became the "nation's anchor."

Over the years, the respect for Brian Williams only grew. *Time* magazine named him one of the most influential people in the world in 2007. Arizona State University awarded him the Walter Cronkite Award for Excellence in Journalism in 2009. Just before he died, Cronkite said he was overjoyed that Williams had accepted the award. Cronkite considered himself one of Williams's "most ardent admirers" and praised him for being a "fastidious newsman" who brought distinct credit to the profession. Williams was the most awarded network news anchor, having won five Emmy Awards, four Edward R. Murrow Awards, the Alfred I. duPont–Columbia University Award and six honorary doctorates. He was chosen to moderate eight presidential debates.

But it could be argued that what distinguished Brian Williams from his competitors was less his ramrod respectability than his sense of humour. It would show itself in flashes on the nightly news—where appropriate—but it was most on display in his frequent appearances on late-night talk shows. When his accession to the *Nightly News* anchor chair was first announced, he was a guest on Jon Stewart's *Daily Show* and demonstrated he could hold his own with Stewart. Then came multiple appearances slow-jamming the news with Jimmy Fallon, trading quips with Letterman and regaling Seth Myers with wry observations. Williams was not only a good storyteller, he was a great straight man. He could move between self-importance and self-deprecation so effortlessly you had to be amused. He clearly relished the opportunity to flex a different muscle on the talk show circuit. He even did a cameo on Tina Fey's *30 Rock*.

Then in 2007, he became the first network anchor in history to host *Saturday Night Live*. One of the more amusing skits follows him on an "average" day at the office. It begins with Williams saying the first thing he likes to do when he arrives at 30 Rockefeller Plaza in the morning is to stand outside the building and wait for people to recognize him. He goes on to say he likes to eat in the NBC cafeteria because it connects him with his fellow workers—where we see him eating alone at a roped-off table guarded by security. We see him giggling while throwing pennies from his window as they rain down on a Matt Lauer interview taking place in the plaza below. It was a very funny, tongue-in-cheek send-up of a top network anchorman. Williams later told Alec Baldwin it took him six months to say yes to Lorne Michaels, explaining, "I worried that I was going to flush fifteen years of my credibility down the toilet." Clearly, he was smart enough to understand the vast difference between humour and comedy. And self-inflicted mockery gives you a hall pass. There was no doubt he enjoyed it.

That love of performing and interest in off-the-cuff banter led him to throw his hat into a very unexpected ring. According to *New York* magazine, Williams began chafing at reading a teleprompter every night. He also felt embraced by the entertainment community in a way he never felt with the old guard at NBC News. When Jay Leno was scheduled to depart *The Tonight Show*, Williams told NBCUniversal CEO Stephen B. Burke he wanted to take over the hosting duties. Burke dismissed the idea. *New York* magazine also reported that Williams pitched CBS chair Leslie Moonves about succeeding David Letterman. Reportedly, Moonves wasn't interested.

The magazine profile said the job of persuading Williams to stay on as network anchorman fell to NBC News president Deborah Turness. At a dinner to celebrate Williams's tenth anniversary in the big chair, Turness presented Williams with a gift: Edward R. Murrow's mahogany writing table. She hoped it would remind Williams he was America's most trusted news anchor— the Murrow of his day. Williams was clearly moved by the gesture and announced—then and there—that he would renew his contract for another five years, surprising his NBC bosses, who broke into spontaneous applause around the table.

Less than two months later, the Iraq trapdoor would swing open under Williams's feet.

When the mainstream press picked up on the chopper story, the brass at NBC News knew they had to act quickly. It was decided Williams would be suspended for six months without pay. The money wasn't really an issue for Williams, who had been earning $10 million annually. Six months in the penalty box was much more humiliating. The CEO summoned Williams to his Upper West Side apartment to deliver the news of his suspension. According to the *New York Times*, only Burke and Williams were present at that meeting. The *Nightly News* crew was told after that night's broadcast. Deborah Turness then issued a memo to staff members on Tuesday, February 10, 2015. She spelled out the terms of the suspension, named Lester Holt as substitute anchor and confirmed an internal review was underway. She said, "While on Nightly News on Friday, January 30, 2015, Brian misrepresented events which occurred while he was covering the Iraq War in 2003. It then became clear that on other occasions Brian had done the same thing while telling that story in other venues." The memo stated unequivocally, "This was wrong and completely inappropriate for someone in Brian's position." Turness said she, her immediate boss Pat Fili and Burke had made the decision together. She told the staff that NBC was bigger than this unfortunate moment and they would all get through it together. There was a message from Stephen Burke in that memo, too: "By his actions, Brian has jeopardized the trust millions of Americans place in NBC News. His actions are inexcusable and this suspension is severe and appropriate."

Burke went on to say, "He deserves a second chance and we are rooting for him. Brian has shared his deep remorse with me and he is committed to winning back everyone's trust."

Before the apology, Brian Williams was ranked the 23rd-most-trusted person in America. Immediately after, he plummeted to 855, on par with Willie Robertson of *Duck Dynasty* fame. But this predicament was about more than journalistic ethics—it was business. The cost of a single thirty-second commercial in Williams's broadcast was $47,500. NBC News had generated over $200 million in ad revenue the previous year. ABC lined up second at $170.6 million, with CBS panting last at $149.9 million. In the news game, credibility equals ad revenue. How many of those dollars would NBC now have to cede to its hungry competitors?

From anchoring the number-one news program in the nation, to commanding the most expensive commercial rates in the news business, to the rarified air atop reputation mountain—the perch from which Brian Williams fell was so high, it was breathtaking.

According to an anonymous insider at NBC News, Brian Williams was always reluctant to go on difficult assignments. He didn't want to leave New York and dispatching him to war zones was almost impossible. So the Iraq assignment takes on another unexpected shading. Unlike Anderson Cooper, for example, Williams wasn't waving his hand for out-of-town assignments. And unlike Cooper, network anchors are held to a higher standard than political affairs talk show hosts. They are expected to be truth tellers. Beyond geometrical face structure and good hair, their perceived credibility and honesty attracts eyeballs. Those eyeballs attract advertisers. Networks bank that revenue and stockpile the prestige. The trusted anchor becomes the face of a network.

When Brian Williams himself became news, all of that reverence for NBC News teetered in the gale force of the blowback. The social media snark soon followed. On Twitter, the hashtag

#BrianWilliamsMisremembers ignited a litany of posts. One showed Williams dressed as an astronaut with the line "It was an honour to be the first man on the moon." Another showed a pic of Williams holding an Academy Award for "Best Supporting Actor, American Sniper. Helicopter pilot #2." Still another had Williams saying, "Hey, if I could handle two years in a Viet Cong prison, I can deal with a six-month NBC suspension." The very late-night talk show hosts who had embraced Williams now strip-mined him for comedic fodder. Even before news of the suspension, Letterman featured a list of the "Top 10 Things Brian Williams Has Said That May or May Not Be True." Jon Stewart, who announced his departure from *The Daily Show* on the same day Williams's suspension was made public, mocked Williams by saying he was suffering from "Infotainment Confusion Syndrome," explaining that the "celebrity cortex" got its wires crossed with the "medulla anchordalla."

One of the first questions that arose about the incident centred around the soldiers on that mission. Why had they remained quiet for so long? And what about Tim Terpak? He must have heard Brian Williams's description of the incident. Why had he remained silent? Well, Terpak wasn't on the helicopter that carried Williams, nor was he on the helicopter that took the ground fire. As a matter of fact, Terpak wasn't on any of the choppers. He was in charge of the ground forces sent in to protect those Chinooks once they landed and his platoon didn't arrive until three days later. Terpak couldn't comment on the accuracy of Williams's report because he wasn't in the air when it happened. Pilot Don Helus was in the chopper that took the enemy fire that day. He says he saw an internet video of Williams telling his story years before the Rangers game and had sent a letter to MSNBC .com alerting the network to the inaccuracies. If true, the network doesn't appear to have taken any action.

Five months into his suspension, Brian Williams agreed to sit for an interview with colleague Matt Lauer. Although it was the home team interviewing the home team, Lauer prefaced the segment saying they had mutually agreed no conditions or guidelines would be placed on the interview. While it could be argued Lauer didn't go all Mike Wallace on Williams, there were definitely some squirmy moments. When asked what the last five months had been like, Williams looked genuinely shaken, saying it had been torture. He said he had been going over and over the last ten years in his mind, looking for clues as to why he went off the rails. He was truly at a loss to explain it. Williams acknowledged something had changed in him. At work, he would treat words very carefully because it was the key to an anchor's credibility and integrity. But when he left the building, he said, something unclicked. He began employing a double standard and saying things that weren't true. When Lauer pushed, Williams said it had to be ego that compelled him to feel he had to be sharper, funnier and quicker than anybody else. When Lauer asked Williams why he hadn't just come out and said he had lied earlier in the process, Williams started repeating himself, reaching for an answer, saying the urge must have come from a bad place. Throughout the interview, Williams oscillated between forceful and lost. He had rehearsed these answers in his mind, but it was the last few seconds of the interview that revealed the complexity of his emotions. One could sense he was genuinely sorry—not that he got caught, as so many high-profile offenders seem to feel when revealed in the glare of the searchlight, but rather that he had allowed this to happen. His disappointment in himself was visceral. His eyes grew heavy, his eyebrows arched, his voice wavered. He said he was now a different man. Part two of the interview took on a different tone as it focused on the future of Brian Williams. He declared, in a penitent moment, that he was now the unofficial spokesman of the second chance club.

A big question still loomed: Was there any way to come back after that RPG tore a hole through his credibility?

After watching Williams questioned by Lauer (who would have his own come-to-Jesus moment a few years later), it was still not at all clear what had happened. Williams seemed as mystified as the viewing audience. There was no closure because there seemed to be no premeditated transgression. Who lies about something over and over again on one of the most-watched programs on network television when the claim can so easily be fact-checked? It was puzzling. Malcolm Gladwell posited a theory in his aptly named podcast, *Revisionist History*. He defended Brian Williams by building an argument that our memory is not infallible. As a matter of fact, it is wholly fallible. Gladwell unspooled a very plausible theory that the mind takes the bits and bytes of our memories and often rearranges the events. Gladwell himself told a story about the morning of 9/11, when he and a downstairs neighbour in his New York apartment building commiserated minutes after the second plane hit the tower. Both remember the moment clearly, but they could not agree where it happened, whether in Gladwell's apartment or in a café. Gladwell believes Williams didn't intentionally lie; rather, his memory altered the details without any real direct involvement from Williams himself. We all fall into this quicksand in our memories. How many times have you recounted an event only to have someone else who was present contradict the details? You may now be thinking, how could Brian Williams's memory of being shot at in a military helicopter—or not being shot at in a military helicopter—be hazy at all? The moment was too big. It was a military helicopter. He was sitting beside an army general, in a war zone. It wasn't inconsequential.

But Dax Shepard recounted an interesting story on his podcast, *Armchair Expert*. He was recalling a dramatic moment of brutality he and his older brother witnessed between his mother and his stepfather. Each remembered the incident clearly because it traumatized them both. Except each brother remembered the incident happening in different houses.

In different cities.

How can an earth-shattering moment—recalled with full emotion—be remembered so differently by eyewitnesses? Back in January 1986, I was working at an advertising agency in Toronto. One day I was sitting in the office I shared with an art director named Steve Chase, and we were working on an ad campaign. Suddenly, someone in the hall shouted the space shuttle *Challenger* had exploded on takeoff. We all ran to a television in the agency and watched the replay in horror. One of our colleagues was Philippe Garneau, brother of astronaut Marc Garneau, who had flown aboard *Challenger* just two years before. The moment was made more acute as Philippe stood behind us watching wide-eyed. When Steve and I went back to our office, we sat in stunned silence. I remember it was hard for us to get back to work. A very consequential, historic day. Recently, I asked Steve how he remembered that time. He said he was in Florida on a golf vacation and actually watched the launch live. He wasn't beside me in the office. He wasn't in Toronto. He wasn't even in Canada. Now Steve has altered my memory of that event.

It was yet another *Rashomon* moment.

But can one mind contain its own *Rashomon* angles?

Could Malcolm Gladwell be right about Brian Williams?

Williams's disgrace wasn't the only tremor at NBC's monolithic *30 Rock* in that period. Three of its on-air talent had left high-profile shows. To steady the ship, Andrew Lack was brought back as chair of NBC News. Lack was a legendary news executive who had run the department back in the nineties. He had also mentored a young Brian Williams. As his exile was nearing its end, Williams suggested to Lack he could return as a breaking-news anchor on MSNBC. It was a way to ease him back onto the airwaves. Breaking news and special events. Lack agreed, and when his six-month suspension ended, Williams returned to on-air duties, often alongside respected MSNBC host Rachel Maddow.

Then in 2016, Lack took Williams out for dinner to propose a new show. Lack wanted to mount a late-night news program that gathered the onslaught of election news that was now continually breaking after the sun went down. It would air Monday to Thursday at 11 p.m. Williams liked the idea. The late-night hour was a humble way for a chastised anchor to re-emerge from purgatory. Williams characterized the show as "self-cancelling"—meaning that once the election was over, so was the show.

But as with so many things in life, timing is everything. *The 11th Hour with Brian Williams* began on September 16, 2016, and it launched into a perfect storm. Election news was coming fast and furious—much of it downloading heavily after 7 p.m. Traditional news cycles were turned upside down. Every day—almost every hour—Donald Trump brashly overturned apple carts as he bulldozed his way through the primaries. As *Vanity Fair* writer Emily Jane Fox put it, 11 p.m. was the new 5 a.m. and news programming was suddenly the hot new reality show. Viewers couldn't get enough. Even MSNBC's Rachel Maddow, who together with her team spends the day meticulously preparing their in-depth hour, was throwing their script out the window minutes before showtime and starting all over again because a thunderbolt had landed on their desk. Into this news maelstrom landed *The 11th Hour*. It was a half hour of thoughtful interviews with White House correspondents, former prosecutors and legal experts talking about the late-breaking news. The ensuing conversation would try to make sense of the day and bring additional colour to the reporting. The show was the perfect containment vessel for exploding news and for catching a policy decision by the tail as it tried to scamper unseen into the late hour.

The show had a tone that separated it from CNN. There was no confrontation. No cage matches between political gladiators at opposite ends of the political spectrum. At the end of the broadcast, the mat wasn't stained UFC red. Instead, Brian Williams navigated a thoughtful half hour. He juggled up to four guests simultaneously. He asked intriguing questions, the kind guests are delighted to be asked—interesting questions that demanded interesting answers. The guests had to be in the moment, because Williams would gather threads and build upon replies. He rarely seemed to rely on the notes in front of him. Williams was a listener. It wasn't just question-to-question, it was question-to-thought-to-question. Then the unthinkable happened. On November 8, 2016, Donald Trump won the election. It was a gift to Brian Williams.

In January 2017, the program was expanded to an hour and in the spring it moved to five days a week. *The 11th Hour* finished 2017 as the top-rated cable news show in its time slot with an average total viewership of 1.5 million. That gave MSNBC its best ratings ever in that time period and *Forbes* pointed out that it was the first time any MSNBC show had finished the year ahead of Fox News among total viewers in prime time since 1999. On many nights, the program was MSNBC's only number-one show. *The 11th Hour* was a bona fide hit.

A year before that, it was almost unimaginable that Brian Williams could even return to air, let alone helm a hit show. He handles the multiple guests with ease. He asks informed questions. In the contentious political talk show universe, his show feels like a calm meeting spot to analyze the day that was. His wit and self-deprecating humour is on full display. In the beginning, it was difficult to book guests, as booking agents, journalists and pundits were tentative about the venture. Now the spots are filled every night. Williams lavishes his guests with splendid introductions and heaps on an additional tablespoon of sugar when thanking them. He says it's his thing. It appears genuine and the guests clearly appreciate it. Those sumptuous welcomes and the verbal goodbye hugs, delivered with a slightly forlorn look in Williams's eyes, feel as if he is really saying, Thanks for allowing me back into the club. At least it does a teeny bit.

But more than anything—more than anything—Brian Williams looks invigorated. He is using his full skill set. He is pulling tools out of his belt he never had the chance to wield while reading a teleprompter. He has Houdinied his way out of that Cronkite straitjacket and juggles the program's various spinning plates with an ease that would interest the talent scout on *The Ed Sullivan Show*. He doesn't shy away from this pivot, either. In a recent instalment, he was asking his panel how they reacted to a spectacular double-back retraction the Trump administration had done that day. Williams said something to the effect of, "I've seen some big walk-backs in my time, commented on them on this show and had a few of my own." The guests chuckled at his self-awareness.

All of this raises the big question: Could it be Brian Williams's monumental mistake has landed him the late-night talk show he always dreamed of?

It has all the elements: A bewitching time slot. Multiple high-level guests. Room to be thoughtful. Ample opportunity to be sharp and funny and quick. He may not be interviewing Tom Hanks about his latest movie, but Williams is narrating a far more important and fascinating storyline—the presidential ride of a lifetime. In 2019, *Forbes* published an article titled "How Brian Williams Made 11 p.m. the Hottest Hour in Cable News." The piece said, "If ever a show was created to perfectly showcase the talents of its star anchor, that would be *The 11th Hour*," and went on to quote Edward R. Murrow, who said of television, "The medium has enormous power . . . but it has no character, no conscience of its own." *Forbes* said Williams gives it both. It was an absolution from a magazine with a long memory. The article also noted that *The 11th Hour* closed 2019 as the top-rated 11 p.m. show in cable news, for the third year in a row, with an average total audience of 1.6 million viewers.

Brian Williams jumped out of that chopper and just may have parachuted into something he had long dreamed of.

It's a reminder to us all—be careful what you wish for.

5.

Billy Joel

They Sit at the Bar and Put Bread in My Jar

On February 6, 1964, Billy Joel experienced a life-altering moment. It would shake his foundation, redirect his career path and be forever underlined, stamped and filed in his memory bank. It was the night the Beatles played on *The Ed Sullivan Show*.

He was fourteen years old, watching television in his Hicksville, Long Island, home. He stared at the four mesmerizing musicians on the tube and saw four average-looking guys with long hair. They played their own instruments and wrote their own songs. They were from a strange place called Liverpool, which he thought sounded even worse than Hicksville. Joel said he and his friends all went "nuts" when they saw the Beatles, because suddenly, the Beatles offered an alternative to a blue-collar working-class life. He remembers thinking that night you could earn a living playing rock music. "This is possible. This can be done."

William Martin Joel was born in 1949 in the Bronx, but his family moved out to Long Island when he was a toddler. They settled in Hicksville, in an area of that town where one of the first real prototypes of planned suburbia was developed, called Levittown. Designed by Abraham Levitt and built by his Levitt & Sons company, Levittown offered postwar vets and baby boomer families of modest means a way to own their own home, a dream that was simply unattainable in big cities. Abraham was a horticulturist who excelled at the landscaping and gardening of instant communities. Son Alfred was an innovator who experimented with progressive ways of designing and constructing houses. Son William later became the public face of the Levitt company, marketing and selling the homes with a Madison Avenue flourish and gracing magazine covers as the "King of Suburbia." The houses, spaced sixty feet apart, were designed to be assembled quickly by on-site workers using twenty-seven production-line steps to erect a structure in a single day. Levittown was also a segregated community, because Levitt refused to sell homes to people of colour. By 1953, with a population of seventy thousand, Levittown was the largest community in the United States with no Black residents. Billy's only exposure to Black people, and especially Black music, came through the radio. From this cookie-cutter world, a young Billy Joel would emerge and run.

His father, Howard Joel, was from a prominent Jewish textile family in Nuremberg. When the Nazis seized their factory in 1938, the family fled Germany and Howard ended up in the United States via Cuba. America had already hit its quota of European Jews, but Cuba's allocation offered a more immediate way in. Billy's mother, Rosalind, had emigrated with her family from England in 1914 so that his maternal grandfather could avoid serving in the First World War. Howard was a brooding man who worked as an engineer for General Electric during the day and was a classical pianist who played Beethoven in his home at night. He met Rosalind when the two of them were performing in a college production of *Pirates of Penzance* and they married not long after. But in 1957, when Billy was eight, Howard left the family and moved to Vienna. He remarried and started a second family (Billy has a stepbrother there who is a well-known music conductor), leaving Billy and·his older sister to be raised by their single mother. As Billy later said, although his father did send a cheque every month, they went hungry often. Rosalind took on a series of odd jobs to survive. He wouldn't set eyes on his father again until 1972.

While it was his father who was the pianist, it was his mother who encouraged Billy to take piano lessons. He began pounding the piano at the age of four and immediately showed a natural ability. His piano teacher, Miss Francis, also taught ballet, so as a teen, Joel was often taunted and beat up by the rough kids down the street who would yell, "Hey Billy, where's your tutu?" So Joel decided to take up boxing at the Police Boys Club. The welterweight won twenty-three of his twenty-six bouts. His boxing skills meant the taunting stopped and the shape of Joel's nose changed forever. In 1964, the year of the Beatles, he joined his first band, called the Echoes. They played their first gig at a local church and Joel revelled in the experience. It was the perfect trifecta: the noise the band made sounded pretty good, a girl he had a crush on actually looked at him and the priest handed the band members fifteen dollars each after the show—which felt like fifteen thousand to a fourteen-year-old. There was never any question after that night. "The door locked behind me," Joel said. "That's it. That's what I'm doing." So he dropped out of high school and course-corrected to rock 'n' roll.

The following year, the Echoes became the Lost Souls; then in 1967, Joel was enticed to join another band. Irwin Mazur, whose father owned a rock 'n' roll club on Long Island called My House, was watching the Lost Souls play there one night, covering Top 40 songs. Mazur didn't like the band, but he liked the keyboard player and asked Joel to join a band he managed called the Hassles.

Joel took him up on the offer and began writing songs with an R&B drift, influenced by Sam & Dave with a liberal splash of the Rascals. The band managed to record two albums, which gave them some local acclaim. (The Hassles' bassist, Howard Blauvelt, would reappear a few years later in the band Ram Jam, best known for its 1977 hit "Black Betty.")

Two years later, Joel left the Hassles with drummer Jon Small to form a heavy metal duo called Attila. They landed a record contract with Epic in 1970 and recorded one self-titled album. The music was interesting, a mix of Deep Purple seasoned with Jethro Tull topped with some Yes keyboard acrobatics. But the album cover foretold the future: it featured Small and Joel in medieval armour standing in a meat locker. Indeed, the record was stone-cold dead on arrival.

With yet another band that went nowhere, Joel felt aimless and needed to find a way to earn money. He became a rock critic for a magazine called *Changes*, writing reviews for twenty-five dollars an article, but became increasingly uncomfortable criticizing other musicians. He tried house painting, he mowed lawns, he worked at a typewriter factory and he even did time on an oyster boat, though he hated getting up at five on cold mornings.

When Joel left Attila he took something with him: Jon Small's wife, Elizabeth. When he told Small he was in love with his wife, Small broke Joel's already-broken nose with one punch. That experience tipped him into despair. Three bands had hit dead ends, his songs were languishing, he had no high-school diploma, he had no money and his good friend had just punched him in the face. He spiralled and slipped down into a very dark place. Not long after, while staying at Mazur's house, he made a half-hearted attempt at suicide by washing down a handful of anxiety medication with some furniture polish (he left a suicide note that would later inspire the lyrics to "Tomorrow Is Today"). When he woke up in the hospital, his first thought was, "Oh great, I can't even do this right." He was put on suicide watch and received treatment for depression.

Attila had pounded the rock 'n' roll star dream out of Billy's system and the record business had pounded the hope out of his dream. He told Mazur he was quitting music. Yet he had written some good songs since Attila folded and Mazur didn't want him to give up. The very thought of getting pulled back in to the record business was exhausting to Billy. He told Mazur he would give him thirty days to find a record deal, but after that he was going to head to the Midwest with Elizabeth and her young son and get a simple bartending gig. He was fed up and done.

Mazur had a brother who worked in the art department of Paramount Records, so the two of them compiled a voice and piano demo of five Billy Joel songs, including "She's Got a Way," "Tomorrow Is Today" and "Everybody Loves You Now." First stop, same address—Paramount. But the head of the A&R department turned him down, saying they were already working with a piano-playing singer-songwriter from England by the name of Elton John. One day, however, while the tape was playing in Mazur's brother's office, a guy named Michael Lang popped his head in to ask who was singing. Lang had been the promoter of Woodstock and ran one of the dozens of small record labels housed under the Paramount banner. He liked what he heard and asked to borrow the tape. Then he left for Los Angeles.

Lang took that tape to Artie Ripp, an L.A.-based independent record plugger. Ripp had learned the trade the old-fashioned way, by "selling a hundred records over the table and a thousand under the table." He had started Kama Sutra Records, then Buddah, signing acts like the Lovin' Spoonful, the 1910 Fruitgum Company and the TV version of the Cowsills—the Partridge Family. He eventually sold those labels to a larger company and stayed on to run the business, but the relationship slowly started to sour. After a clash with the owners, Ripp left to start yet another label called Family Productions and made a deal with Gulf & Western to distribute the records.

So it was that Lang played Billy Joel's tape for Artie Ripp that night. He listened, then asked Lang three questions: Does the kid singing also play the piano? Did the kid write the melody? And did the kid also write the lyrics?

When he heard yes three times in a row, Ripp leaned in. Lang told him nobody was interested in the singer and he had been turned down by just about every label in the country. But Ripp heard something on that tape. He heard a songwriter who didn't just write bubblegum lyrics like "Yummy, yummy, yummy, I got love in my tummy." To Ripp's ear, this kid was more like a poet or a painter. He asked Lang for the name and number of Billy Joel's manager and reached for the phone.

Lang said, "You're not going to call him now, are you? It's four in the morning in New York!"

Ripp was already dialling, saying, "Of course I'm calling him now. This kid is just waiting for a call like this. He's waiting for a call where somebody says, 'I love Billy Joel and I want to sign him!'"

Somewhere on Long Island, a phone rang in Irwin Mazur's bedroom in the middle of the night. When he answered in a groggy voice, Ripp yelled, "Whaddya want for the kid?" Which must have been a jarring moment for Mazur. Ripp said he loved Billy Joel's sound and wanted to sign him to a record deal; he would guarantee him one album and one single and give him a monthly allowance so Joel could concentrate on writing more songs and polishing his performance chops. Now Mazur was sitting up, wide awake. He told Ripp he wanted an album budget for Billy. Ripp told Mazur not to play the tape for anybody, not to

54

talk to anybody and to meet him on Tuesday morning in front of the Gulf & Western building.

As promised, inside the thirty-day deadline, Irwin Mazur had found twenty-year-old Billy Joel a record deal. Then Mazur and Joel made a classic mistake.

Artie Ripp knew his way around the record business and he really knew his way around the four corners of an artist contract. Probably due to Mazur's desperation to find a deal for Billy inside thirty days and Billy's lack of business savvy as a young musician, they signed away all the critical deal points that an artist lives on: future publishing rights, copyrights and royalties. Billy didn't know anything about contracts and years later said he probably would have signed anything to get a deal at that point. He just wanted to write songs for other artists and not be a front man for a band anymore.

It was the age-old record deal quicksand: Billy Joel was certainly not the first artist in history to sign away all his rights. The music business is littered with similar stories. But unlike most of those stories, this particular mistake would have a positive effect on Billy's career to this very day.

With lopsided record deal in hand, Billy recorded his first album for Family Productions, titled *Cold Spring Harbor*. But a strange thing happened when Artie Ripp was mastering the record. Unbeknownst to Ripp and his sound engineer, the tape machine they mixed the master recording to was running slow. At the start of recording sessions and especially during mastering sessions, the absolute rule of thumb is to do speed tests on all studio tape machines. Like guitar strings, they go out of tune with heavy use. (The Beatles often sped up recordings to put an interesting effect on vocals, as Lennon did with "Lucy in the Sky with Diamonds"—creatively and on purpose.) But for some reason, the speed test was not done in Billy Joel's mastering session. Because the album was slow when mastered, the songs sped up when played at regular speed on a turntable. This made Billy's vocals a half-octave higher. When he excitedly put the new record on the turntable at an album-listening party for his friends, Billy discovered he sounded like one of the singing Chipmunks. He was so upset and humiliated, he smashed the LP against the wall. With a few thousand records already pressed, it would cost serious money to fix the album at this late stage and the small label seemed reluctant to cough up the money. Then the original tape and acetate mysteriously went missing.

The only thing Ripp could do to salvage the situation was to send Billy out on a European and U.S. tour to play for the music press, radio people and retailers. The songs were good even if the record wasn't. Billy and the band travelled with a little camper trailer and survived on peanut butter and jelly sandwiches and a minuscule allowance. Most of the time they opened for other acts: some were a good match; others were terrible. It was a difficult time. Joel had never wanted to be the front man for a band, and now here he was, centre stage as a gigging solo artist.

While out on the grinding tour promoting the record, he wasn't hearing his songs on the radio and he wasn't seeing the LP in record stores. As it turned out, people couldn't buy the album even if they wanted to. Gulf & Western was having financial problems and the records weren't being distributed. That lack of liquidity starved Artie Ripp's company and the money Ripp was sending to underwrite the tour slowed to a trickle. Then it simply stopped coming. Billy Joel spent six months on the road promoting an album that wasn't available and came back with absolutely nothing to show for it. Ripp owed them money and Billy wanted to figure out a way to get out of the onerous contract.

So Billy, along with Elizabeth and her son, and Mazur and his wife, decided to move to L.A. in late 1972. Rather than trying to wrangle results long distance, being near Ripp in L.A. would allow them to quietly sniff out the money trail. Los Angeles was the epicentre of the recording industry and Billy needed a west coast lawyer and accountant to (hopefully) extricate him from Ripp's contract. Plus, as Mazur said at the time, "It was easier to be broke in L.A. than in New York." It was a very thorny situation: Joel and Mazur needed paycheques, Ripp was chained to a contract with Gulf & Western, Gulf & Western wasn't letting Ripp out of the contract and the corporation wasn't distributing Ripp's records.

Meanwhile, Billy needed to support Elizabeth and her son, so he decided to find work with the only real skill he had—playing piano. He auditioned at a few bars, got a couple of job offers and took the one at the Executive Room lounge at 3953 Wilshire Boulevard. He chose that gig because it was the closest one to the shabby motel he was living in. The bar (long gone) was a hole in the wall with a sign promising cocktails and entertainment. It was frequented by a crowd of regulars, from businessmen and real estate agents to folks who didn't have anywhere else to be. Billy didn't want Family Productions to know he was in L.A. trying to find a way out of the contract and he certainly didn't want the record label trying to slice a commission out of his piano bar earnings. So he used his middle name and billed himself as Bill Martin, performing nightly at the keyboards, 9 p.m. until 2 a.m. He got union scale and it was the first steady money he had earned in a long time. That temporary, desperate gig would inspire a profound moment in Billy Joel's life.

A song.

Not just a good song, not just an excellent song, but a song that would become a showstopper. His encore song. His audience sing-along-that-shakes-the-foundations-of-the-stadium song. The song everybody waits for in a forest of hit songs. Five and a half minutes that elicits an automatic standing ovation at every performance. A song that today has close to 150 million views of its official video on YouTube.

That song, of course, was "Piano Man."

It's a story song, done in 6/8 waltz time. The lyrics were all drawn from his six months playing piano incognito at the Executive Room. Each line is a finely sketched character study of the people who find solace in a dimly lit bar, watching the ice melt in their drinks as the dreams melt in their lives. Bill Martin studied their faces night after night while playing tunes for tips. The piano sounded like a carnival, the microphone smelled like a beer and the people were all real. There was John, the yearning bartender, Paul, the real estate agent writing a novel that would never be published, and Davy, who never meant to spend a career in the navy. The feisty waitress practising politics was none other than Elizabeth, who had also landed a job at the lounge. And, of course, there was the piano man.

The imagery so vivid, the hopelessness so palpable, the microphone so pungent. Billy was slumming it in the Executive Room and even the regulars could sense it. But the gig was a lifeline and, as Artie Ripp had realized on that first listen, Billy could paint an unforgettable picture.

Meanwhile, one of his stops on the *Cold Spring Harbor* promotional/non-promotional tour in Philadelphia had been recorded by the sponsoring radio station there. WMMR-FM started playing a song from that performance called "Captain Jack." It was a moody song with biting lyrics Billy had written while living in Oyster Bay, Long Island. Across from his apartment there was a drug dealer named Captain Jack and Billy would watch suburban kids lining up for their fix. The song captured the apathy of an aimless rich kid using drugs to escape the bleakness of the suburbs. Captain Jack wasn't about Jack Daniel's; it was about heroin ("Captain Jack" rhymes with "smack"). Unbeknownst to Billy, "Captain Jack" became the most requested song in WMMR's history. A local A&R guy from Columbia Records told head office in New York that the most-requested song in Philadelphia was by a new singer-songwriter. Nobody seemed to know who he was, but the A&R guy suggested they track him down. When Clive Davis, the legendary record executive, was told the mysterious singer was Billy Joel, he remembered seeing Billy at a music festival and, when he put two and two together, wanted to sign him. Through the recording industry grapevine, Columbia learned Billy was managed by Irwin Mazur and set up a meeting at the Beverly Hills Hotel. There, Davis told Mazur that Billy Joel belonged on the Columbia label. Mazur agreed.

Meanwhile, Atlantic Records had also caught wind of "Captain Jack" and approached Artie Ripp to talk about a deal. That brought Ripp back into Billy's orbit before Billy could find a way to squirm out of their contract. Ripp actually negotiated a lucrative deal for Billy with Atlantic head Ahmet Ertegun. Of course, Ripp didn't know Mazur was talking to Columbia, and when he found out, he wasn't happy. Suddenly, Billy Joel went from struggling musician to having two major record labels vying for his services. When presented with the two options, Billy wanted to go with Columbia because it was the home of Bob Dylan. Ripp tried to convince him to go with Atlantic, but Billy was firm. That meant Ripp had to backtrack on his handshake deal with Ertegun.

Piano Man, the album, would be released on Columbia Records in 1973. Although it cracked the Top 30, it didn't attain gold record status until much later, when the immense success of *The Stranger* ignited sales of all Billy's previous albums. Artie Ripp's hermetically sealed contract meant he would get twenty-eight cents per album on the sales of the next ten Billy Joel albums, which over time would net Ripp an estimated $20 million. Years later, the powerful and volatile CBS Records president Walter Yetnikoff threatened to blackball Artie Ripp right out of the music business unless he sold Billy's publishing rights to CBS, rights that included *Piano Man*. Ripp had no choice but to acquiesce and Yetnikoff gave the rights back to Billy as a present on his twenty-ninth birthday.

To date, Billy Joel has sold over 150 million records worldwide and has recorded thirty-three consecutive Top 40 hits, twice as many as Bruce Springsteen, the Eagles or Fleetwood Mac. He is the sixth-best-selling recording artist of all time and the third-best-selling solo artist. Since 2014, Joel has had a residency at Madison Square Garden, where he performs once a month, nearing seventy-five consecutive sold-out shows at the time of this writing. He has won six Grammy Awards including the prestigious Grammy Legend Award, just one of many honours bestowed on Joel over the years.

Piano company Steinway & Sons has honoured him with a painted portrait that hangs in the fabled Steinway Hall in Manhattan. Of all the chart-topping songs Billy Joel has written, it was "Piano Man" that was selected for preservation by the U.S. Library of Congress National Recording Registry, cited for being "culturally, historically and aesthetically significant." When Ray Charles inducted him into the Rock and Roll Hall of Fame in 1999, the piano great referred to Joel as "the piano man."

So many young recording artists sign away their futures and come away with nothing but bitterness and crippling legal bills. While there's no doubt Billy Joel's towering talent would have eventually surfaced, it was his mistake and the subsequent trip to Los Angeles to fix that mistake that led to arguably the greatest thing he will always be remembered for.

His classic, career-defining signature song.

6.

Steve Madden

The Shoe of Wall Street

Born in 1958, Steven Madden grew up in Long Island, New York, the youngest of three boys in a family that was half Irish, half Jewish. His father owned a textile business, and although Madden says he was a smart entrepreneur, he wasn't a risk-taker. He was filled with the fear of going broke as a result of growing up during the Depression. It was the constant subject of talk at the dinner table. But despite that fear, his father provided a solid middle-class life for his family.

Madden describes his younger self as small in stature with a big mouth and that obnoxiousness often made him a leader. He got into trouble at school frequently because he had undiagnosed attention deficit disorder. While school was not easy for him, Madden was a reader. His favourite subject was entrepreneurs who began with nothing but achieved great things in life. He marvelled at the stories of Hollywood moguls like Louis B. Mayer and Samuel Goldwyn. Looking back, he was drawn to the intersection of art and commerce.

The drive to succeed was instilled early and his lust for money burned hot even at a young age. He envied his friends' fancy ten-speed bikes, which the Maddens could never afford. He dreamed of one day flying first class. When he turned sixteen, he found a job that would forever alter the direction of his life. It was a shoe store called Toulouse. What began merely as a high school job soon turned into a passion. Madden discovered he loved the creativity of shoes, and he learned what women want. It was the mid-seventies and platform shoes for men were big sellers. The owner of Toulouse was a twenty-seven-year-old named Lance Rubin. Because he was innovative and designed many of the shoes his store sold, wholesalers would often tap him for input on new designs. Madden became obsessed with shoes, hungry to understand which shoes became popular and which didn't. He learned a lot about the shoe business from Rubin, who was unlike any of the old-school businessmen Madden had seen around his father's textile company. Rubin was young, he had long hair, he drove a Mercedes, he was bold and creative. He ignited a big spark in sixteen-year-old Steve Madden.

When he graduated high school, Madden went to the University of Miami in Florida, but he didn't enjoy his time there. He dropped out and went back to Long Island to work as a salesman at another shoe store. But Lance Rubin called him out of the blue. He had just opened a wholesale business in New York called L.J. Simone and wanted Madden to join him. Madden happily reunited with his old boss and together they grew the company to over $40 million in sales. Rubin designed shoes and sourced product from factories around the world. Madden learned the shoe business top to bottom there, from designing shoes to shipping shoes to going out on the road selling shoes to retailers and department stores. Rubin taught Madden how to use different types of shoe construction and how to market a product. It was a heady eight-year period for Madden.

He was single and making a lot of money. Because he was working so hard during the day, he felt he deserved to do some hard partying at night to let off some steam. He began drinking heavily and doing a lot of cocaine, which eventually started to affect his work. Some friends knew he needed help, sat him down and steered him to Alcoholics Anonymous. As Madden says, AA saved his life.

After he got sober, he re-evaluated his life. He was thirty years old and the thought of starting his own business was beginning to tug at him. So he scraped together $1,100 to start Steve Madden Ltd. in 1990. He designed and manufactured five hundred pairs of shoes and paid the doorman at his apartment building $60 a day to drive him around New York because Madden didn't have a licence. He sold the shoes out of the trunk of the doorman's little red car for $16 a pair, and retailers sold them for $24. His aim was to design shoes for his contemporaries, people in their thirties. But Madden noticed a strange thing happening. His chunky-heeled boots and platform shoes caught on with teenagers. His big hit was the Mary Lou, a big-toed Mary Jane–style patent leather shoe inspired by the glitter rock he loved in the seventies. Teens, whose mothers and grandmothers wore stilettos, gobbled them up. It was a surprise to Madden. But he quickly realized the teen market had been ignored by shoe manufacturers and was completely underserved, so he redirected his company to focus on the Gen X market. These teens had their own style, their own music and their own attitude; Madden had a good sense of their vibe and was able to tap right into it. Teens loved Steve Madden's shoes because they offered quirky high fashion they could afford. By catering to that very large youth market the shoe industry had essentially abandoned, Madden did about $500,000 in sales his first year alone. He opened his first retail store in SoHo in 1993.

Madden was providing, and in some ways pioneering, high fashion design at an affordable price. Teens had never had this kind of product offering in the shoe department. All of a sudden, kids could buy a pair of sexy shoes for $70 that looked just like $800 Manolo Blahniks. Madden carved out a niche somewhere between Christian Louboutin and 9 West. However, upscale stores like Barney's refused to carry Steve Madden shoes, even though all the employees were wearing them. Madden also wasn't welcomed into the exclusive club of high-end shoe designers. His peers in the Council of Fashion Designers of America did not acknowledge him. He hadn't apprenticed at any of the top fashion houses or spent any career time in Paris or Milan. Madden had not even studied design; he was just a brash upstart with a great flair for footwear. That outsider feeling would both wound him and fuel Madden's desire to succeed wildly in an industry that shunned him.

His company's revenues were growing, but most of that revenue was being reinvested in the business. Although Madden was becoming a rock star in the shoe business, holding court at his SoHo store and sitting courtside at Knicks games, the reality of his existence was very different. He didn't have a lot of money in the bank. He carried a constant anxiety, inherited from his father, that his business could go under any day. As Madden describes it, he was successfully living hand-to-mouth. He needed capital to grow.

That's when he ran into Danny Porush.

Porush was a childhood friend who now worked for a brokerage firm called Stratton Oakmont, which he had cofounded with Jordan Belfort. Porush told Madden the firm was in the business of raising money for small companies. Because he believed in Madden's creativity, he could take the company public and raise $6 million. At first, Madden didn't believe him. He only had one store in SoHo at that point, which is not the typical size of business that goes public. But Porush disagreed, saying, "No, we're like dream makers." He also said the initial public offering could put over half a million dollars in Madden's pocket. That got his attention.

Although the pitch sounded amazing, the reality was less glamourous. While the name on the door sounded like a highly polished Wall Street company, Stratton Oakmont was actually a phone bank boiler room located in Long Island. Belmont and Porush had figured out a way to circumvent Securities and Exchange Commission regulations and make a killing with stock schemes. The firm with the country club name was actually a "pump and dump" joint. Essentially, they'd pump up a stock price artificially, take it public then dump it on unsuspecting investors for a big profit.

Here's how the SEC enforcement attorney who would eventually be assigned to the case described the scheme. First, Stratton Oakmont needed a company with a good story that Stratton salespeople could use to seduce investors. Then that company would be converted into publicly traded shares through a Stratton initial public offering, or IPO. However, these shares were not really sold to the public, but to Stratton. Since it's illegal for an underwriter to buy more than a small percentage of the IPO stock it issues, Stratton employed "flippers"—selectively recruited friends who bought all the IPO shares and sold them back to Stratton for a small, prearranged profit. For example, if the flippers purchased shares for $4 each, they would sell them back to Stratton for $4.25, resulting in a nice little risk-free profit for the flippers and a handy smoke screen for Stratton.

Second, Stratton Oakmont would attract and groom investors by letting them in on stocks that consistently provided small profits. Once they gained investors' trust, they would tell them that a really hot IPO was coming down the pike and the clients could get in on the ground floor at (say) $4 per share.

Stage three was a bait and switch. Shortly before the IPO, Stratton brokers would tell investors that the stock was so hot, they could only offer a small block of shares at the $4 price. When investors started to get cold feet, the Stratton brokers would pressure them to stick with the plan, saying, "I made money for you before—now you don't trust me?" Many investors were persuaded to stay in, committing hundreds of thousands of dollars and sometimes their life savings, assuming Stratton would buy them the hot shares as close to the $4 price range as possible.

Step four was market manipulation. Say 1 million IPO shares had been issued and Stratton knew it had $12 million of investors' money ready to invest. Stratton now needed the stock to go from $4 per share to $12 before selling to the investors. So the firm simply bought and sold shares between Stratton accounts or to and from flippers, with each trade incrementally increasing the price: $4.25, then $4.50, then $4.75, all the way up to $12 per share. These price increases would happen in minutes, a common first-day trading pattern for hot IPOs back in the nineties, so the manipulation wasn't obvious. If investors tried to buy the stock before it hit $12, their orders were conveniently "lost" or Stratton simply didn't return their calls.

The fifth and last step was to sell high and move on. When the stock hit $12, Stratton finally executed its customers' buy orders and pocketed the $12 million, since Stratton was the only seller. These were the same orders Stratton had promised their investors they would buy somewhere around the $4 mark. To avoid SEC scrutiny, Stratton would support the $12 stock price for about a month before letting it drop like a stone on the market. At that point, they had stolen millions of dollars from their investors, who were left with worthless stock nobody else wanted to buy. Then it was on to another IPO and a new list of lambs to slaughter. And that's how Stratton Oakmont bilked many investors out of their bank accounts.

So it was that Stratton Oakmont offered to take Steve Madden Ltd. public. The company fit the profile. The business had a good product, it had a good story and owner Steve Madden, who always feared his business was about to go bust and who was driven to prove he could succeed in an industry that snubbed him, was all in.

That decision would turn out to be a fateful mistake.

As per the well-oiled scheme, Stratton Oakmont inflated the Steve Madden stock price before selling it to unsuspecting investors. On the day of the IPO, the shares went from $4 to $18 in about sixty minutes, generating about $7 million. At the end of the day, Madden netted half a million bucks. Flush with that success, Madden become a Stratton flipper. He used his windfall to start buying and flipping Stratton stocks whenever Stratton called. He used the profits to expand his shoe company. Sales went from $5 million in 1993 to $83 million by 1998. Madden says the change in his life was extraordinary, going from an eviction notice to a private jet in less than two hundred days. Over seven years, he participated in twenty-two pump and dumps with Stratton. By the year 2000, Madden had used those ill-gotten gains to build a $240 million shoe empire. He knew in his heart it was all too good to be true, as well as wrong, but the thrill of getting away with it was exhilarating. He lied to himself that there were a lot of grey areas in the world of stock trading. Part of his greed was rooted in Madden's constant fear of going broke. He believed money was the holy grail. When money is everything, you'll do anything to get it. As Madden says in hindsight, money is a powerful drug. And he was addicted.

Eventually the SEC started to investigate Stratton Oakmont. In early 2000, founders Jordan Belfort and Danny Porush were put under house arrest. Faced with overwhelming evidence and long jail sentences, they cut deals with the government and began ratting on their friends. One of those friends was Steve Madden. After being implicated in Stratton's stock manipulation scheme, Madden was charged with securities fraud and money laundering. He pleaded innocent initially and was brought to trial, where he faced both civil and criminal charges. Refusing to cop a plea, he was eventually found guilty. He was ordered to repay $4 million to settle claims and received two forty-one-month prison terms that ran concurrently. Belfort, the master schemer, got only twenty-two months; Porush served thirty-nine. Through the pressure of the ordeal, Madden had an addiction relapse. The press gobbled up the story, ripe with stock schemes, SEC investigations, trials and a famous shoe designer who was headed to the clink. The entire Stratton Oakmont story, including Madden's participation, was so juicy, it was made into a Hollywood motion picture titled *The Wolf of Wall Street*, directed by Martin Scorsese.

Madden was sent to a minimum-security prison in Florida. He was forty-five at the time and his only concern was how to survive. It was a uniquely painful time for someone who had been riding high—he now had no good food, no sex, no privacy and no family. He shared a small living area with two other inmates. It was a spartan existence. He attended court-ordered alcohol rehab. Deciding to try and use the time constructively, he read an average of four books a week. He taught business classes to other inmates. He pumped iron daily, transforming his body over the next two and a half years. He also learned it was impossible to run a business from prison. Sales dropped without his leadership. The footwear become dressier, more expensive and less quirky. Although the business lost customers, the higher prices kept the company profitable. His management team took care of him financially by paying Madden $700,000 in yearly consulting fees. Work colleagues visited often.

When Madden was eventually released in 2005 after thirty-one months, he was barred from serving as an officer of his company until 2008. But he considers this time a pivotal moment in his company's history. "When I got out of prison, it was a moment with a lot of energy and a whole lot of grit," he says. "It took the company to another level. Bet you don't hear that a lot, right?" Madden feels both he and his company bounced to next-level achievements immediately after his prison release. He continued designing shoes and became the company's "creative and design chief." Within four years of his release, Steve Madden's company revenues soared to over half a billion dollars, with more stores opening and explosive sales growth online. Madden says that huge growth came from realizing his own limitations. When the company was small, he had been a good CEO. But once the company crossed a certain threshold through growth and acquisitions, he wasn't detail oriented enough to be CEO anymore. So he hired a better CEO and assembled a smart management team. Through all that expansion, the company stuck to Madden's founding philosophy: great design, great prices, great value.

When people go to prison, most wish it never happened to them and try to forget. But Steve Madden maintains he wouldn't change a thing about his life and doesn't regret a single day in jail. While he's not proud of all his choices, he believes everything he's done to date has brought him to where he is today. His abrasive personality softened. He's more empathetic. On prison visiting days, he watched other inmates surrounded by their families, while he was visited only by employees. He developed a longing for stability. Over time, he fell in love with one of his staff who came to visit him regularly. He proposed to Wendy Ballew in 2004 near a vending machine in the visiting room. He maintains he would never have married his wife and had his children had he not gone to prison.

When he was released, Madden says he was stronger physically, mentally and spiritually than he had ever been before. Incarceration made him sharper and more conscious of time. When he went back to work, he had to sit back and catch up because he had been disconnected from pop culture for such a long time. But he was patient, not a trait he had exhibited prior to his jail term. His colleagues saw a different man with a new perspective. When the company faced a problem, Madden would often say things like, "Seven years ago I was sitting in a jail cell. We aren't going to die if this shoe doesn't sell." Pre-jail, he was known to throw shoes across the room when things didn't go well.

Madden also developed a strong urge to give back. He started a program called Self Made, dedicated to supporting and promoting young entrepreneurs. He employed the inmates he did time with, giving them jobs at Steve Madden distribution centres around the country. He continues to work one-on-one with convicts as a mentor and is an active supporter of the Doe Fund, a nonprofit that provides paid transitional work, counselling and education to people with a history of homelessness and incarceration. Madden also does work with Defy Ventures, another nonprofit that helps ex-convicts get a second chance, because Madden knows a thing or two about second chances. When he ran into Martha Stewart shortly after she was released from prison for serving time for a stock trading scheme, he sensed a bond between them. Both had made mistakes, but the great thing about America is that you get another shot.

He is philosophical about mistakes now. During an interview with Guy Raz, Madden said mistakes can be a very good thing. Many of his company's mistakes eventually led to great things. If you are afraid of making mistakes, you get gun shy. And if you're gun shy, you'll never make the leap to big, brilliant ideas. Madden believes there are necessary mistakes in life. If you're not willing to fail, that means you are not reaching.

Today, his company has reached a market capitalization of over $3 billion. He is now divorced but loves spending time with his children. While he is a very wealthy man, Steve Madden says he has finally learned the hardest lesson of his life.

Money isn't everything.

Swanson's TV Dinners

The Problem with Leftovers

When Carl Swanson arrived in America in 1896, he had a tag around his neck that said, "Carl Swanson. Swedish. Send me to Omaha. I speak no English." The authorities did just that and soon seventeen-year-old Carl found himself standing in Nebraska. Carl was an enterprising man, and just three years later he had built up a wholesale food company handling eggs, milk and poultry. The sum total of his delivery apparatus comprised one wagon and a horse. But he clearly had a gift for the food business because by the late 1920s, Carl had seen the future of the industry and moved into food processing. He became the first midwestern dealer to recognize the potential of the newly patented quick-freezing technology. He was the first to automate the plucking and gutting of chickens and the first to mass-produce separated and powdered eggs. He parlayed his original $456 investment into a $60 million corporation that he christened C.A. Swanson & Sons. The Swanson family name would become the biggest, most recognizable name in Omaha, adorning libraries, schools and a university.

Carl's sons, Gilbert and Clarke, inherited their father's ability to anticipate opportunities. After his death in 1949, the brothers introduced a frozen chicken pot pie that was a runaway success. The company continued to thrive and grow.

Then, in 1953, they made a colossal mistake.

It was Thanksgiving and the Swanson brothers had massively overestimated the demand for frozen turkeys.

As a matter of fact, Swanson had 260 tons of unsold turkeys. On top of that, the company didn't have enough refrigerated space to store the surplus. So the panicked Swanson executives came up with a solution. They filled ten refrigerated boxcars with the frozen gobblers. Since the compressors worked only when the train was moving, Swanson had to keep the rail cars going back and forth between its headquarters in Nebraska and the east coast. The turkeys criss-crossed the country over and over again. It was a race against time to figure out how to save all that turkey.

Then Swanson salesman Gerry Thomas—who was probably feeling the heat of a white-hot poker coming from all that unsold inventory—had an idea.

He had just flown on Pan American Airways and noticed the airline served food in a three-compartment aluminum tray. He sent a sample tray to headquarters and suggested they sell the surplus turkey as a frozen dinner. Thomas drew up a quick diagram on a napkin showing one compartment for sweet potatoes, one for peas and another for turkey and gravy. Next, the Swanson kitchen experts had to figure out a way for all the food to cook at the same rate. Since it all had to go into the oven at the same time, synchronization was critical. Convenience was also a major marketing factor, so the cooking time was set at twenty-five minutes. As a pièce de résistance, the foil-topped tray could serve as both a cooking pan *and* a dinner plate.

This wasn't the first frozen food on the market. Clarence Birdseye had invented a system of flash-freezing and packaging frozen food back in 1923. Swanson wasn't even the first company to offer frozen dinners in compartmentalized trays. That innovation is credited to the One-Eyed Eskimo brand, started by two other brothers named Albert and Meyer Bernstein, who rolled out packaged frozen dinners in aluminum trays in 1949. But what would make Swanson so successful was its incredibly innovative marketing.

Because Swanson trademarked the name "TV Dinner."

The Swanson TV Dinner packaging itself was novel: it was designed to look like an actual TV set, with faux wood panelling, a screen and tuning knobs. And the tray was small enough to fit comfortably on someone's lap. The timing was perfect. In 1954, America was in the grip of a futuristic wave. The war was over and the country was now enjoying the many innovations developed in the war, from aerosol cans to nylons. Science fiction was all the rage. In particular, the public was gaga over a brand-new piece of transformative technology. The television set was the latest in the line of entertainment centrepieces families would gather around, which had begun with the upright piano, then progressed to the radio. Thirty-three million TVs were purchased that year and soon 56 percent of the population owned one.

Then Swanson made its second big mistake. Although the company was desperate, they were initially skeptical about the idea of frozen dinners. So they hedged their bets by ordering only five thousand trays, then recruited a small assembly line of women armed with spatulas and ice-cream scoops to fill those trays. The new TV Dinners hit the grocery shelves priced at ninety-eight cents. The initial five thousand units were a slight miscalculation. Families would gobble up over 10 million TV Dinners by the end of the first full year of production alone. It was an out-of-the-park home run for the company. Thomas received a thousand-dollar bonus and a promotion.

Full-colour print ads ran in magazines showing stylish moms pulling Swanson TV Dinners out of a shopping bag with the headline: "I'm late—but dinner won't be." And it only made sense to advertise Swanson TV Dinners on TV. The first commercial featured a pitchman talking about how Swanson TV Dinners helped his harried wife:

> *You gals think you're lucky to get Swanson TV Turkey Dinners, but I say Swanson TV Turkey Dinners are a bigger break for husbands! You take me. I can be early, I can be late, I can bring pals to dinner anytime I please and—get this—my wife never panics! She just takes Swanson TV Turkey Dinners from the freezing compartment of our refrigerator when I am a little off schedule.*

Aside from the blatant sexism, it was a persuasive pitch. As soon as all that surplus turkey was gone, Swanson expanded to include fried chicken, Salisbury steak, meatloaf and desserts. Attaching a food product to a hot new entertainment medium turned Swanson TV Dinners into a phenomenon. Families all over the nation heated up their TV Dinners and sat down to watch their favourite TV shows, like *The Jackie Gleason Show* and *I Love Lucy*. Today, one of the original aluminum trays has a place of honour in the National Museum of American History.

A cultural icon created as a result of a nearly catastrophic mistake.

Bill Maher

The Problem with Being Politically Incorrect
on Politically Incorrect

On September 17, 2001, Bill Maher was hosting what would be a consequential episode of his talk show, *Politically Incorrect*. The weekly program had an interesting premise. Maher wanted to bring together people with opposing viewpoints and give them a place to chew over current events. People who would rarely sit across from one another or even want to sit across from one another. Maher called it a "designed train wreck."

The program premiered on Comedy Central in 1993. Based in New York, Maher could pluck guests from the heart of east coast intelligentsia. They included pundits like Fran Lebowitz and Jimmy Breslin. The ensuing sparks, set against a Roman coliseum backdrop, made for revealing entertainment. Maher's steely-eyed refereeing was often the most amusing element of the show. He was clearly left-leaning but didn't toe a party line. More than anything, he possessed a rare DNA aberration few people share.

He wasn't trying to be liked.

He didn't seem to care if his guests liked him. Or even if the audience liked him. He called out people on both sides of the aisle. If he heard something false, or inconsistent, or merely insipid, he would rail against the guest. Liberal or conservative. Man or woman. Revered or moronic. He took no prisoners. (The only exceptions seemed to be an elite club of fellow comedians he respected.)

There's a lot of freedom in not caring. As a matter of fact, it's hard to imagine that kind of intoxication. Sure, he cared about ratings, but there never seemed to be a whiff of pandering to his guests, to the audience or even to his corporate overlords. Then again, those overlords were Comedy Central, which allowed a lot of latitude in the service of funny. At the time the show launched, Maher felt we were being smothered by the relatively recent "politically correct" blanket that was being thrown over virtually every aspect of society. He believed the elevation of sensitivity over honesty was killing important debate and narrowing the discussion. It was taking important subjects off the table, like race, partisan divides, gender and sex. He felt this fear of frank engagement was fake and damaging. But above all, Maher believed it was stifling truth. He said he was much more offended by lies than by brutal honesty and thought the antonym of politically incorrect was "bullshit." So he created a show that not only aspired to jump the moat of political correctness, it was the show's raison d'être. Lest anyone forget along the way, they need only look to the show's title.

William Maher Jr. grew up in River Vale, New Jersey, a commuter suburb for people working in New York. His father, William Sr., was a news editor and radio announcer at NBC, and his mother, Julie, was a nurse. Bill was raised in his Irish-American father's Roman Catholic religion and didn't realize until his early teens that his mother was Jewish. His father strongly disagreed with the Catholic Church's stand on birth control and stopped taking Bill and his sister to Sunday mass when Bill was thirteen, which may have influenced Bill's antireligion stance years later. William Sr. was a very funny man who could also go on angry tirades against Richard Nixon. He tried to instill an interest in politics in his son and young Bill was imprinted by that cocktail of outrage and humour. In his own words, Bill was "an intense, serious, adult-like kid" who was later "crushingly" unpopular in high school. He went on to double-major in English and history at Cornell University in Ithaca, New York, graduating in 1978. Maher says selling pot allowed him to get through college and make enough float money as he tried to make inroads in his preferred career, comedy.

Most first stand-up gigs are both exhilarating and humiliating. Maher experienced that one-two punch as his first stand-up routine was in a Chinese restaurant on Route 17 in Paramus, New Jersey. Not long after, he moved to Manhattan and started hanging around the Catch a Rising Star comedy club to watch the seasoned comics at work. "I was their little mascot," Maher says. Larry David, the emcee there at the time, saw some potential in Maher and gave him his first onstage break. Eventually, Maher was named the emcee at the club and honed the stage authority he would exhibit later in his TV hosting duties. His longtime hero was Johnny Carson. Maher liked his style. His monologue delivery. His easygoing control. Eventually, Maher got his first booking on his idol's show in 1982. Jerry Seinfeld went with him for moral support. Maher made Carson laugh with a joke about being half-Catholic and half-Jewish, saying he used to bring a lawyer into confession: "Bless me, Father, for I have sinned. I think you know Mr. Cohen." He would eventually appear on *The Tonight Show* over thirty times. Those appearances eventually caught the attention of Steve Allen, who cast Maher as his sidekick in his 1984 cable series, *Steve Allen's Music Room*.

Around that time, Maher moved to California to try acting and landed small roles in single episodes of a few TV sitcoms, including one full-season role in Geena Davis's short-lived show *Sara*. Maher also tried his hand at movies, acting in such fare as *D.C. Cab*, *Ratboy* and *Cannibal Women in the Avocado Jungle of Death*, but he never found his groove. Secretly, he knew what that groove was. He had dreamed of being a talk show host ever since he was twelve years old. In a sense, his sitcom and movie failures would lead to the promised land. Comedy Central hired him to co-host an irreverent program covering the 1992 presidential election. Then Maher pitched Comedy Central on a new show idea. One year later, his hosting dream came true when *Politically Incorrect with Bill Maher* hit the air. As Maher said, he wasn't trying to create a politically important talk show; he was just trying to create a job. It worked. But it meant Maher had to move back to New York.

The show was a big hit for Comedy Central. For three years, Maher grabbed a chair and a whip and unleashed guests with opposing points of view while America watched the spectacle. Then in 1996 two things happened. First, Maher moved the show from New York to Los Angeles. The guest list obviously altered as the Hollywood celebrity quotient rose (although A-list celebs seemed wary to appear because Maher coddled no one and agents kept their less-informed clients away). Second, *Politically Incorrect* became a politically incorrect top-rated show on Comedy Central, winning four CableACE Awards. That heat eventually attracted the attention of ABC. In the relentless search for ratings, ABC lured Maher over to the big leagues in 1997, scheduling his show to follow Ted Koppel's *Nightline*. The network thinking was that the audience would already be in a political state of mind and the lead-in could give Maher a bigger audience with an additional heaping helping of prestige.

It was a strange pairing but it seemed to work. *Nightline* passed the baton to *Politically Incorrect* each night (although Koppel never did it directly, to Maher's constant consternation), ratings climbed and ad revenue surged north. *Variety* magazine called the show "the main propeller of growth in late-night ad sales," and the "edgy" program was positioned to blast a hole in the Letterman/ Leno armada.

So it was on September 17, 2001, six days after the planes flew into the twin towers, crashed into the Pentagon and plowed into a Pennsylvania field, that Maher uttered a line that would lead to a career catastrophe. Actually, he was agreeing with guest Dinesh D'Souza, who didn't buy into President Bush's view of the suicide terrorists as "cowards." D'Souza maintained the terrorists were the opposite of cowards because they all were willing to smash into concrete for their cause and none of them backed out. That's when Bill Maher agreed, saying, "*We* have been the cowards, lobbing cruise missiles from two thousand miles away. *That's* cowardly. Staying in the airplane when it hits the building, say what you want about it, it's not cowardly."

Here's where Bill Maher gets filed into the same "careful what you wish for" folder as Brian Williams. The desire to have a hit show on a major network viewed by millions wheeled on Maher. The blowback wasn't immediate. First, conservative radio hosts began discussing Maher's comment. Then those talk shows invited the public to weigh in. Then they began asking their listeners to call advertisers and urge them to stop advertising on Maher's show if they wanted to avoid boycotts. Not long after, FedEx, General Motors and Sears all withdrew their sponsorships of *Politically Incorrect*. Some pundits suggested it was a $10 million loss for ABC.

There's nothing like the sound of the door slamming shut as advertisers vamoose to sober you up. Maher knew he was in the barrel on this one. Within days, he appeared on *The Tonight*

Show and *The O'Reilly Factor* to apologize to "anyone who took it wrong." But anyone watching knew he wasn't exactly contrite. As advertisers fled, seventeen ABC affiliates refused to air future episodes. Then came the rebuke from White House press secretary Ari Fleischer, who stated Maher's comments were "a terrible thing to say." Fleischer then ominously added that people have to "watch what they say and watch what they do." The White House addressed the issue again later by saying Maher's comments were no different from intolerant people shouting that all Muslims should be rounded up in the wake of the September 11 attacks. In a telling moment, Fleischer said that while it is always the right of an American to speak out, people still had to be thoughtful as the nation moved toward a wartime stance.

Interestingly, other prominent folks expressed views not unlike Maher's. Later that September, *Slate* posted a similar opinion, and writer Susan Sontag had expressed as much in a short piece in the *New Yorker* magazine. But Maher's audience was much larger, national advertisers were involved and the impact of his remarks reverberated well beyond the *New Yorker*'s 800,000 subscriber base.

One other factor exacerbated the situation for Maher. ABC was owned by Disney, the bastion of squeaky-clean entertainment. From the get-go, wooing a program called *Politically Incorrect* into the fold was an odd move for the house that Uncle Walt built. Maher would later say the Disney brass probably never even watched the show—until there was trouble. As September rolled into October, the calls for Maher's head didn't subside. He continued to seem annoyed and confused by the reaction. He wasn't just a First Amendment advocate, he was a First Amendment zealot. He had defended comments by people he deplored because he believed everyone in America had the right to speak their minds and that free speech was the bedrock of democracy. He also maintained he wasn't criticizing the military; he was criticizing White House policies. And his show was called *Politically Incorrect*, for chrissakes.

For their part, ABC and the mouse mothership were going through their own existential crises. To cut Maher loose would bring back advertisers and calm affiliates down, but it would also look as if they were buckling under. As a former *Politically Incorrect* producer observed, affiliates are not the bravest bunch, but they are ABC's bunch. And what would the optics be if the network cancelled a show called *Politically Incorrect* for being, well, politically incorrect? It was the kind of moment you see in Tarantino movies—where five guys all pull guns on each other and it's a completely weird Mexican standoff. Meanwhile, Maher soldiered on. Political commentator Barbara Olson, who died in the 9/11 attacks, was actually travelling to L.A. for a taping of *Politically Incorrect* when her plane was overtaken by the terrorists and crashed into the Pentagon. Maher left a seat on the panel open for a week in her memory.

As things appeared to cool down—a tad—nine of the seventeen affiliates tiptoed back on board. Maher's average weekly audience was a still very healthy 2.8 million, as large as it had been in the months leading up to his fateful remarks. The controversy may have even attracted some curious new viewers. While advertisers were still nervous about buying time on the show (FedEx and Sears vowed never to return), the audience numbers held.

Inside ABC, opinions were split on Maher. He was professional but prickly. He didn't play the expected smiley game when network executives toured the set shaking hands. His sarcasm was not reserved for air-time. He thought drugs were good. As a matter of fact, he was a weed aficionado and often said he wanted all drugs to be legalized, which was a stone in Disney's shoe. The two subjects most people avoid to preserve careers—politics and religion—were his two favourites. He loved to call out politicians and he thought all religion was bad. So when it came time to defend him and defiantly throw up the deflector shields, ABC's reflex time was slow and the buttons were sticky.

Finally, on May 14, 2002, ABC announced *Politically Incorrect* would be cancelled in January and replaced by a new show hosted by Jimmy Kimmel. It would be a more traditional talk show, with a monologue, guests and a desk. Just over a week later, Maher appeared on *The Larry King Show*. *Politically Incorrect*, although cancelled, was still airing, so this was Maher's first interview since the announcement. First of all, he told King he had begun cleaning out his office on September 18. In other words, even though he had been in trouble with the network before, he knew this time was different. He knew the fateful call was coming. Maher complained the show had never received any real promotion from ABC over the course of its five-and-a-half-year run. Nor did it ever get any direct lead-in help from Ted Koppel. But what really rankled Maher was that the press said the reason for the cancellation was sinking ratings, when, in fact, the ratings were as strong as they were before Maher's comment.

In a *Playboy* interview, Maher said most people in show business will never know what it feels like when the white-hot glare of negative scrutiny is turned on them. It got to the point where Maher was afraid to leave his home. He feared people would assault him. Because the enemy was nebulous and hard to define, America needed a target for their rage. Maher provided that target.

He did take some comfort in the fact that he had proved his initial point with *Politically Incorrect*. He didn't sell out when he made the move to ABC. He didn't lose his edge. As Maher said to Larry King, "If I had to choose between losing my soul or losing my show, I'm glad I chose losing my show." He didn't pander on network TV. And he got fired for it. Ironically, six days after the cancellation, Maher received an award from the Los Angeles Press

Club for championing free speech, followed by a Hugh M. Hefner First Amendment Award.

Bill Maher was a man of principle. He spoke his truth.

And he was now a man without a show.

For the next seven months, Maher tried to keep busy. He went out on a stand-up tour. He published a book titled *When You Ride Alone You Ride with bin Laden: What the Government Should Be Telling Us to Help Fight the War on Terrorism*. But privately he worried the damage was irreparable.

Then in mid-December 2002, Bill Maher made an announcement. He was returning to television—only this time he would be on HBO. The new show would be a kind of "that was the week that was" wrap-up in a one-hour format, airing on Friday nights.

Real Time with Bill Maher debuted on February 21, 2003. As with *Politically Incorrect*, he was going to host a revolving panel of guests that included actors, activists, politicians and comedians, but the new show had two big differences. First, it was filmed before a live audience and broadcast live with no tape delay, and second, HBO was commercial-free. With no sensitive advertisers to worry about and the free-range nature of cable, Maher was able to say whatever he wanted. He revelled in that freedom.

Real Time with Bill Maher has been a resounding success. It averages around 4 million viewers per episode. As of this writing, it is beginning its eighteenth season.

Like Brian Williams, Maher hit the mother lode with the Trump era. With a scandal a day, trying to contain the show to one hour was the challenge. He railed against Trump with both glee and deep concern. But he also understood the dichotomy at work:

"There's a contradiction between what's good for my country and what's good for my living."

But in an era when people are careful about what they say, he has maintained his provocations. Maher told *Vanity Fair* that his show's content was completely contradictory to what you were hearing everywhere else. He had been a guest on other shows and he knew the drill: Don't say anything to upset the audience, make them cheer. Maher had no interest in playing that game. He felt it lacked integrity.

So Maher keeps his truth phasers on stun. The guests are interesting and the conversations often get feisty. Maher invites both Democrats and Republicans and arbitrates with his trademark sarcasm. The show's format includes a topical opening monologue and a short one-on-one interview with a special guest. Then Maher moderates a panel of three people, a fourth guest joins the table for an interview, followed by a comedy segment, and the show culminates with a biting rant-of-the-week. All within an uninterrupted commercial-free hour. There is an after-show continuation on YouTube in which Maher asks his guests questions submitted by viewers. Like *Politically Incorrect* before it, it is neither light talk fare nor is it a cable political talk show.

It is original.

As contentious as Maher is, he has survived on television for over twenty-five years, which is no easy feat. He lives in Ben Affleck's previous home in Beverly Hills, he was a minority shareholder in his beloved New York Mets baseball team until recently, he was an early investor in Twitter and he had enough cash to donate a million bucks to Barack Obama's re-election campaign.

It's also important to note Maher didn't change when he got a second chance. Many people might have felt chastised or once-burned-twice-shy, but he still doesn't pander. He still doesn't tolerate rote campaign talk or easy applause points from anyone. As

Martin Short remarked in *Real Time with Bill Maher: Anniversary Special* (celebrating fifteen years of the show), you get a sense nothing has been altered to get a rating. As someone else noted, Maher has the rare ability to get the unguarded green room conversation out onto the set. He still challenges his guests *and* his audience. In one recent episode, when some rowdy audience members began shouting down the guests, an angry Bill Maher actually jumped into the audience to deal with the hecklers personally until security finally ejected them from the studio. Maher also holds the dubious distinction of being nominated for forty-one Emmys over the years but only winning one for *Vice*, a seven-part series he produced. As he says, tough love never gets awarded.

With all the delicious political *sturm und drang* happening on CNN and MSNBC, one wonders if he might be tempted to jump into one of those two arenas. He admits he did have extensive talks with MSNBC, but when it was all said and done and they looked around the room, everyone knew they would never be able to make it work because they had advertisers to worry about. The irony is not lost. Maher's terrorist comment peeled advertisers from his show and led to his dismissal. But in the end, he had to peel his own sponsors to succeed. That infamous incident led to the ideal situation for Bill Maher—a weekly talk show that mixes humour with politics, framed with the ability to go free range with any opinions using any kind of language. Damn the torpedoes.

He's never been happier.

But it didn't always feel that way. Maher said being cancelled "seemed like the worst thing in the world at the time," but added that in hindsight, "it was the best thing." What seemed like a career-ending mistake dragged Maher through hell, but he emerged out the other side with the perfect vehicle.

Pretty good, considering the only celebrity to lose their job after 9/11 was Bill Maher.

9.

The Dixie Chicks

On Getting Dixie-Chicked

Back in 1989, sisters Emily and Martie Erwin formed a four-piece band with friends Laura Lynch and Robin Lynn Macy. Emily, sixteen, played five-string banjo, Martie, nineteen, played fiddle, Laura played the stand-up bass and Robin was on guitar. Raised in Addison, Texas, the Erwin sisters began their music career busking on street corners in Dallas. They wore prairie skirts with fringed blouses and played a mix of bluegrass and traditional country. When people would inevitably ask the name of the band, the girls didn't have an answer. One day while they were throwing potential names around, a song came on the radio. It was a Little Feat tune called "Dixie Chicken" and the chorus went, "If you'll be my Dixie chicken, I'll be your Tennessee lamb." The sisters named their group the Dixie Chickens in a kitschy hat-tip to the tune. A week later, Martie suddenly worried some cute boy she had a crush on might stroll by and spot her in a ten-gallon hat and fringe and wonder why she was calling herself a "Dixie Chicken." So they shortened "Chickens" to "Chicks," had a "chick" tip jar and—hilariously—their first business card featured a chicken with eyelashes.

The goal of the Dixie Chicks was to get off the street corner and start landing real gigs. Real gigs with roofs. Slowly but surely it started to happen. Martie began making enough money to quit college, and Emily was earning money so young she never really had another job. They started gigging at small music venues and bluegrass festivals and set their long-term sights on Nashville. In 1990, a friend who was the daughter of a Texas senator wrote them a cheque for ten thousand dollars, and with that, the Dixie Chicks recorded their debut album, *Thank Heavens for Dale Evans*. The group's cowgirl look reflected the album title and a 45 rpm record was put out in time for Christmas, titled "Home on the Radar Range." They landed an appearance on the Grand Ole Opry and one of their songs was played on Garrison Keillor's radio show, *A Prairie Home Companion*. They also won a "best band" award at the Telluride Bluegrass Festival, which created opportunities for the Dixie Chicks to open for big acts like Garth Brooks, Reba McEntire and George Strait. But none of it led to any national airplay.

Two years later, the Dixie Chicks moved toward a more contemporary sound on their second album, *Little Ol' Cowgirl*. The group enlisted seasoned studio musicians, and as a result, the album featured richer arrangements. Macy wasn't pleased with the change in direction and chose to leave the band to pursue a purer bluegrass sound. The remaining trio, with Lynch now handling lead vocals, released a third album in 1993 titled *Shouldn't a Told You That*. While their albums didn't yield any hits, they eventually did yield another chick.

Legendary steel guitar player Lloyd Maines played on the second and third Dixie Chicks albums and slipped the sisters a cassette tape of his daughter, Natalie. He promised he wasn't pitching her as a singer, but just suggested they check it out. Natalie had grown up in a musical household in Lubbock, Texas, and had shown an interest in singing at three years of age. In high school, she was a cheerleader, performed in the school choir and played in a short-lived band. When she moved on to college, her musical tastes were rock 'n' roll, alternative rock and R&B. One of her college professors described Natalie as opinionated, and she would often get into political arguments at the largely Republican, conservative college. Natalie herself said she was a college rebel with strong convictions. She sent an audition tape to the Berklee College of Music, which led to an audition and eventually a full vocal scholarship. (This was the same tape her father Lloyd would give to the Dixie Chicks.) School never did sit right with Natalie and she dropped out of Berklee before she finished the course. But music certainly did sit squarely in her sights, and she began doing background vocal sessions for albums her father was producing.

Meanwhile, the Erwin sisters found a new manager named Simon Renshaw. He saw a group of talented and attractive women with potential. They just needed to up their game. Renshaw began to strategize their next move and secured a deal with Sony's Nashville division. But, by some reports, vocalist Lynch was weary of the touring and wanted to spend more time with her family. When she decided to leave the group, the sisters found themselves in the market for a new lead singer. One full year after Lloyd Maines had given the cassette to the Erwins, they finally listened to it and liked what they heard. When the three of them got together, Natalie's voice blended beautifully with the sisters' soprano and alto tones. With that, the duo became a trio again and twenty-one-year-old Natalie Maines officially became a Dixie Chick.

With Natalie's arrival in 1995, Renshaw convinced the group to undergo some urban renewal. To appeal to a broader audience, they dropped the cowgirl look and infused their rootsy sound with Natalie's rock influences. Prior to joining the band, Natalie wasn't a country music listener, didn't have any chops in Western music and didn't follow bluegrass. But she admired the talent that oozed so effortlessly from Emily and Martie and loved that they played their own instruments. Plus, she really dug the band's name. Like any entity that changes 33 percent of its elements, the Dixie Chicks began to shapeshift. Natalie Maines was a spark plug. She was bold and comfortable centre stage and the change in the band's attack was felt instantly. The lead vocal and three-part harmony had a new urgency, and there was an additional undercurrent of shrewd humour at work. The band's three tumblers clicked into place when they recorded their first major-label album, *Wide Open Spaces*, in 1998. It was a new sound for the Dixie Chicks and they were excited about it. They had no idea how massive that album would become.

The first single, "I Can Love You Better," became the group's first Top 10 country hit. Two more singles hit the top of the country charts. *Wide Open Spaces* would open the doors in the country music industry and become their breakthrough album. It sold 14 million copies worldwide and was designated Diamond status by the Recording Industry Association of America (RIAA). At the Forty-First Grammy Awards, it was awarded Best Country Album as well as Best Country Performance by a Duo or Group with Vocal for the song "There's Your Trouble." By the end of 1998, the Dixie Chicks had sold more CDs than all other country groups combined that year.

Next came *Fly*, released in 1999. On an album containing fourteen new tracks, an astounding eight songs were released as singles. The album was a major crossover success, debuting at number one on the Billboard 200 as well as the Billboard Top Country Album chart. Like *Wide Open Spaces*, *Fly* would attain Diamond status, shipping 10 million units by 2002 and making the Dixie Chicks the only female band in any genre to release two RIAA-certified Diamond albums back-to-back. The lead single, "Ready to Run," reached number two on the Billboard Hot Country Singles &

Tracks chart. Two of the songs foreshadowed the kind of controversy that would hunt the Chicks a few years later—for the first time, the group was removed from some radio station playlists. The song "Goodbye Earl" was about killing an abusive husband, but the black humour and accompanying comedic video took the curse off it. The lyrics to "Sin Wagon" talked about leaving a boring relationship behind and doing a little "mattress dancing." That term ended up being more troublesome in the conservative country music world than the murder song. The album was fun and bold, earning four nominations and winning two awards at the Forty-Second Grammys: Best Country Album and Best Country Performance by a Duo or Group with Vocal for "Ready to Run." They headlined their first successful tour. The Dixie Chicks were flying high.

After the release of their second album, the band had gotten into in a lawsuit with Sony over accounting irregularities. The case was settled privately and the Chicks were given their own record label imprint, named Open Wide Records. The group released their sixth album in August 2002, the third with Maines, titled *Home*. Produced by the band and Lloyd Maines, it had a different sound from the last two records: less polish, more traditional up-tempo bluegrass. The trajectory of the Dixie Chicks continued skyward, as the album garnered six nominations at the Forty-Fifth Grammy Awards, winning four, including Best Country Album, Best Recording Package, Best Country Instrumental Performance for the song "Lil' Jack Slade" and Best Country Performance by a Duo or Group with Vocal for "Long Time Gone." The album shot to the top of the Billboard 200 and stayed at number one on the Billboard Top Country Album chart for twelve non-consecutive weeks. The record was a landmark for the group because it yielded their first two Top 10 pop chart hits, "Long Time Gone" and a soulful cover of Fleetwood Mac's "Landslide." To promote the album, the group announced a major concert schedule dubbed the Top of the World tour. Tickets sold out six months in advance and major sponsor Lipton came onboard to underwrite the tour.

The Dixie Chicks were now a bona fide superstar group on their way to selling 30 million albums. They were the biggest-selling group in America over the past eight years and they had set a record as the best-selling female group in history. Country Music Television produced a special titled *CMT 40 Greatest Women of Country Music* that ranked the Dixie Chicks number thirteen. On top of that, the trio had just signed a deal reportedly worth over $20 million to each member with a rare 20 percent royalty rate. They were one of the best-selling groups in country music history after only three albums. It really did feel as if the Dixie Chicks were on top of the world.

The year 2003 began with 88 million viewers watching the Dixie Chicks sing "The Star-Spangled Banner" at Super Bowl XXXVII in San Diego, California. Like all Super Bowl anthem performances, it was a massively patriotic moment, with fireworks and jets flying overhead as the Chicks hit their last note. At the time, political tensions were escalating between the United States and Iraq. American intelligence agencies maintained Saddam Hussein was obstructing United Nations inspectors and hiding weapons of mass destruction. As March approached, President George W. Bush and three ally nations sent troops and warships to the region. The United States was moving into a state of mission readiness and the public was told to brace for war. Protests against the military action began in eight hundred cities around the world. Over in England, a million protestors gathered in the centre of London to denounce the American plans for war.

On March 10, nine days before the invasion, the Dixie Chicks were in London, England, getting ready for the first show on their Top of the World tour. Just before hitting the stage at the

Shepherd's Bush Empire—a name that would prove ironic—
Natalie asked her team for a war update and was told President
Bush was moving troops into position. When the Chicks hit the
stage, they were welcomed with a huge ovation from the crowd of
two thousand and launched into their opening number, "Goodbye
Earl." The sixth song they played that night was their current
number-one hit, "Travelin' Soldier," an emotional song about a shy
soldier who meets a girl on his ship-out day and writes her letters
from Vietnam. When the song ended, Natalie told the crowd that,
like the protestors, the Dixie Chicks were also against the war. She
said, "Just so you know, we're on the good side with y'all. We do
not want this war, this violence." Then she uttered thirteen words
that would jump across the ocean and whipsaw back to sideswipe
their careers: "And we're ashamed that the president of the United
States is from Texas." The crowd gasped, then roared, and the
band counted into the next song on the set list, "Am I the Only
One (Who's Ever Felt This Way)." It was a great opening show;
the Dixie Chicks were in fine form and the crowd loved them.
Backstage, Renshaw and his team raved and celebrated. Then it
was on to Munich, Germany.

Little did they know what awaited them.

Two days later, British journalist Betty Clarke filed a three-star
review of the concert for the *Guardian* newspaper. She called
the Dixie Chicks the renegade ladies of country, saying they were
unrepentant about bucking the cowgirl/big hair imagery that country fans love and they had no problem courting controversy. In the
second paragraph, she quoted Natalie's line about being ashamed
of President Bush, saying that in a country music industry where

other artists were releasing pro-war anthems, this statement was "practically punk rock." The review didn't dwell on the twenty-eight-year-old's remark at all, just plucked it out as yet another example of the group's charming and rebellious nature.

The anti-Bush statement got picked up by the Associated Press and quickly became headline news across America. At first, the Dixie Chicks were surprised to hear there was any kind of controversy brewing back home. It had been such an insignificant moment in their show that Martie had to be reminded of what Natalie had said. Manager Renshaw downplayed it, saying it would soon blow over. But as reports kept coming in, it was becoming clear this wasn't going to just blow over. Adhering to the adage that any publicity is good publicity, Renshaw rubbed his hands with glee at one point, saying it would be great if people started burning their records. The thought of that kind of notoriety didn't sit well with the Chicks, especially when they started to get calls from family saying people back home were starting to trash their CDs and were even bulldozing them in protest.

Back in 1966, John Lennon found himself in a similar hot seat, and the parallels are striking. In a series of four interviews with the *London Evening Standard* titled "How Does a Beatle Live?" journalist Maureen Cleave interviewed each of the Beatles. The twenty-six-year-old Lennon casually told her, "We're more popular than Jesus now." He was making the point that the world worshipped pop culture more than the deeply meaningful things in life, as church attendance was in steep decline. It was a criticism, not a boast. England didn't even notice the statement in the two-thousand-word article. In fact, the next line in Cleave's article was about shopping. The quote wasn't deemed worthy of a headline or even a highlight in the layout. When the article was syndicated to other publications, including the *New York Times*, it passed without comment. But when Beatles press officer Tony Barrow offered the four interviews to *DATEbook*, a U.S.-based teen-oriented maga-zine that published racy stories on pop stars, the Vietnam War and the generation gap (sample headline: "The Ten Adults You Dig/Hate the Most"), the editors put a different Lennon remark from Cleave's interview on the cover; "I don't know which will go first—rock 'n' roll or Christianity!" McCartney was on the cover of that issue with his own quote calling the U.S. a "lousy country" for its racist leanings. He even used the N-word. It didn't make a ripple. Lennon's Christianity remarks got all the attention.

Not surprisingly, they were picked up first in the southern Bible Belt. A conservative radio DJ named Tommy Charles, who worked for station WAQY in Birmingham, Alabama, said he was appalled at the "blasphemous" line and instigated a "Ban the Beatles" campaign. The station refused to spin any of the band's hits and Charles urged listeners to trash their Beatles records. United Press International picked up on the boycott and it went viral, sixties-style. That was a pivotal moment for the Beatles, as it led to protests, mass record bonfires, death threats and eventually the end of the band's touring career. If you look at photos before and after that incident, Lennon rarely smiles again.

The Dixie Chicks were feeling the same kind of heat from the fire of the backlash. At each concert stop, Renshaw would update them on the escalating fallout stateside. The group knew it was getting bad when Renshaw informed them he had closed down both the band's website and chatroom. "Travelin' Soldier," their number-one single, did a freefall to number sixty-three. Soon, they discovered that a well-organized right-wing group called Free Republic was mobilizing through boycotts to convince country music radio stations to stop playing their music. The fire-storm was getting so hot, Renshaw went into full crisis mode and proposed putting out an apology as soon as possible. Natalie was against that idea and wanted to stand by her words. She issued her first non-apology apology on March 12, saying the band had been overseas for several weeks and was astounded by the amount of anti-American sentiment there. She felt the president was ignoring the opinions of many Americans and was alienating the rest of the world. But while she said her comments were made in frustration, she also said that one of the privileges of being an American is the right of free speech. She wrapped up by saying the band supported the troops but were frightened of the notion of going to war with Iraq.

As the heat back home intensified, Natalie issued a second statement on March 14:

> As a concerned American citizen, I apologize to President Bush because my remark was disrespectful. I feel that whoever holds that office should be treated with the utmost respect. We are currently in Europe and witnessing a huge anti-American sentiment as a result of the perceived rush to war. While war may remain a viable option, as a mother, I just want to see every possible alternative exhausted before children and American soldiers' lives are lost. I love my country. I am a proud American.

Not everyone was buying the apology. While most felt it was unpatriotic to criticize Bush in a post-9/11 crisis—his approval rating was still very high—many Americans were also highly offended Natalie had voiced her criticism on foreign soil. Then the radio station boycotts got traction. A company called Cumulus Broadcasting with 270 stations in fifty-five cities wiped the Dixie Chicks right off their playlists. Station managers said their decisions were prompted by the surge of calls from irate listeners who threatened to boycott the stations if Dixie Chicks songs continued to be played. Advertisers stuck a wet finger in the wind and considered pulling their campaigns off country radio stations, prompting one manager to say that continuing to play the Dixie Chicks was simply "financial suicide." A Houston station yanked the group's music off the air after 77 percent of the listeners polled on its website supported a ban. One Kansas City radio station held a Dixie "chicken toss" party where listeners were encouraged to dump their Dixie Chicks tapes, CDs and concert tickets into trash cans. A poll by an Atlanta radio station revealed that 76 percent of its listeners agreed with the statement "If I could, I would take my CDs back." Fellow country star Toby Keith performed concerts with a big-screen projection of Natalie Maines being embraced by Saddam Hussein.

While the reaction to the Bush statement may seem over the top, the context was significant. First, it was only a year and a half since 9/11. President Bush was still riding a spike in approval ratings, from over 90 percent directly after 9/11 to over 70 percent leading up to the Iraq invasion (that approval rating over Iraq would completely invert by 2007). Bush even acknowledged the situation in April during an interview with NBC's Tom Brokaw:

The Dixie Chicks are free to speak their mind. They can say what they wanna say. And just because—they shouldn't have their feelings hurt just because some people don't want to buy their records when they speak out. Freedom is a two-way street. But I don't really care what the Dixie Chicks said. I want to do what I think is right for the American people and if some singers or Hollywood stars feel like speaking out, that's fine. That's the great thing about America. It stands in stark contrast to Iraq, by the way.

Second, there was an element of misogyny here. Other male artists had spoken out against the Iraq invasion without a scintilla of pushback. Martie put it this way: "I'm saying if the criticism of us for what was said hadn't been wrapped in this misogynist rhetoric of 'You're sluts because you said that,' to me, that is definitely geared towards a female—women are still treated like the second-class citizens in country music." Emily continued, "All of the sudden, we're bimbos because we differ with their political views. I think they like to put us in our place. Yeah, I do." Country artist Maren Morris told *Rolling Stone*, "It was completely unfair treatment of a group of women just voicing an opinion, like any dude has in the history of time." There is a theory that when the Dixie Chicks fell from grace, the collateral damage wiped out the opportunity for other female musicians to receive the airplay they deserved. In 2003, when their album *Fly* was atop the charts, female-led songs represented thirty-eight of the hundred top country songs that year. Since then, just 18 percent of the songs on country radio had a female vocalist. Years later in 2015, a top radio consultant said, "If you want to make ratings in country radio, take females out." He called female country artists "the tomatoes in our salad"; in other words, they were merely a garnish. (That remark would come to be referred to as "saladgate.")

Under the promotional contract with Lipton, the beverage company had agreed to air a certain number of commercials promoting the Dixie Chicks tour. When the controversy started to reach a boiling point, Lipton was barraged by consumers threatening to boycott its products, as well as those of parent companies PepsiCo and Unilever. According to the Dixie Chicks, Lipton honoured the contract but dumped the commercials into the middle of the night or in regions that were "less angry." Even the band's tour bus driver resigned in protest over Natalie's remarks.

The first stop on the three-month U.S. leg of the tour was in Greenville, South Carolina. It would be a litmus test for the Chicks. The venue had sold out long ago but protestors marched outside with signs saying things like, "If you're supporting the Dixie Chicks, you're supporting traitors." When the group hit the stage, Natalie Maines shouted, "They said you might not come, but we knew you'd come. Because we have the greatest fans in the whole world!" There was a sprinkling of boos, so she added, "If you're here to boo, we welcome that. Because we welcome freedom of speech, so we're going to give you fifteen seconds to get whatever you have out, so here we go, on the count of three you can start booing." There were a few boos, but they were instantly drowned out by the roar of the crowd and the Chicks began their opening tune.

The Dixie Chicks' previous two albums had sold 10 million copies each, but the boycott and controversy immediately stalled *Home* at 6 million. The U.S. leg of the tour was already sold out before the incident occurred. Promoters offered refunds, but according to reports, there were more requests for tickets than for refunds. While crowds filed in to hear the group, there were some protestors making noise outside the venues. Then, paralleling the Lennon controversy thirty-seven years earlier, death threats surfaced. One in particular, in Dallas, was considered credible by the FBI and the Texas Rangers because it specified a date, location and weapon. A scene in the 2006 documentary about the controversy, titled *Shut Up and Sing*, shows the Dixie Chicks' security team providing Natalie with a photo of the man who allegedly made the death threat. Local police were stationed outside the suspect's Dallas house during the concert to track his movements. Not long after, a newspaper printed Natalie's home address in Austin, forcing her to move, first outside the city, then to Los Angeles. Meanwhile, right-wing commentators on Fox dialled up the misogynistic rhetoric, with Pat Buchanan saying, "I think these are the Dixie Twits, these are the dumbest, dumbest bimbos, with due respect, I have seen." Bill O'Reilly piled on, saying, "These are callow, foolish women who deserve to be slapped around." It was a chilling moment for the entertainment industry, making people afraid to speak up—especially female artists—lest they be banned or "Dixie Chicked." Yet in spite of it all, the Top of the World tour would end up being the top-grossing country tour of the year.

On May 2, 2003, the Dixie Chicks appeared on the cover of *Entertainment Weekly* magazine. Against the protests of their publicist, the Chicks conceived of a bold idea for the photo shoot. The three were photographed naked with words strategically scrawled across their bodies—very specific words that had been hurled at them over the last month and a half. Words like "patriot" and "boycott," "proud Americans" and "Saddam's Angels," "Dixie sluts" and "hero." The photo attracted a lot of attention. Natalie defended the cover, saying, "We don't want people to think that we're trying to be provocative. It's not about the nakedness. It's that the clothes got in the way of the labels. We're not defined by who we are anymore. Other people are doing that for us."

The first interview the group gave after the inflammatory comment was with Diane Sawyer, who asked the sisters if they were angry about Natalie's remark the night she made it. Emily told Sawyer she felt a rush of heat from her head to her toes in that moment on the stage, not because she didn't agree with Natalie, but because she knew it was a heavy statement. Martie said she had no reaction whatsoever. In an interview with Bill Maher, Natalie made the point that the entire controversy proved free speech is something you can't take for granted and you have to keep fighting for. It was later revealed that the American Red Cross had turned down a million-dollar donation from the Dixie Chicks because the band asked the Red Cross to endorse their 2003 tour. As a spokesperson for the organization explained, the political controversy made it impossible for the American Red Cross to associate itself with the band because such association would have violated two of the founding principles of the organization: impartiality and neutrality. Then there was that other tiny issue Renshaw pointed out—George W. Bush happened to be the honorary chair of the Red Cross.

Over the next two years, the Dixie Chicks performed occasionally for various causes like the Vote for Change tour, they appeared with James Taylor for a few dates and they contributed a song to a compilation album released to benefit the Human Rights Campaign. A lot changed in that time. All three Chicks were married now with kids. Life slowed down a bit. But even after it turned out Saddam Hussein wasn't hiding a stockpile of weapons and Bush's approval rating had plunged to 29 percent as a result, the incident still stuck to the trio.

Then, like the sun slowly rising in the morning, a new horizon appeared for the band. First, renowned, in-demand record producer Rick Rubin reached out and wanted to produce their next album. He had a different take on the "incident." He felt it was a momentous moment that rattled and changed the band. Rubin believed it was the start of a new phase of their career. An important phase. Up until then, people loved the Chicks, but loved them in a surface way. Now people talked about them in a different tone and cared about what they thought and what they said. In one fell stroke, the Dixie Chicks had become serious artists.

It was a perceptive insight. The group had now been through an ordeal, they were scarred, they had survived, they were emboldened and they stood for something. Like Muhammad Ali after he lost for the first time to Joe Frazier, they were suddenly more interesting; the struggle for redemption was an alluring storyline. Rubin instantly saw all that potential. He had made his reputation on hard-rock bands like the Red Hot Chili Peppers and hip-hop acts like Public Enemy and the Beastie Boys. He had resuscitated the career of Johnny Cash with a series of meaningful albums near the end of Cash's life. Rubin wanted the Chicks to address the pain that was still lingering. He felt they had a lot to say and believed there was "a lot of power and energy and talk around them" and the time was right. He wanted them to write about their experience in a raw, truthful way. It was a huge opportunity for the Dixie Chicks: someone like Rubin might never have knocked on their door in any other universe. They accepted his offer and Rubin encouraged their creativity, challenging their lyrics often through the writing process and eventually convincing them to experiment with their arrangements.

The resulting album was *Taking the Long Way*. Released in 2006, it was an unapologetic record that opened with a song titled "The Long Way Around." It referenced the infamous 2003 tour with lines like "It's been two long years now since the top of the world came crashing down." It was the first time the Chicks had cowritten every track on an album. Some songs were intensely personal, like "So Hard," which spoke of the struggles of Emily (now Robinson) and Martie (now Maguire) with in vitro fertilization (they had each given birth to twins). The track "Silent House" dealt with Natalie's heartbreaking experience caring for a grandmother with Alzheimer's disease. But the feistiest track, which got the most attention, was "Not Ready to Make Nice." The title let the world know the band was still angry. The lyrics said, in no uncertain terms, that the band was not about to back down and was still "mad as hell." Also, tellingly, the lyric said it was too late to make it right, but that the band probably wouldn't make it right even if they could.

The album went straight to the top of the charts, making the Dixie Chicks the only female group in history to have three albums debut at number one. An important point has to be made here: they hit number one without any traditional radio support.

This reception was a huge validation for the band. They were now reaching a new audience fuelled by the music and the band's hard-fought battle to stand their ground. After all they had been through—the death threats, the bans and the boycotts—the record would be a Grammy triumph, taking home all five awards it was nominated for that year: Album of the Year, Best Country Album, Song of the Year, Record of the Year and Best Country Performance by a Duo or Group with Vocal for "Not Ready to Make Nice." As the group stood on the stage with an armful of awards, Natalie smiled and proclaimed, "I'm ready to make nice!"

But lurking within the grooves of that album was one line in particular in "Not Ready to Make Nice" that hinted at a new freedom: "It turned my whole world around and I kinda like it."

In interviews to this day, with the benefit of clear-eyed hindsight, the Chicks, as they have been known since 2020, maintain the incident was the best thing that ever happened to them. It left them unshackled. Unbound to corporate interests. Free to say **exactly** what they wanted to say.

MARTIE: *It's the best thing that ever happened to me, it was the best thing that happened to our career, we'd never change it. It was a huge way for us to grow and none of the three of us would go back and want to change it because it's opened our minds and made us more passionate about what we say and that our music needs to say something and mean something. So in so many ways it's such a positive for us.*

NATALIE: *We have no regrets and I would never take this statement back, we would never have this record, we grew closer, we grew as women, it was positive in so many ways.*

EMILY: *It's been a blessing. I truly feel that . . . I feel like it was better for the longevity of this band, believe it or not, to have gone through something like that . . . it makes you even stronger.*

The Chicks felt the entire experience had given them a new superpower. Natalie calls it "a true ability not to care." Suddenly, the country music machine had lost its power over them. They could do anything they wanted now, musically, without the pressure of having to answer to radio gatekeepers. The incident that threatened to make the Dixie Chicks the first casualty of the future cancel culture actually, in the end, made them a household name. The Chicks got their fire back. They attracted top producers. They wrote with more fearlessness. What they had to say mattered. They landed on the cover of *Time* magazine. They won more Grammys than ever. As the *New York Times* put it, they were witches who could not be burned.

In July 2006, the Dixie Chicks returned to the scene of the crime: a sold-out show at Shepherd's Bush Empire in London, England. That night, Natalie Maines took to the stage, looked out over the crowd and said, "Just so you know, we're ashamed the president of the United States is from Texas."

Seth MacFarlane

The Gate Is Now Closed

At the age of nine, Seth MacFarlane got his first paying job. He began publishing his own comic strip, titled *Walter Crouton*, in the local *Kent Good Times Dispatch* newspaper. One cartoon showed a man receiving Communion and asking, "Can I get fries with that?" It generated his first piece of hate mail, from the local priest. The MacFarlane family laughed it off and young Seth experienced the rush of aggravating the status quo for the first time. It wouldn't be the last.

Seth Woodbury MacFarlane was born to parents Ronald and Ann MacFarlane in Kent, Connecticut, on October 1, 1973. Dad was a teacher and Mom was an academic administrator. She clearly had a sense of humour, as Seth's middle name, Woodbury, was her homage to Kent's town drunk. Their son was a very bright and aware child. At the age of two, he began drawing Woody Woodpecker and Fred Flintstone pictures. When little Seth could string his first complete sentences together, he asked, "How are cartoons made?" and "How can I do one of these?"

When he was eleven, another local newspaper, the *Litchfield County Times*, wrote a feature about the prepubescent "working cartoonist." The young man had his future clearly in focus, telling the reporter he planned to "publish books, draw comic books, do TV specials and pursue his latest passion—animation." An eight-millimetre camera given by his parents fuelled a desire to make short films, and his passion for animation continued through high school, where he won the top art prize in his senior year. That led to the Rhode Island School of Design, where he studied video and animation. His thesis film was titled *Life of Larry* (remember that title). Seth's professors were enthusiastic in their support while being simultaneously horrified by his brand of brilliant, often scatological humour.

Upon graduating in 1995, MacFarlane headed straight to Los Angeles after one of his professors sent his *Life of Larry* film to some animation companies there. Although he had his sights set on Disney, it was Hanna-Barbera Productions that offered him his first full-time job. MacFarlane worked as both an animator and a writer on a series that included *Cow and Chicken* and *Johnny Bravo* (for which our company did voice casting). While he worked on a number of animated shows, his heart still lay with *Life of Larry*. He continued to tweak and polish it on the side and created a short sequel called *Larry and Steve*.

The development head at Hanna-Barbera introduced MacFarlane to the executives at Fox as part of an effort to convince Fox to broadcast animation in prime time. While that deal eventually fell through, MacFarlane stayed in touch with the network. When *King of the Hill* became an animated success, Fox was suddenly looking for a new animated property to add to its schedule. MacFarlane approached them with an idea, pitched a little scene and did all the voices. Mike Darnell, the president of alternative programming at Fox, said he thought MacFarlane was either crazy or a genius. He gave MacFarlane $40,000 to make a rough two-to-three-minute pilot with the hope it might lead to a new prime-time series.

MacFarlane knew it was a big opportunity. He took the $40,000, cashed out every credit card he had and worked day and night, hand-drawing every cel of the animation at his kitchen table. As MacFarlane later said, he had no life for six months. He slept, ate and breathed the idea. When he finally met again with Fox, he actually presented them with a fully formed animated film—not a rudimentary animatic of stills set to a soundtrack. Fox was incredibly impressed with MacFarlane's bold irreverent humour and took comfort in the fact he was an "an equal opportunity offender." Fox was also impressed that MacFarlane had put it all on the line to produce a fully realized pilot. The network decided to not only broadcast it but give it the best launchpad possible—a slot after the Super Bowl in 1999. Fox aired a Super Bowl–themed *Simpsons* episode right after the big game, then segued right into MacFarlane's pilot as 22 million people watched. That night *Life of Larry* officially turned into *Family Guy*.

At the age of twenty-four, Seth MacFarlane was the youngest showrunner in Hollywood history. The animated series centred on the dysfunctional Griffin family of Quahog, Rhode Island. The show was instantly polarizing. It took joyous stabs at such taboo subjects as sex, handicapped people and eventually even 9/11. The headmaster of the high school MacFarlane had graduated from in 1991 was outraged that MacFarlane had borrowed the name Griffin from the surname of the headmaster's longtime personal assistant. MacFarlane's mother, who had worked at the school for fifteen years, got into an argument with the headmaster over the issue and ended up resigning. The headmaster, who was also a minister, then wrote letters to advertisers urging them to boycott the show, calling it anti-Semitic, demeaning and obnoxious.

It clearly wasn't the first time MacFarlane got pushback from the clergy. The Parents Television Council also repeatedly objected to the program's "oblique sexual innuendo, incest, bestiality and pedophilia." None of this seemed to bother MacFarlane in the least, as he often maintained his show had room for both high- and lowbrow humour.

MacFarlane was not only *Family Guy*'s creator, executive producer and head writer but also voiced three of the show's six main characters: Pete, Stewie and Brian Griffin. He has said the show found its comedic inspiration in the odd-couple combination of Woody Allen and Jackie Gleason, with more than a dollop of *All in the Family*. But the humour was bold and uniquely MacFarlane. While the show developed a small but loyal cult following, it never did well. Because Fox executives believed in the show and thought it was very funny, they shifted the show all over the schedule, trying eleven different time slots, looking for a sweet spot. That hide-and-seek scheduling made it difficult for loyal viewers to keep up and be counted in the ratings. After trying every trick in its toolbox, Fox finally announced that *Family Guy* would be cancelled in the fall of 2000. The network brought the show back sporadically a few months later, but it suffered further in the ratings and was finally cancelled a second time.

In 2003, *Family Guy* was given its first syndicated run on Canada's Teletoon network, where it quickly gained massive popularity. A few months later, the show was syndicated to the Cartoon Network, essentially for free, in return for promoting *Family Guy* DVDs. Fox was having difficulty convincing retailers to stock the DVDs and hoped the promotion would ignite sales. The episodes that ran on the Cartoon Network were specially edited by MacFarlane and were far edgier than what had originally run on Fox. As *Fast Company* reported, even though the *Family Guy* audience had been ignored at every turn, they dug in on the

Cartoon Network, swelling the numbers and giving the channel some of its highest viewership. The show regularly beat Letterman and Leno, delivering the prized demographic of men aged eighteen to thirty-four. Fans bought the DVDs in record numbers. The set containing the first season sold 2.8 million copies and became the best-selling TV-based DVD in 2003 and the second-highest-selling TV-based DVD in history. Against all odds, *Family Guy* was quietly becoming a pop culture phenomenon.

Then a very rare thing happened.

Gary Newman was the head of Fox business affairs at the time. MacFarlane, who was trying to develop other comedic ideas for Fox, would often pop his head into Newman's office to talk about resurrecting *Family Guy* on the network. Newman understood the obstacle: Fox just didn't want it. But Newman was a fan and believer, and he persisted. Whenever he had update meetings with his boss, Newman would eventually find a way to say, "I know I'm a broken record, but I just want to talk one more time about *Family Guy*, given the huge DVD sales and the show's popularity on the Cartoon Network." Newman took every opportunity to bring it up until his boss wheeled on him one day and said that if he brought *Family Guy* up one more time, he'd fire him. Weeks later, in another update meeting, Newman held his breath and brought it up yet again. That was the moment his boss looked at him and said, "Okay, if you're prepared to get fired over this and you're staying with it, maybe we should consider it." Lo and behold, three years after being cancelled, *Family Guy* was miraculously put back on the air. The original writers had all dispersed, so new writers were brought onboard, with MacFarlane encouraging them to give the show an even sharper edge. The season premiere attracted over 12 million viewers. Newman's job stayed secure.

And thus began the MacFarlane empire.

Family Guy brings in an estimated $200 million per year in ad revenues for Fox. It attracts the most desirable advertising demographic. It is often the highest-ranked scripted show in all of television. It is among the most downloaded shows on iTunes. The franchise is estimated to be worth over $1 billion (*Fast Company* puts it closer to $2 billion). MacFarlane's production company now oversees a herd of hits that include *American Dad!*, *The Cleveland Show* and *The Orville*. In 2009, Seth MacFarlane signed a $100 million three-year deal with Fox, making him the highest-paid writer/producer in television. His net worth is estimated to reside in the $200 million neighbourhood. He not only receives revenues from the episodes his company creates and syndication, but he also pockets lucrative royalties from DVDs and merchandise. Animation is incredibly profitable when it comes to merch. While few people might sport a *Friends* T-shirt, millions wear shirts bearing Stewie's scheming face. There are animation action figures, posters, ring tones and video games. MacFarlane has won the Outstanding Character Voice-Over Performance Emmy four times, tying animation heavyweights Dan Castellaneta and Hank Azaria from *The Simpsons*.

MacFarlane's success has allowed him to do something else very rare in Hollywood—he has jumped out of his animation silo. He has directed three motion pictures, *Ted*, *Ted 2* and *A Million Ways to Die in the West*. *Ted* earned $54 million in its opening weekend, a record for an R-rated comedy. It eventually brought in $214 million in box office receipts, making it the eighth-highest-earning R-rated movie ever. A song from *A Million Ways to Die* was nominated for an Oscar. MacFarlane hosted *Saturday Night Live* in 2012. He hosted the Oscars in 2013. He struck a deal with Google to produce Seth MacFarlane's *Cavalcade of Cartoon Comedy* and shares lucrative advertising revenue as an equity partner with Google and a media finance company. He has emcee gigs on Comedy Central. He has released five records where he sings lushly orchestrated American standards, and his album *Music Is Better Than Words* received two Grammy nominations. He has sung at the Royal Albert Hall in London and Carnegie Hall in New York. He has won a prestigious Peabody Award. Harvard bestowed him with the Humanist of the Year award. And in the ultimate sign of his Hollywood status, MacFarlane received a star on the Hollywood Walk of Fame in 2019. And he is wealthy. Seth MacFarlane is not just a brand, he is an industry.

And none of his remarkable twenty-year career would have happened if he had not made a life-altering mistake in September of 2001.

On September 10, 2001, Seth MacFarlane was at his alma mater, the Rhode Island School of Design, giving a keynote talk about his success with *Family Guy*. After the speech that night, he went out with some of the faculty and got drunk. The next day, he was booked on American Airlines Flight 11 to Los Angeles. Because he was severely hungover, he overslept, and he didn't get to Boston's Logan Airport in time to make his 7:59 a.m. flight. That mistake was compounded by a second mistake—made by his travel agent—who had told him the flight departure was ten minutes later. When MacFarlane got to the ticket counter at 8 a.m., the agent told him he was too late and the gate had closed. So he decided to take the eleven o'clock flight, headed for the lounge and promptly fell asleep.

He woke up forty-five minutes later to commotion in the lounge. A plane had hit the north tower of the World Trade Center in New York at 8:46. He sat there with all the other travellers in horror, then watched as the second plane crashed into the south tower. When CNN announced the first plane was American Airlines Flight 11, MacFarlane turned to the person beside him and said, "Oh my God, that's the plane I was supposed to be on. I was late. I missed it."

Had Seth MacFarlane not made a mistake and overslept, he would have caught that fateful flight. If he had been on that plane, we would have only two seasons of *Family Guy* in the vault. And the vast MacFarlane animation empire would have never happened.

Steve Jobs

The Second Bite of the Apple

There was a time when Apple Computer Inc. was ninety days away from declaring bankruptcy. Then a man saved the company. He made an unpopular decision and that decision would ultimately save Apple. His name was Gil Amelio.

Bet that wasn't the name you were expecting. I'll make a further bet you have never heard of Gil Amelio. But he is an important footnote in the history of the game-changing company. As a matter of fact, there might be no Apple today without Amelio. Let's take a little trip back in time.

Steve Jobs was raised by adoptive parents Paul and Clara Jobs. His birth parents, Joanne Schieble and Abdulfattah "John" Jandali, met in college in Wisconsin and were unwed at the time of his conception. Abortions were not an easy option in 1955, so Schieble travelled to San Francisco and found a doctor who helped unwed mothers. He delivered the baby boy and arranged for an adoption. Schieble had one stipulation: the adoptive parents had to be college graduates. The doctor arranged for her baby to be adopted by a lawyer and his wife, but at the last minute, they backed out and opted for a baby girl instead. The doctor then found a second couple who were happy to adopt a baby boy. Paul Jobs was a high-school dropout who loved cars and mechanics. His wife, Clara, was a bookkeeper. When Schieble found out neither had even graduated high school, she refused to sign the papers, even though the baby was already in a nursery in the Jobs household. Eventually, Schieble consented to the adoption but demanded the Jobses sign an agreement stating they would create a college fund savings account. They agreed, signed and the adoption went through.

Paul Jobs was a handyman who loved building things in his garage workshop and had a special fondness for repairing old cars. Young Steve would observe him closely as he negotiated prices for cars and parts, then fix up the cars and sell them for a small profit. That profit would go into the college fund. Paul taught Steve that design was important, pointing out the small, almost hidden design features on the cars he worked on. He also taught Steve to care about the details. For example, if Paul built a wooden cabinet, he would put good wood on the back of the cabinet, instead of the usual plywood. He told Steve that a true craftsperson even cares about the part of a design that no one might ever see. He also got Steve interested in electronics when repairing cars. While Steve wasn't that interested in old cars, he was fascinated by technology.

The Jobs home was in Mountain View, California. It was an interesting neighbourhood to grow up in, as many residents were employed by high-tech companies that had factories in the area. Companies like Lockheed, Westinghouse and Hewlett-Packard—as well as the National Aeronautics and Space Administration—were building missile systems and innovative components for both industrial and consumer use. It was the early days of Silicon Valley. One of the most important breakthroughs to come out of the valley was the semiconductor, and by the sixties over fifty companies in and around Mountain View were manufacturing the silicon elements. Steve befriended a neighbour down the street who worked for one of those companies. He was always tinkering in his garage and was happy to show Steve what he was working on. One day he gave Steve a Heathkit, a DIY assembly set containing low-end parts, detailed line drawings and soldering tips that let hobby-ists build amateur radios and other small electronic equipment. It was right up Steve's alley and it fuelled his fascination. That same neighbour arranged for Steve to join the Hewlett-Packard Explorer's Club, a group of fifteen or so students who would meet in the company's cafeteria once a week to hear HP engineers talk about their latest creations. One of those engineers took Steve on a tour of the HP lab and it was on this tour that Steve laid eyes on his first computer. He also spotted a desktop prototype that night that made a lasting impression. The club encouraged students to tackle their own projects. In a scenario that would come to exem-plify Steve's chutzpah, one day when he needed parts for a project, he looked up Bill Hewlett's home phone number, called the HP founder and actually asked him for help locating the parts. Hewlett was impressed by the kid's confidence and not only helped Steve but got him a job on the HP assembly line.

In his last few years of high school, Steve Jobs attended an elec-tronics class where he met a shy student named Steve Wozniak. Five years older than Jobs, Wozniak already had a big reputation among the students for his technical knowledge and aptitude. The diametric opposite of Jobs, Wozniak was a socially awkward wunderkind who liked to stay in the shadows working on cir-cuit boards, whereas Jobs liked to be out front, asking questions and defying authority. Wozniak's father was a brilliant engineer who would go on to become a rocket scientist at Lockheed, and he taught young Wozniak about circuitry and resistors while Woz was still in the second grade. Because complex algebra came so eas-ily to Wozniak, he marvelled at how simple these new computers were. The day Jobs met Wozniak, they shook hands after class and sat on a curb talking for a few hours. Wozniak told Jobs about the kinds of things he'd like to design and Jobs understood instantly and completely. The introverted Wozniak had finally met a friend who understood his passion. Jobs had finally met someone who knew more about electronics than he did.

Their first collaboration would define their relationship. Wozniak devised a little contraption, called a Blue Box, capable of replicating the tones that triggered long-distance signals on the AT&T network. The device essentially tricked AT&T's system into making long-distance calls for free. Woz thought the Blue Box was naughty fun, but Jobs figured it could actually be sold. He estimated a Blue Box required about $40 worth of parts, then brazenly decided they could sell them for $150 each. So Woz made a hundred Blue Boxes and Jobs sold them all. The Blue Box proved that their complementary skills of engineering and marketing vision could actually be worth something. It was from this seed that Apple would eventually sprout one day.

Not long after, Wozniak headed to Berkeley, and Jobs's parents kept their promise to Joanne Schieble and sent him to Reed College in Oregon. But Jobs became bored with the classes, eventually dropped out and went back to Mountain View. He saw an ad for a low-level job at Atari, marched over to the office and told the receptionist he wasn't leaving the lobby until they gave him a job. Even in his salad days, Jobs was a force to be reckoned with. Wozniak would never have dreamed of pulling that stunt in a million years. But it worked and Jobs found himself working at Atari—first on the day shift, though he was moved to the night shift after other Atari staff complained about his abrasive personality and lack of basic hygiene. Jobs loved the friendliness of Atari's games. They were designed so simply they didn't even come with a manual. He particularly loved the "never take no for an answer" attitude of Atari founder Nolan Bushnell. Both aspects would inform Jobs's perspective going forward.

The January 1975 issue of *Popular Electronics* was a turning point in history. The cover featured a picture of the first personal computer. Called the Altair, it was a $495 pile of parts that hobbyists could solder together. The resulting computer couldn't do much, but it caught the attention of four very specific people: Bill Gates and Paul Allen up in Washington State, as well as Steve Jobs and Steve Wozniak down in California. Little did the world know how that unassuming article would forever alter the future. Gates and Allen were inspired to work on a BASIC computer language, while Wozniak began contemplating the potential of computer hardware. Three months later, a group in California who were also taken with the *Popular Electronics* article organized the Homebrew Computer Club in the neighbouring Menlo Park area. The first ad for the club said, "Are you building your own computer? Terminal? TV? Typewriter? . . . If so, you might like to come to a gathering of people with like-minded interests." That was a dream come true for Wozniak, who anxiously attended the first meeting. At that first gathering, Wozniak saw a specification sheet for a microprocessor, a single chip that contained an entire central processing unit, and a historic light bulb went off in his mind. He had been busy designing a terminal with a keyboard and a monitor that would connect to a remote mini-computer. But if he were to use a microprocessor, he could put some of the capacity of the mini-computer inside the terminal itself. That meant it could become a small, standalone computer on a desktop. In that moment, the entire vision for a personal computer assembled itself in his mind. He took that thought and sketched it out on paper. That sketch would one day become the Apple I.

Woz was employed at Hewlett-Packard and after work each day, he would return at night to quietly tinker on his side project.

He soldered the pieces to a motherboard and then wrote the software that would hopefully trigger the microprocessor to display images on the screen. After a few months, he was ready to test his creation. He typed a few characters on the keyboard and, magically, they appeared on the screen. Wozniak stared at the screen in amazement. It was milestone moment, because it was the first time in history anyone had typed on a keyboard and watched the characters show up on the computer screen in front of their very eyes without accessing a remote mainframe. It was June 29, 1975.

When Woz showed his friend, Jobs was wide-eyed as he contemplated the potential. He peppered Woz with questions. From that point on, Jobs accompanied Wozniak to the Homebrew meetings. The ethos of the club was to share knowledge and Woz was open and welcoming. But Jobs was firmly against that altruism. He wanted Wozniak to stop giving his schematics away for free and, instead, build printed circuit boards Jobs could sell. Wozniak said, "Every time I designed something great, Steve would find a way to make money for us. It never crossed my mind to sell computers."

And there was the partnership in a nutshell.

Wozniak was the programming genius, Jobs the visionary. They pooled their money, managed to scrape together just over a thousand dollars and started a company. When it came to naming that company, Jobs had an idea. He had just come back from an apple farm. He was experimenting with a fruit-based diet and wondered if the name Apple might be simple and friendly. Attached to the word "computer," it would induce a memorable double-take of something organic colliding with technology. Wozniak agreed and a company was born.

But there was still one problem. Wozniak was hesitant to join Apple full-time. He liked his job at Hewlett-Packard and was loyal to the company. Not only that, he felt he had to offer his breakthrough to HP first, since it had been built at their facility and he was their employee. Jobs disagreed completely, but Woz believed it was the right thing to do. When he presented his idea to his HP superiors, they were impressed, but thought it was ideal for hobbyists and didn't fit into Hewlett-Packard's corporate strategy.

That's what you'd call a teeny mistake, in hindsight.

But with that, Wozniak was free to join the partnership. Jobs managed to land a $25,000 order from a local electronics store, but the store wanted fully assembled circuit boards. It was a big order for a production line that was still working out of the Jobs garage. Not long after, Jobs came to the conclusion that personal computers should come in a complete package—with a case and a built-in keyboard as well as software and a power supply. Woz began to work on that idea, which would eventually become the Apple II.

To fill that $25,000 order, they needed significant working capital. So Jobs pitched the rights to the Apple II to the president of Atari. He turned it down. Then Jobs pitched to Commodore. They weren't interested, either. Jobs then went back to Atari to ask CEO Bushnell if he would personally put in $50,000 in return for one-third of the company. As Bushnell now says looking back, "I was so smart I said no. It's kind of fun to think about that, when I'm not crying." But Bushnell did do Jobs a favour by introducing him to a venture capitalist named Don Valentine. Valentine was intrigued by what he saw in that garage and would eventually invest in Apple, but told Jobs the company first needed to find a partner who knew how to write a business plan and who understood marketing and distribution. Valentine then introduced Jobs to Mike Markkula, a wealthy ex-Intel manager who had semi-retired at the age of thirty-three. Jobs and Wozniak liked him instantly. A deal was struck: Markkula guaranteed Apple a line of credit for $250,000 in return for an equal share of the company. They would each own 26 percent, with the rest put in reserve for future investors. The company could finally fulfill its orders now that it had working capital. Jobs secretly thought Markkula would never see his money again.

Markkula drafted a business plan that aimed way beyond hobbyists. He wanted a product that appealed to the masses. Markkula believed you should never start a company with the goal of getting rich. Your goal should be making something you believe in and building a company that will last. He wrote up "The Apple Marketing Philosophy," which stressed three main points. The first was empathy, an intimate connection with the feelings of the customer. The second was focus, to prioritize the important opportunities and eliminate all the unimportant things. The third was to position Apple in a creative, professional manner so people would perceive the company as creative and professional. Jobs would absorb and internalize those three principles and apply them throughout his entire career.

In April 1977, the Apple II was introduced at the West Coast Computer Faire in San Francisco. The computer looked sleek in its sculpted beige case and was sexier than anything else on display at the event. They landed three hundred orders. It was official: Apple was now a fully fledged business with a dozen employees and a line of credit. Time to move out of the Jobses' family garage and into rented offices in Cupertino.

Markkula held the role of chair, but he wanted to bring someone else in to run the day-to-day business of the company. Jobs wasn't happy about that. Even though he was only twenty-two and knew he wasn't experienced enough to run a company, relinquishing control was agonizing for him. That septic feeling would be shades of things to come. Markkula brought in a colleague from his Intel days named Mike Scott to fill the president position. Markkula assigned Scott one priority over all:

To manage Steve Jobs.

Scott was one of the few people in Jobs's life who could easily resist the sheer, hypnotic force of his will. Even though the volatile relationship threw off sparks, it somehow seemed to work as the company became more and more successful every day. Apple II sales rose dramatically, from 2,500 units in 1977 to 210,000 in 1981. While Jobs was driven to evolve their product line, he hit some stumbling blocks along the way. The Apple III would fail, as would the Lisa. But that streak of bad luck would all change the day Jobs took a walk through the offices of Xerox.

The Xerox Corporation had a very inventive research facility located in Palo Alto, California, far away from its head office in Connecticut. That geographical distance gave the group a great amount of freedom. When the Xerox venture capital division showed an interest in investing in the second round of Apple's financing in 1979, Jobs said he would allow Xerox to invest $1 million—in return for getting a look at its latest technology. The engineers at Xerox PARC were hesitant to open their kimono, but at the same time wanted to show off their latest advances, especially since head office seemed to show little interest in them. When they unveiled the graphical interface they were working on, Jobs was stunned. He knew in an instant he had just seen the future of personal computing. As an added bonus, he was convinced Xerox had no idea what it had on its hands. The technology was based on another Xerox PARC innovation called bitmapping. At the time, computers were limited to rudimentary characters and numerals. But bitmapping used pixels, much smaller bits that could be manipulated to create beautiful fonts and graphics as well as breathtaking onscreen displays. As per their agreement, Xerox purchased 100,000 Apple shares at $10 each. (One year later when Apple went public, that investment would be worth over $17 million.) Apple, in return, borrowed and/or stole that graphical interface concept and kicked it through the goalposts in a way not even the minds at Xerox could have imagined.

Jobs had a philosophy (by way of Markkula) that if you chase profit, you skimp on quality. But if you chase quality, profits will chase you. He also wasn't a believer in consumer research. He didn't think the public knew what they wanted until you gave it to them, subscribing to Henry Ford's dictum that if he had asked the public what they wanted, they would have said a faster horse. Apple's mission was to invent the future. On the day Apple went public, the company was valued at $1.79 billion. Three hundred people became millionaires. Twenty-five-year-old Steve Jobs was suddenly worth $256 million. Profits certainly did come chasing after Apple.

When Apple was developing the Macintosh, Jobs insisted the computer not only be friendly to use, but look friendly. He even had his team design the front of the Mac to resemble the contours of a human face. He insisted that the circuit boards and interior design be beautiful, even though no one would ever see inside a Mac— the lesson he had learned from his father. When the Macintosh was finally finished, Jobs had all forty-five of his engineers sign a document and had all those signatures engraved inside every Mac. Artists sign their work and he wanted his team to think of the Mac as a piece of art.

The Macintosh computer was a runaway success. It altered the personal computer industry forever. That success fuelled huge growth for the company. But along the way, Mike Scott's management of the company became erratic and he was eventually relieved of his duties. Mike Markkula had never wanted to be president, but reluctantly took on the role again while they searched for a replacement. When Jobs made noises about possibly running the company, Markkula told him he still wasn't ready. He was too inexperienced and too prickly. Again, Jobs was faced with giving over control to somebody outside the company and it irked him. But Markkula insisted. They agreed to hire a top corporate headhunter to scout out potential candidates, widening their search beyond the technology industry and instead looking for someone who understood marketing. Someone Wall Street would like.

At the top of the list was John Sculley. He was president of the Pepsi Cola division of PepsiCo, and his Pepsi Challenge campaign was the talk of the industry. Sculley was raised in a prominent family on the Upper East Side of Manhattan. His father was a Wall Street lawyer, and Sculley had an undergraduate degree from Brown, topped with a business degree from Wharton. His innovative marketing ideas had accelerated his rise through the ranks at Pepsi. He was on a career track to maybe one day run PepsiCo, so when he was approached by the headhunter about Apple, he wasn't enthusiastic. Until, that is, he mentioned the opportunity to his kids, who gushed because they thought Jobs was a celebrity. Their reaction intrigued Sculley, who agreed to a tentative, exploratory meeting the next time he was in California.

When Sculley finally did walk through the doors of Apple's headquarters, he was immediately taken aback by how casual the offices were. They were sparse and shockingly unassuming for the hottest tech company in the Valley. The staff dressed less formally than the Pepsi janitorial staff. But those hesitations evaporated when he spent time with the evangelical Jobs. His enthusiasm and vision for the future was bewitching. But Sculley's heart was still firmly rooted at Pepsi.

When Jobs was in New York a short time later, Sculley agreed to meet with him again. Over dinner, Sculley walked Jobs through the Pepsi Generation marketing strategy, telling him they weren't selling a liquid; they were selling an energetic and optimistic lifestyle. He explained how to generate buzz. He told Jobs Apple had an opportunity to create an Apple generation. Jobs was fascinated and told Sculley he could learn much from the Pepsi marketer, saying the dinner was one of the most exciting conversations he had ever had. Jobs was in a sly seduction mode. Sculley was still wed to Pepsi, but he was open to flirting. As author Walter Isaacson says in his definitive biography of Steve Jobs, Sculley was now playing hard—but not impossible—to get.

Jobs called Sculley often, keeping the embers burning. The next time Jobs was due to fly out to the east coast, he arranged to meet with Sculley again. Sculley took him to the lavish Pepsi headquarters with its sprawling lawns and manicured grounds. To Jobs, the ostentation clearly symbolized the difference between the polished Fortune 500 establishment and the feisty digital upstarts of Silicon Valley. He chose to overlook the warning signal.

The courtship continued on both coasts. In Cupertino, Jobs was excited to show Sculley the development of the Macintosh and brought him into the inner sanctum. Sculley was more than impressed, both with the Mac and with Jobs's showmanship skills. In New York, they toured the Metropolitan Museum together, with Sculley giving Jobs a tutorial in the evolution of art. Jobs lapped it up. The teacher had found what he felt was a brilliant student. The student knew the teacher was smitten.

One night in New York, Jobs made a move to consummate the relationship. He offered Sculley a $1 million salary and an additional $1 million signing bonus, a $1 million golden parachute, options on 350,000 shares of Apple stock and the difference in cost to buy a home in California equivalent to the one he owned in Connecticut. Sculley demurred, saying maybe they should just remain friends, with him quietly coaching Jobs from the sidelines. That's when Steve Jobs made one of the most persuasive pitches in business history. He looked at Sculley and asked, "Do you want to spend the rest of your life selling sugared water, or do you want a chance to change the world?"

Sculley has since said that sentence was like a punch to the gut. It was both an insult and a challenge. It haunted him. It wouldn't let him sleep. It became the pea under the mattress from that moment on. For the first time in the four-month courtship, Sculley finally admitted to himself that he couldn't say no. He was willing to walk away from a big, assured fast-track future at Pepsi to join Apple. He realized, once and for all, that he was willing to resign from the navy to join the pirates.

Hiring Sculley would turn out to be a huge mistake for Jobs. The decision would eventually shred both men. It would be years before Jobs would heal. Then benefit.

Sculley assumed the role of president at Apple in May 1983 and Mike Markkula shifted to the board. It was more of a culture shock than Sculley had anticipated. He watched in horror as the Apple staff constantly bickered and sniped at Jobs in meetings. No one would have ever dared do that to the chair of Pepsi. Sculley sometimes recoiled at the rudeness Jobs would inflict on his staff. In the early months, Jobs and Sculley talked multiple times a day as Sculley slowly found his sea legs. They seemed to be on the same wavelength, finishing each other's sentences. Sculley was amazed at how alike they seemed, if not in temperament, then at least in philosophy and vision. Sculley said he sometimes thought he was watching Jobs play him in a movie. But something else was happening just under the surface.

Jobs would tell Sculley that he was the only one who truly understood what Apple was trying to achieve. He would heap praise on Sculley and confide in him. He made Sculley believe they were soulmates. But Jobs was manipulating him. That meant even though Sculley was managing the company, Jobs could still manage Sculley. Over time, the easier the manipulation became, the more contemptuous Jobs would become of Sculley. One astute Apple employee observed that Jobs was projecting on Sculley attributes Sculley didn't really have. That lit a long slow fuse that only grew more dangerous as time went on.

Their first big disagreement came when pricing the Macintosh. Jobs wanted to keep it under the important $2,000 threshold, at a price point of $1,995. Sculley wanted to add $500 to the tag to cover marketing costs. Sculley, the experienced pragmatist, told Jobs he could have the $1,995 price or he could have a big marketing launch budget, but he couldn't have both. Behind Sculley's back, Jobs began quietly telling his team he wouldn't let Sculley get away with it. But in the end, Sculley got his way. Later, Jobs would point to this decision as the reason the initially strong Macintosh sales eventually slowed and Microsoft grabbed the opportunity to dominate the market. But in that moment, in the clash of wills with Sculley, Jobs began to feel he was losing control of his company and his pet product.

It was a feeling that would begin to fester in Steve Jobs.

The Macintosh was a revolutionary personal computer and Jobs wanted a revolutionary commercial to launch the computer. Apple's advertising agency, Chiat/Day (pronounced Shy-It/Day), was arguably the most creative firm in the industry (I worked there from 1988 to 1989). The agency was cofounded by New Yorker Jay Chiat, who was the mirror image of Steve Jobs in the personality department. Driven, bold, blunt and chronically unwilling to take no for an answer, he dared to build a powerful ad agency on the west coast in an industry that huddled in the east. He believed in "ads with a jolt" that broke through the public's indifference toward commercial messages. Like Jobs, he was propelled by an odd disdain for any objective he managed to attain, as if his ability to accomplish it diminished the inherent value of the achievement. Also like Jobs, he didn't suffer fools and preferred aggressive agendas. He set impossibly high standards and drove his people hard, but the award-winning campaigns that made brands famous, and resulting accolades, made the gruelling sacrifices worthwhile. Internally, the company was known as "Chiat/Day and night." The shop's president and executive creative director, Lee Clow, was the antithesis of Chiat. He was a tall, bearded Los Angeles–born surfer who personified the laid-back Cali vibe. He had a perpetual white sunglasses stripe across his eyes. His daily uniform was Hawaiian shirts, shorts and sandals—even in formal presentations to new clients. But Lee Clow was an advertising genius. He held strong convictions on what made for effective advertising, and he had an uncanny ability to understand a client's branding problems and inspire great ideas to solve them. He also possessed a superpower Chiat needed: Clow was adored by his creative teams. Chiat was mercurial and cracked a stinging whip. Clow placed his body between the combustible Chiat and his creative department, creating a safe space for his people to consistently exceed Chiat's nosebleed standards. Not unlike Jobs and Woz, the odd-couple partnership was formidable.

Jobs gave Clow complete freedom to present any idea to him, no matter how crazy or bleeding edge. For the agency, it was a relationship you would never find at IBM. To answer Jobs's demand for a show-stopping, jaw-dropping commercial for the Macintosh launch on January 24, 1984, Clow and his crew came back with an intriguing theme line: "Why 1984 won't be like 1984." It was a reference to George Orwell's dystopian novel of the same name, which featured a society under the mind control of Big Brother. And in Jobs's mind, Big Brother was IBM. Chiat/Day then presented an idea for a sixty-second TV commercial titled "1984." The storyline begins with a rebellious young woman being pursued by armed Orwellian storm troopers. She runs toward a huge screen, where Big Brother is lulling a crowd into a spirit-crushing stupor with something called the Information Purification Directives. She runs into the room, halts suddenly, swings a sledgehammer and releases it with an urgent scream, destroying the screen. Then a calm voice-over intones: "On January 24th, Apple Computer will introduce Macintosh. And you'll see why 1984 won't be like *1984*." Jobs loved the idea and gave Clow the go-ahead to shoot the commercial. The agency hired Ridley Scott, who was fresh off the futuristic film *Blade Runner*, to direct the ad. The resulting commercial was awe-inspiring; the advertising industry would eventually come to regard "1984" as the best commercial of the twentieth century. It would change the ad business forever by altering the scale of the industry's thinking. It showed Madison Avenue that commercials could have the same production values as a major motion picture—a notion that could only have come from an ad agency based next door to Hollywood.

The commercial wasn't only highly creative and jaw-dropping —as per Jobs's original request—it also positioned Apple, and by extension, Jobs, as rebels, pirates and slayers of IBM. The commercial was set to run during the Super Bowl in January 1984. Jobs excitedly screened the commercial for the Apple board of directors in December.

It didn't go well.

When the final frame of the commercial dipped to black, the board sat in stunned silence. Markkula was the first to speak, saying, "Who wants to move to find a new ad agency?" Other board members hung their heads. Several said it was the worst commercial they had ever seen. It didn't even show the product. Where the hell was the Macintosh? Surprisingly, the master marketer in the room, Sculley, didn't side with Jobs and ordered Chiat/Day to sell off the two expensive Super Bowl time slots Apple had purchased—one sixty seconds, the other thirty seconds. The decision was made: the commercial would not run.

Jobs was fit to be tied. It was another tremor in the fault line of his relationship with Sculley and he raged at the board, making matters worse. He later showed the commercial to Woz, who loved it. When Woz asked what the cost of the commercial time was, Jobs told him $800,000. Woz said he would happily pay half the tab if Jobs paid the other half. Later, Jobs huddled with Chiat/Day. The agency strongly believed it was their best work ever. (Interestingly, the agency had put the ad through research, where it failed dramatically, scoring a 5 against a norm of 29. Chiat paid for the research but never showed it to Jobs. Chiat/Day executive Fred Goldberg has since said it wouldn't have changed Jobs's mind. He knew it was great the second he saw it. He preferred intuition over science.) So Chiat/Day and Jobs devised a plan. The agency sold off the thirty-second Super Bowl time slot, but told the board they couldn't find a buyer for the pricier sixty-second spot so close to game time. In reality, Jay Chiat had told his media department not to try too hard to sell the longer spot, or risk losing their jobs. Now believing they were up against the wall and facing the possibility of losing half a million dollars, the board resigned itself to running the only commercial they had in the expensive Super Bowl slot. They weren't happy.

Jobs smiled that pirate smirk.

The "1984" commercial aired in the third quarter of Super Bowl XVIII, which featured the Los Angeles Raiders playing the Washington Redskins. Ninety-six million people were watching. When CBS cut back to the game, the colour commentator actually said "Wow!" The commercial was a grand slam in a football game. Switchboards lit up at Apple, Chiat/Day and CBS. All three major networks did stories on the ad. Over fifty local stations covered it. The commercial generated an estimated $5 million in free publicity as hundreds of newspapers and magazines wrote about it. "1984" did more than launch the Macintosh; it launched an ideal, a mission statement that continues to propel Apple to this day. It also launched the era when Super Bowl commercials became spectacles unto themselves, signalling the beginning of ads as news. On the following Monday, 200,000 people flocked to stores to view the Mac, driving $4.5 million in sales within six hours. Seventy-two thousand Macs were sold in the first hundred days, exceeding Apple's most optimistic estimates by 50 percent. It was an empowering moment for Steve Jobs. And a comeuppance for the board.

At the Macintosh launch to shareholders on January 24, Jobs began the event by quoting Bob Dylan's "The Times They Are a-Changin'," before Sculley took to the stage to report on the company's earnings. He concluded by saying, "The most important thing that has happened to me in the last nine months at Apple has been a chance to develop a friendship with Steve Jobs. For me, the rapport we have developed means an awful lot." Jobs returned to deliver a cryptic story about how IBM wanted total domination in the computer world—but maybe Apple could be the one company to stop Big Blue. Then the lights went down and "1984" hit the screen. When the line "And you'll see why 1984 won't be like *1984*" rang out, the entire audience jumped to its feet and cheered. Jobs then walked dramatically over to a small table and removed a cloth bag to reveal the Macintosh. As the theme from *Chariots of Fire* thundered through the packed auditorium, the Mac came alive. The crowd gasped as beautiful fonts and incredible graphics floated across the screen. Jobs then invited the Mac to speak for itself. With that, a digitized voice said, "Hello, I am Macintosh. It sure is great to get out of that bag." The crowd roared. "I'd like to share with you the maxim I thought of the first time I met an IBM mainframe. Never trust a computer you can't lift." The crowd went ballistic. The ovation lasted for five full minutes.

The wild success of the Macintosh and all the attendant cover stories gave Jobs a new level of celebrity. Though Sculley had been brought in to manage Jobs, he rewarded Jobs with even more authority. Jobs threw a one-year anniversary party for Sculley and invited the board and some key shareholders. Making a toast, Jobs said the last year working with Sculley had been the absolute best of his life. Sculley returned the toast, saying Apple had one leader, "Steve and me." Concerned looks darted between board members. They appreciated the camaraderie, but clearly Sculley was too eager to please Jobs. The board knew Jobs had to be controlled or else he would do the controlling. The entire evening didn't sit well with the members. It seemed forced. It seemed dangerous.

The seams in the relationship really began to tear in 1985. It was becoming more and more apparent Sculley didn't have any real interest in the details of the components Apple was producing. That was unforgivable to Jobs. For his part, Sculley felt Jobs's obsession with the smallest, seemingly inconsequential details were a monumental waste of his valuable time. He was also having increasing difficulty with Jobs's offensive behaviour toward his staff. The two men started to bristle around each other and the troops were picking up on the turmoil.

Meanwhile, sales of the Macintosh began to slow down. After a year, the honeymoon was over. Flaws in the Mac were becoming more noticeable as time went on. The machine was gorgeous but underpowered. It needed connectivity to other computers. It desperately needed business software, dubbed Macintosh Office, but it was slow in coming. At the same time, IBM had slashed the price of its PCjr from $1,698 to under $900 and was stealing market share. Dealers found themselves with an excess of Apple inventory. Sculley had to shut down four of the company's manufacturing plants for a week to slow production. Wall Street analysts began cutting Apple's earnings estimates and the stock fell to new lows each day. It was becoming increasingly obvious that most people couldn't afford to spend over $2,000 on a computer just to play video games, balance a chequebook and file recipes. The average consumer simply couldn't do anything useful with a computer yet.

Members of Jobs's staff secretly told Sculley that no one on the team really knew what the next generation of the Macintosh would look like. Jobs was in a funk with the lowering Mac sales and was constantly changing his mind when issuing direction. Staff couldn't keep up with him and bridled at his management style. Morale was eroding. Key executives and middle managers were starting to leave Apple. Other executives voiced concerns that the company had two drivers fighting for control of the steering wheel. They challenged Sculley in meetings, saying if he was the CEO, why was Jobs telling everybody what to do? But the more Sculley challenged and questioned Jobs, the more they butted heads.

Meanwhile, the Apple board was increasingly alarmed at the toll the turmoil was taking on the company. Both Sculley and Jobs were called on the carpet. Sculley was told to focus on managing the company with more authority, and Jobs was told, in no uncertain terms, to focus on fixing the Macintosh division. But the more sales plunged, the more erratic and mercurial Jobs became. Apple managers began to complain more loudly to Sculley. Staff felt Apple was now a car racing down the highway with a brick on the gas pedal and the brake lines were cut. Jobs's behaviour was becoming more and more indefensible. He was now calling Sculley a bozo behind his back, "bozo" being the word Jobs reserved for the people he held most in contempt. Jobs also created an unhealthy competition between his Macintosh group and the Apple II division. The Apple II was still selling more units than Macintosh, but Jobs referred to that division, too, as bozos. The Macintosh people even began wearing buttons with a line running through the face of Bozo the Clown. As Sculley later said, "I had given Steve greater power than he had ever had and I had created a monster."

Sculley did not relish a showdown with Jobs. It wasn't his style and Jobs was a wild card in a confrontational situation. Finally, Sculley called a meeting with Jobs and told him that while he thought he was brilliant, he had lost confidence in Jobs's ability to run the Macintosh division. He also called Jobs out for badmouthing him to staff. Jobs felt ambushed and laid into Sculley, telling him he knew nothing about computers and that he had been a huge disappointment since coming to Apple. Sculley didn't back down, saying he was going to recommend to the board that Jobs be relieved of his position running Macintosh. Jobs said, "I don't believe you're going to do that." Sculley said, "Yes, I am." Jobs was incensed. What was left of their friendship was now irretrievably shattered. Jobs had brought Sculley to Apple and now Sculley was telling Jobs to step down.

At that board meeting in April 1985, Sculley said he wanted Jobs to relinquish his responsibilities as head of the Mac division and instead focus on new product development with a small team in a separate building. He told the board it had become impossible to run the company with Jobs in dual roles as chair and Macintosh general manager. As chair, he was over Sculley; as head of Macintosh, he was under Sculley. Jobs—and the company—had to accept Sculley as the sole chief executive. Then he left the room so Jobs could address the board. Jobs told them Sculley knew nothing about computers and that the entire problem sat squarely in Sculley's lap. But the board wasn't having any of it. They tore into Jobs. They told him he had been acting foolishly for over a year and had frittered away his right to head the division. Jobs was speechless. When he left the room and Sculley was brought back in, he simply told the board they could either back him with full authority or find another CEO. He was fully prepared to resign. On the other hand, if supported, he would transition Jobs to the new position in an orderly and respectful manner over a short period of time.

The board sided unanimously with Sculley.

Jobs seethed at the betrayal.

Subsequent meetings between Jobs and Sculley devolved into yelling sessions. When Apple received approval to sell computers in China, Sculley was to travel there to formally sign the deal. Jobs secretly planned to stage a coup in his absence, but word leaked to Sculley and he cancelled his trip. At an executive meeting the very next day, Sculley confronted Jobs in front of everyone and demanded to know whether Jobs was scheming to throw him out of the company. Jobs was caught off guard yet again. Sculley then asked the executives, in a show of hands, to vote for either him or Jobs. It was a calculated risk, as the executives were well aware of the escalating conflict. When the last hand was raised, all had sided with Sculley.

Jobs left and slammed the door.

A few days later, Jobs asked Sculley to reconsider his decision and let him retain his position overseeing Macintosh. Sculley was unmoved. Then Jobs actually asked Sculley if they could run Apple together. You can only imagine Sculley's face in that moment. Sculley had to make a definitive move, so he double-checked with the board to make sure he still had their full support. He did. He moved Jobs to the position of board chair with no operational responsibilities—a purely ceremonial role.

Essentially, Jobs was out.

Not long after, Jobs asked to be added to the agenda of a board meeting. Wary of his intentions, the board braced for another showdown. But instead, Jobs said he wanted to leave Apple and start a new company, building computers for the educational and research market. He told the board he wouldn't compete with Apple and that he would take only a handful of low-level staffers with him. At first, Mike Markkula demanded to know why Jobs would take *any* Apple staffers with him, citing a breach of fiduciary duty. Jobs told him those staffers were planning on leaving anyway. Then word leaked Jobs was actually taking five key members of Apple's staff. The board was livid and sued Jobs for secretly starting a company that would, indeed, compete against Apple and for recruiting key staff members while still an executive with Apple. Jobs delivered a resignation letter to Markkula and sold his 6.5 million Apple shares for over $100 million, keeping one solitary share just so he could attend Apple shareholder meetings if he chose to. When the Apple staff went to sweep out Jobs's empty office, they found a picture of Jobs and Sculley smashed on the floor.

They would never speak again.

The idea of creating computers for the education and research markets was exciting for Jobs. He named his new company NeXT and paid famous designer Paul Rand (who had designed logos for Westinghouse, ABC and even archenemy IBM) the sum of $100,000 to create a logo. There was definitely a gap in the market and Jobs was eager to market to the gap. He wanted to use the same product designer who had a contract with Apple, but he needed the lawsuit to go away first. So, through lawyers, he negotiated. Apple agreed to drop the suit with the following stipulations: The NeXT product would be positioned as a high-end workstation, it would be marketed directly to colleges and universities and it would not ship before March 1987. Lastly, and most importantly, the NeXT machines could "not use an operating system compatible with the Macintosh." That condition, meant to protect Apple, would be the very reason Jobs would one day return to the company.

The NeXT workstation was designed as a perfect black cube, echoed in Rand's cube-shaped logo design. While the Mac was revolutionary due to its graphical interface, NeXT was to be the next evolution to object-oriented programming based on an optical disk. Jobs sent a team to talk to universities like Harvard and solicit opinions and desires for their future computing needs. Jobs then built a bleeding-edge factory with his usual obsessive colour schemes. He put in $7 million of his own money, but that cash was flying out and nothing was flying in yet. Jobs needed to find additional funding. He offered venture capital firms 10 percent of NeXT for $3 million. He had no takers until Ross Perot, founder of Electronic Data Systems, came to the rescue. He loved the idea of NeXT and had always regretted passing up the chance to invest in Microsoft in the early days when a young Bill Gates came knocking. He didn't want to make the same mistake twice, plus he saw a little bit of himself in the brashness of Jobs. Years ago, he had used a loan from his wife to build EDS, which he eventually sold to General Motors for $2.4 billion. Perot purchased 16 percent of NeXT for $20 million.

But in the end, the NeXT computer was just too expensive. Jobs had promised academia a price between $2,000 and $3,000, but the NeXT came in at $6,500. The optional printer was another $2,000, and the slow speed of the optical disk meant an external hard drive that cost an additional $2,500. On top of all that, the delivery deadlines were constantly missed. The NeXT factory was set up to produce ten thousand units per month, but by the time NeXT finally arrived in 1988, the hype had evaporated and sales were just four hundred a month. The company bottom line continued to bleed. Eventually, Jobs realized he had to license the NeXT operating system in order to survive. It went against every pixel of his being to do it, but it was a necessary loss. He also gave up producing hardware, one of his passions. Soon after, he sold his pristine factory.

Jobs also seethed from a distance as he watched Apple's market share slowly erode. When he left, Jobs believed Apple had a ten-year lead over Microsoft, but that head start had been frittered away due to a lack of innovation. Under Sculley, Apple actually had its most prosperous period, growing from $600 million in net sales in 1983 to over $8 billion ten years later. But in 1992 Apple's earnings began to drastically decline in response to deteriorating Mac margins and fierce price wars with competitors. Sculley had begun to get involved in politics, helping Bill Clinton with his campaign, and it was diverting Sculley's attention. He had also bet the farm on his pet project, the soon-to-be-much-maligned personal digital assistant, the Newton MessagePad. When Apple declared its first quarterly loss that year, over twelve hundred Apple employees were laid off, representing one-fifth of its workforce. Just as they had with Jobs, the board eventually lost faith in Sculley, who resigned as CEO on June 13, 1993. The head of Apple's European operations, Michael Spindler, then took over the reins. Market share plunged further from a high of 16 percent to an anemic 4 percent by 1996. Spindler tried and failed to sell Apple to Hewlett-Packard, Sun and then IBM. He was ousted in 1996 and replaced by a board member by the name of Gil Amelio, ex-CEO of National Semiconductor.

Remember that name?

During Amelio's first year as CEO, Apple lost over a billion dollars. But he had an even bigger problem on his hands than the freefalling share price. Apple was betting heavily on a new operating system called Copland, but Amelio quickly discovered the system was ineffective and didn't solve Apple's various networking and memory problems. It was also nowhere near being ready to meet the promised 1997 launch date. Amelio desperately needed to find an alternative. He flirted with a few other operating systems and even considered Microsoft's Windows NT. But none seemed to fit the bill. There was one more option out there.

But would Amelio dare make the call?

In December 1996, Jobs stepped foot in the Apple offices for the first time in over a decade. He pitched NeXT as a perfect solution to Apple's problem and told Amelio that once he did his due diligence, he would probably want to buy not just the operating system, but the entire company. Jobs sensed an opportunity to save his failing business and also get back inside Apple, sit on the board and maybe, just maybe, claim the CEO chair. NeXT was, in fact, the perfect solution for Apple, but Amelio knew that bringing Jobs back would be a dangerous move. Colleagues warned that NeXT was a Trojan horse and that Jobs would come bounding out with his troops, sights set on Amelio's job.

But Amelio needed a solution and decided to buy NeXT. He and Jobs got together at Jobs's house to negotiate the acquisition. The two went back and forth before settling on a price of $400 million. Jobs wanted cash, but Amelio wanted Jobs to take cash and stock, so he would have "skin in the game." Jobs eventually agreed, then made a pitch to sit on the Apple board. Amelio resisted, but the pitch was a check on the chessboard. Amelio didn't know it, but he was about to surrender his queen. He offered Jobs a position overseeing the operating system group. Even though Jobs was quietly insulted, he told Amelio to announce to the company he was coming back as an "advisor to the chairman."

Jobs slowly started putting his NeXT people into the power positions at Apple. He badgered Amelio to shut down the Newton. It wasn't doing well, but more than that, it was a Sculley product and Jobs wanted it jackhammered into the ground. By all accounts, Amelio wanted a relationship with Jobs and felt they were on a similar wavelength. In reality, Jobs thought Amelio was not only in the wrong position, but breathtakingly ineffective. The chair of the Apple board, Ed Woolard, former CEO of DuPont, who had taken over for Markkula, was alarmed after Amelio gave a speech at the shareholders meeting. Amelio didn't seem to be in control of the situation and didn't handle the questions well. Woolard then contacted Jobs and asked him what he thought of Amelio. Jobs hesitated as he quickly did the math in his head. Telling the truth would damage his (temporary but necessary) relationship with Amelio, but holding back would damage Apple. He chose to spill.

Amelio had to go.

Woolard asked Jobs to return to Apple as CEO. Even though Jobs had been gunning for control, surprisingly, he demurred. He had purchased Pixar from George Lucas, who needed money because of a costly divorce. Jobs had assumed the role of Pixar CEO and didn't want to leave that company high and dry. But the real reason Jobs hesitated to take the steering wheel was that he didn't want to fail. He needed time to figure out whether Apple could, indeed, be salvaged. Meanwhile, Woolard advised Amelio he was fired. The following Monday, the senior Apple employees were assembled in the company auditorium. Amelio announced he was leaving the company and the interim CEO, Fred Anderson, said he would be huddling with Jobs. With that, twelve years after he had been unceremoniously dumped, Steve Jobs walked back onto the Apple stage. The open door on the Trojan horse swung in the wind. Gil Amelio had brought Jobs back because he wanted the NeXT operating system. Now he was out and Jobs was in again.

When he spoke, Jobs asked the audience a question: "Okay, tell me what's wrong with this place?" Before the crowd could answer, he yelled, "It's the products!" Then he lobbed another question that appeared to be aimed at the crowd. He said, "So what's wrong with the products?" Before anyone could blink, he blurted out the answer to his own question again: "The products *suck*! There's no sex in them anymore!"

While Jobs stressed he was assuming the CEO role only on an interim basis—hence the title iCEO—until a permanent person could be found, he dove right into the weeds. He got involved in product design and supplier negotiations, chose where to invest and where to cut, and rehired Chiat/Day (now TBWA/Chiat/

Day). He was able to exert that control because he had the backing of the board. Then in another Jobsian swing of the machete, he actually asked the board to resign. He wanted fresh blood. He asked only Woolard and one other member to stay on. That meant Mike Markkula, the man who had been with him since the Jobs family garage days in 1976, the man who had floated the company with his own money, was out, too. Jobs understood the significance of the moment, so he drove to Markkula's house to talk to him and accept his resignation personally.

Jobs began Apple's turnaround. He approved TBWA/Chiat/Day's new grammatically challenged but powerful "Think Different" campaign, featuring icons like Picasso, Einstein, Lennon and Jim Henson. The TV commercial was a manifesto celebrating the "crazy ones who push the human race forward." The posters featured the famous faces with just the tagline and the Apple logo. Jobs wasn't equating Apple with genius; he was equating Apple users with great creativity. His friend Larry Ellison, CEO of Oracle, said Jobs created the only lifestyle brand in the tech industry. He was creating an "Apple generation"—maybe the only lasting gift Sculley bestowed upon Jobs. Apple's advertising just got better and better, as Jobs was the only CEO of a multibillion-dollar company who spent three hours with his advertising agency every Wednesday afternoon. Every week. That kind of access to the CEO meant a direct line to the decision maker. No bureaucracy, no layers of people with the power to say no but none to say yes. No minions to pull the plug on daring ideas before they got to the C-suite.

After hours, Jobs would wander the halls of Apple, snooping in offices to try and get a sense of what was going on in the various groups. One night, he spotted a few ignored but interesting prototypes sitting in the office of a young product designer named Jony Ive. When he asked to see Ive the next day, the designer tucked a resignation letter in his back pocket, ready to pluck it out before

Jobs could fire him. Instead, Jobs told him he liked his thinking and that they were going to do great things together. Ive was shocked. The letter stayed in his jeans. Jobs was true to his word. Ive was, in fact, a brilliant product designer who only needed support. He now happened to have the ear of the CEO. Together, they would produce the colourful iMacs, the iPod, the iPhone, the iPad, AirPods and the various Mac computers and laptops. The Apple we know today was reborn with Jobs's second coming. He would revolutionize six industries in the coming years: personal computers, music, phones, tablet computing, digital publishing and animated movies.

You could add a seventh industry to that list: retail stores. As author Kevin Ashton insightfully says, what made Jobs unique wasn't genius, passion or vision. It was his refusal to believe that having sales and customers meant nothing was broken. He created Apple retail stores because he didn't want lame middlemen between him and his customers. When Jobs announced the launch of the stores, the press and most competitors rolled their eyes and predicted their quick demise. Today, Apple retail stores generate the most revenue per square foot in virtually every mall they inhabit. While Apple was enjoying a surge in sales, Jobs refused to believe it couldn't be better. Like Jay Chiat, he drove his staff hard, but they knew Jobs was after world-changing products, so the sacrifice seemed more than worth it. The wavering Jobs of the mid-eighties had given way to a crisp decisiveness in product and software design, saying no to many features his staff presented to him. Jobs had the uncanny ability to put himself in the shoes of customers who don't care a whit about the minutiae of the software industry. He wanted simple, elegant solutions. When asked how the iPod worked, he once said, "Plug it in. Whirrrr. Done."

When Steve Jobs returned to Apple in 1997, the company was ninety days away from declaring bankruptcy. When he died in

2011, the share price of Apple had risen over 1,300 percent. A tribute to Jobs was the fact the company share price didn't sink like a stone on the news of his passing. In 2018, Apple became the first publicly traded U.S. company to hit a market cap of $1 trillion. Just two years later Apple became the first to pass the $2 trillion mark. The operating system Jobs developed at NeXT laid the foundation for OS X, which Apple continues to build on to this day.

The mistake Jobs made of wooing John Sculley to Apple wasn't just an unfortunate clash of personalities; it eventually caused Jobs to lose the company he founded. The loss was catastrophic and devastating. But those twelve years away from Apple were transformative. Apple board member Arthur Rock said in hindsight, "The best thing ever to happen to Steve is when we fired him [and] told him to get lost." That tough love made him wiser and more mature. Jobs himself later said, "It turned out getting fired from Apple was the best thing that could have ever happened to me. The heaviness of being successful was replaced by the lightness of being a beginner again, less sure about everything. It freed me to enter one of the most creative periods of my life."

Walter Isaacson writes, "Jobs' NeXT company created a series of spectacular products that were dazzling marketing failures. This was the true learning experience. What prepared him for the great success he would have in Act III was not his ouster from his Act I at Apple, but his brilliant failures in Act II." All of which would not have happened had Jobs not made the mistake of hiring John Sculley. He had to lose his company in order to regain it. He had to leave in order to build another company Amelio would want to purchase.

Gil Amelio, a forgotten footnote in Apple's story, made one of the best decisions in business history.

Kellogg's Corn Flakes

Supressing Your Desires since 1896

J ohn Harvey Kellogg was a man with a vision. In the late
nineteenth century, he transformed the staid Western Health
Reform Institute into an extremely popular health destina-
tion, renamed the Medical and Surgical Sanitarium. The new word
was a play on the word "sanatorium" and John Harvey wanted it to
be defined as "a place where people learn to stay well." According
to the excellent book *Cerealizing America*, John Harvey's health
complex was a "combination of medical boarding house, hospital,
monastery, country club, spa and revival camp." He had a staff of
over eighty doctors, with hundreds of nurses, cooks, masseurs and
bath attendants. Patients were certainly put through their paces,
beginning with early morning calisthenics, followed by laughing
exercises (!) and gymnastics class. They suffered through mechanical poundings with chest beaters and stomach punchers and they
stood on vibrating platforms to stimulate their vital organs. They
were made to bathe endlessly and often, with salt baths, steam baths,
hot water baths, cold water baths, showers, douches and fomenta-
tions. The real treat was a steam-powered enema that could (stand

back) put fifteen gallons of water through the bowels in a matter of minutes. John Harvey was especially giddy to apply a mild form of total-body electro-shock therapy. At the end of every withering day, the patients were made to parade in step as a drill team to a piece of music called "Battle Creek Sanitarium March."

John Harvey was born in Tyrone Township, Michigan, in 1852. His father, John Preston Kellogg, was a strict, religious (and very fertile) man who fathered fifteen children. The family eventually moved to Battle Creek, Michigan, where John Sr. opened a company to manufacture brooms. As Adventists, John Preston and his second wife, Ann, were so convinced the world was going to end any minute, they believed school was a waste of time for their children. Young John Harvey left school at the age of ten to work in his father's broom company. When he got older, he went to work as a printer's assistant for a publication owned by the Adventist Church. He was a quick study and by the time he was sixteen, he was writing editorials for the church's main newspaper, the *Advent Review and Sabbath Herald*.

John Harvey would go on to become a teacher, then was encouraged to study medicine. He studied and received degrees from the Hygeio-Therapeutic College, Michigan State Normal, the University of Michigan Medical School and Bellevue Hospital in New York City. He was an incredibly hardworking student who read the latest scientific journals in French and German—remarkable in an era when even the Harvard Medical School didn't give exams because so few students could read and write. He returned to Battle Creek when he agreed to take charge of the Western Health Reform Institute for one year. He would end up staying sixty-seven years. His work in surgery, his writings and his promotional abilities made him one of the most well known people in late-nineteenth-century medicine. John Harvey had strong convictions when it came to vitality and well-being. He firmly believed the key to happiness lay in the digestive tract and urged people to avoid alcohol, drugs, tobacco and meat, observe a low-calorie diet and get moderate exercise. This advice may sound mild by today's standards, but it was radical advice for the times.

While he could be forgiven for his strict bodily therapies, he had some odd mental ones, too. Patients were required to attend musicals, Shakespearean plays and lectures by leading scientists. Women were warned that reading novels was "one of the most pernicious habits to which a young lady can become devoted. When the habit is once thoroughly fixed, it becomes as inveterate as the use of liquor or opium." So reading was out. He didn't allow alcohol, tobacco or caffeine. Mr. Fun also believed feeding his patients bland food would prevent horrible lust from building up in their loins, which would otherwise lead to the devil's playground—the dreaded masturbation.

Then one day, on August 8, 1894, John Harvey Kellogg and his younger brother, Will Keith Kellogg, made a mistake. They left some cooked wheat uncovered in the kitchen when they left to attend to more pressing matters.

That moment would change their lives.

When the brothers returned, they discovered the cooked wheat had gone stale. Not wanting to waste anything, they put it through a roller, hoping to salvage long sheets of dough. Instead, they were left with flakes. So they roasted those flakes and served them to the patients. The flakes turned out to be very popular. Will Keith told his older brother that he wanted to apply for a patent and was eventually granted one for "Flaked Cereal and a Process for Preparing Same" on April 14, 1896. Will Keith, who served as the business manager of the sanitarium, decided to try and mass-market their discovery. So he experimented with other grains and started the Battle Creek Toasted Corn Flake Company in 1906.

By 1922, the business was renamed the Kellogg Company. The brothers eventually had a falling out because Will Keith wanted to add sugar to the cereals. John Harvey completely opposed the idea, believing sugar would create sexual stirrings in their patients. So Will Keith Kellogg went it alone. He turned out to be a smart entrepreneur in those early days of modern marketing.

In the twenties, he created a mail-in promotion where millions of kids mailed in Kellogg's box tops for prizes. That made Kellogg a household name. In the thirties, during the Great Depression, Will Keith made another remarkable decision. Just as everyone was cutting back on their advertising in those tough times, he doubled his—and Kellogg's sales increased. He also groomed his next generation of customers by sponsoring *The Singing Lady* with Ireene Wicker, the first radio show for children. During the Second World War, Kellogg manufactured packaged K-rations for the troops, which created breakfast routines the soldiers would take back home with them.

In 1951, Will Keith Kellogg died at the age of ninety-one. In an ironic footnote, one of his biggest competitors was Post Cereals, started by C.W. Post—a former patient of Kellogg's at the Battle Creek Sanitarium. But in spite of the competition, the Kellogg's company continued to grow. In 1957, the Corn Flakes brand got its own mascot, a big green rooster named Cornelius, or Corny, for short. Kellogg's Corn Flakes even went to the moon with the Apollo 11 astronauts on their historic mission in 1969. It's been on breakfast tables ever since.

From that one mistake in the Battle Creek Sanitarium kitchen back in 1894, Kellogg's Corn Flakes is now marketed in 180 countries around the world.

Rob Lowe

Sex, Lies and Videotape

Hard to believe, but there was a time when Rob Lowe was not catnip to females. The girls at his high school had no time for him. He didn't surf, he didn't glisten while playing beach volleyball and he wasn't a dark, interesting enigma. He was one of the "uncool" guys. A theatre nerd.

Robert Hepler Lowe was born in 1964 in Charlottesville, Virginia, and grew up in Dayton, Ohio. His dad, Chuck, was a lawyer, and mom Barbara was a former high school teacher. When Rob was eight or nine months old, he lost all hearing in his right ear due to an undiagnosed virus. When he turned four, his parents divorced. At the age of eight, Rob saw his future at a theatrical production of *Oliver!* He was mesmerized and decided he wanted to be one of those kids up there on the stage. With his cute mug and the pockets in his short pants full of ambition, he began landing commercials, which turned into acting jobs on local TV and radio. Those led to onstage roles in summer stock and college productions.

Not long after divorcing her second husband, Barbara met a therapist who worked in Los Angeles. He would become her third husband and that change in marital status would also result in a change of geographical status. Barbara moved Rob and his younger brother, Chad, to Malibu. It was a tough move for twelve-year-old Rob, who was leaving all his friends and theatre group behind in Dayton. As he later said, "It didn't matter to me that it was sunny, it was Hollywood, there were palm trees and no snow. It was not an ideal move at all."

Back in the seventies, Malibu was just a middle-class beachside community, a very different place than it is today. But the occasional celebrity did dot the neighbourhood. Martin Sheen lived four doors down the street, and Rob became friends with his sons Charlie and Emilio. While Rob's family cut corners to save money, life was decidedly different at the Sheen residence. It was filled with brand-new BMWs, lagoon pools with underwater tunnels, batting cages and a fully lit professional-grade basketball half-court. Lowe also became friends with neighbours Sean and Chris Penn, and they would all float in the Sheens' pool, dreaming of becoming actors. At Santa Monica High School, Rob became classmates with Robert Downey Jr. and Cary Grant's daughter, Jennifer.

But Lowe did take advantage of Malibu's proximity to acting work. After school, he would take the two-hour bus ride into Hollywood a few days a week to audition for roles, interview with talent agents and generally hang around hoping to be discovered. He managed to get cast in two ABC Afterschool Specials in 1980, and at the age of fifteen, he landed a co-starring role in a sitcom called *A New Kind of Family*. The cast was led by the hilarious Eileen Brennan and the show lasted exactly eleven episodes. When that was cancelled, Lowe was about to give up on his dream and walk away from Hollywood. But then he decided to go for one last audition.

Francis Ford Coppola was casting for a new feature film titled *The Outsiders*, from a book written by a then-fifteen-year-old

Serge Savard—the man the Canadiens once forgot all about—who would later become captain, general manager and Hall of Famer.
(*Above*: Bruce Bennett/Getty Images; *below*: Sportswire/Newscom)

One of the earliest advertisements for Corn Flakes. The breakfast cereal created to brighten your mornings and quash your desires. (Smith Archive/Alamy Stock Photo)

An elderly Frank Epperson enjoying one of his creations with a fan. He wasn't much older than this young girl when he invented Popsicles. (Bettman/Getty Images)

Taken the night at Madison Square Garden when Brian Williams arranged a special tribute to U.S. Army Command Sergeant Major Tim Terpak (right). The anchorman's career trouble would begin soon after. (James Devaney/GC Images/Getty Images)

The fateful night the Dixie Chicks played Shepherd's Bush Empire in London, England. Natalie Maines would utter a few words that would forever alter their careers. (Brian Rasic/Getty Images)

FIRST TIME IN MEMPHIS!

W.C. HANDY THEATRE

2 DAYS ONLY - SAT. & SUN. APRIL 7 - 8

ON STAGE! ----- IN PERSON

★ **JACKIE BRENSTON** ★

THE TERRIFIC **ROCKET "88"** SENSATION

WITH

★ **IKE TURNER** ★

"THE KING OF THE PIANO"

AND

★—**"HIS KING OF RHYTHM"**—★

JACKIE IS GONNA TEAR THE HOUSE DOWN

ADMISSION_____ 60c Tax. Incl.

"Rocket '88'" was a milestone record. The band damaged their only amplifier on the way to the studio, Sam Phillips loved the strange sound it made and rock was born. (Michael Ochs Archives/Getty Images)

Gil Amelio (right) looking at Steve Jobs. Amelio brought Jobs back to Apple against everyone's warnings. It is considered one of the best business decisions of all time. (Michael Rondou/MCT/Newscom)

The genius of the TV Dinner was the fact Swanson chose to tether it to the newest technology in 1950s living rooms—the television set. (Everett/Shutterstock)

Director Steven Spielberg was looking into the jaws of a failure when Bruce the shark kept malfunctioning. What a stroke of luck. (Collection Christophel/Alamy Stock Photo)

The first snowmobile built by Joseph-Armand Bombardier in 1959. A spelling error changed the word "Ski-Dog" to "Ski-Doo" and the rest is brand-name history. (Museum of Ingenuity J. Armand Bombardier Archives)

The classic moment in Ellen's sitcom where she admits she's gay over the airport paging system. Neither Ellen DeGeneres nor Laura Dern would get any work for a long time after this episode. (Everett Collection Inc/Alamy Stock Photo)

The lounge where Billy Joel observed the clientele that inspired his opus, "Piano Man." The "waitress practicing politics" was his girlfriend (soon-to-be-wife), Elizabeth Weber. (Anne Laskey/Marlene & Anne Laskey Wilshire Boulevard Collection/Los Angeles Photographers Collection/Los Angeles Public Library)

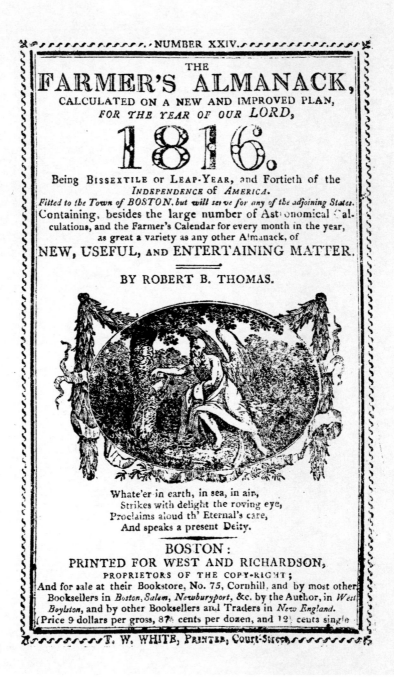

The mistake that put the Almanac on the map. This issue mistakenly predicted snow in July—then it came true. (Old Farmer's Almanac/YPI)

S.E. Hinton. For this coming-of-age story, Coppola was casting his net far and wide. Usually an audition is a private affair with just a few people in a small room, but Coppola had a different dynamic in mind. He wanted groups of twenty or more actors auditioning together on a giant soundstage. Auditioning for a role in front of nearly two dozen hungry competitors is an unnerving situation for actors. To add to the anxiety, Coppola told the young actors they would be switching roles; in other words, they would be performing sections of the script they had not prepared for. It was a brutal cattle call with Coppola hunting for chemistry and every young stud with ambition snapping into kill-or-be-killed mode. Everyone there understood the immense opportunity. Being anointed by Coppola could change an actor's life forever, which created a pressure on that soundstage that was almost unbearable. The list of actors *not* chosen would become as famous as the list who eventually were—people like Mickey Rourke, Dennis Quaid and Timothy Hutton were shown the door. But Coppola's shrewd eye chose many young actors who would become Hollywood's top stars: Tom Cruise, Patrick Swayze and Matt Dillon. The cast would also include C. Thomas Howell and Ralph Macchio. In the darkness of that soundstage, Lowe spotted one familiar face, Emilio Estevez.

When he was finally called, after hours of standing against the wall watching some actors nail the audition and others blow it, Lowe had to perform a scene with two actors he had never met before and convince Coppola they were his brothers. As he said in his autobiography, *Stories I Only Tell My Friends*, Lowe felt like an Olympic skater approaching the moment in his program where he has to land a triple axel—because at the end of this particular scene, he had to break down and sob. It's the moment all actors fear. What if they get to the end of the scene and they can't do it? What if all their tears are spent rehearsing? It's enough to make an actor break down and cry just thinking about the fact he has to break down and cry. When it came to the big moment, Lowe saw fellow actor Thomas Howell's eyes begin to well up in the emotion of the scene. That's all Lowe needed. He completely broke down while the other two actors held him as he wept.

Weeks went by with no word from the Coppola camp. Meanwhile, Lowe made a quiet, internal decision: If he didn't get this role, he would enroll in the University of Southern California to study film. If he couldn't be in front of the camera, he would spend a rewarding career behind it. He applied to the film school. Finally, his agent called to tell him he didn't have the role—yet— because he had to audition again, this time in New York with a roomful of east coast actors. He flew to New York, shared a room with a laser-focused Tom Cruise and, when it came to the moment of truth in the scene, he stuck the axel. Not long after, Lowe told USC he wouldn't be enrolling. He had landed his film debut in a movie directed by Francis Ford Coppola.

In two weeks, he would turn eighteen.

The film was shot in Tulsa, Oklahoma. When Lowe finally attended a private studio screening of *The Outsiders* many months later, he was crushed. Most of his scenes had been cut, even his crying scene. The studio had demanded Coppola shorten the film for a teenage audience's attention span and Lowe's character, Sodapop Curtis, was the sacrificial lamb. He felt blindsided and humiliated. But when Howell and Lowe snuck into an opening-day screening at the famous Mann Theatre in L.A.'s Westwood Village in March 1983, young girls packed the seats. They screamed from the first frame to the last. They stared breathlessly at the bevy of good-looking young actors up on the screen, including the now diminished Sodapop Curtis. They especially reacted to the scene where Lowe comes out of the shower barely covering himself with a towel. As the movie ended and the lights went up, the crowd of girls suddenly spotted Lowe and Howell—and swarmed. The two were pinned into a corner as security guards tried to hustle them out of the theatre. They were chased all the way to Howell's vehicle, as girls grabbed their clothes and pulled their hair. Even though twenty minutes of his role had been snipped, Lowe suddenly realized an incredible upside. He was now officially a teenage heartthrob.

As a matter of fact, all the actors in *The Outsiders* were now hot young movie stars. Within the year, C. Thomas Howell would go on to make *Grandview, U.S.A.* and *Red Dawn*. Patrick Swayze would join Howell in *Red Dawn* and soon after hit the jackpot with *Dirty Dancing*. Matt Dillon would make *Rumble Fish* (with Coppola and *Outsiders* co-star Diane Lane) and *The Flamingo Kid*. Tom Cruise cruised to stardom in *Risky Business*, and Ralph Macchio would waltz right into *The Karate Kid*. Lowe's career rocketed, too. He starred in *The Hotel New Hampshire*, *Oxford Blues* and importantly, *St. Elmo's Fire* and *About Last Night*. Those last two appearances would lead to his inclusion in the infamous Brat Pack.

An obvious play on Sinatra's Rat Pack, the term Brat Pack was coined by journalist David Blum when he was tasked with writing an article on Emilio Estevez for *New York* magazine in 1985. One night, Estevez invited Blum to join him at the Hard Rock Café in L.A., along with Judd Nelson and Rob Lowe. With that eye-opening experience, Blum decided to change the focus of the piece from Estevez to this whole group of cocky young emerging actors. It wasn't a particularly complimentary piece. Blum called them a "roving band of famous young stars on the prowl for parties, women and a good time." The article described how the three studs constantly toasted themselves while eyeballing the parade of girls who slowly walked by their table. When Estevez made fun of one girl's intelligence, they all laughed. They gossiped maliciously about other Brat Packers. Blum also snidely wrote that this new generation of actors had happily skipped the prerequisite of older actors like Brando, De Niro and Pacino, namely, years of acting study. He referred to them as Brats, long on ambition but short on talent and already accustomed to too much privilege and attention. The Brat Pack would come to have a revolving list of members. But the core group consisted of Estevez, Lowe, Ally Sheedy, Molly Ringwald, Judd Nelson, Demi Moore, Andrew McCarthy and occasionally Sean Penn. A starring role in any John Hughes movie was an instant club pass. The group disliked the label and found it demeaning, yet to the world at large, it just made them hotter. There's nothing Hollywood loves more than a heat-radiating celebrity. And Rob Lowe was the red-hot Brat. He dated starlets, supermodels and Princess Stephanie of Monaco. People broke into his house to steal his underwear. Alcohol and drugs were plentiful.

It was in this swirling vortex of fame and easy distractions that Rob Lowe would make a nearly catastrophic career mistake.

In July 1988, the presidential campaign was starting to pick up momentum before the November election. Rob Lowe was twenty-four and was campaigning for the Democratic Party's front-runner, Michael Dukakis. He was into politics at the time and it was also an interesting way to fine-tune his image, moving from *Tiger Beat* cover boy to a more serious film star. The Democratic National Convention that year took place in Atlanta, Georgia. The night before the convention, he attended a party hosted by CNN founder Ted Turner, then went on to trendy downtown Club Rio on Luckie Street (yep!) along with fellow Brats Ally Sheedy and Judd Nelson. At the club, Lowe was sequestered in a roped-off

VIP section enjoying a flow of free champagne. According to a waitress, two eager young women waiting outside the VIP area asked to meet Lowe. So the waitress asked Lowe if he wanted to say hello and he said, "Send them in." Lowe was first introduced to Jan Parsons, who then introduced him to her friend Tara Siebert. Around 2 a.m., Lowe invited both girls back to his suite at the Atlanta Hilton & Towers and the three of them hopped into a cab. In that hotel room, the girls hopped into bed and consented to have videotaped sex with Lowe. According to the aforementioned waitress at Club Rio, twenty-two-year-old Siebert returned the next day boasting of her celebrity conquest, saying that when Lowe eventually passed out, the girls stole two hundred dollars out of his wallet, pocketed a bottle of pills and took the videotape out of the camera. The waitress knew Jan Parsons from a hair salon where they both worked and said Parsons had taken the tape to the salon where her boss made two VHS copies. Parsons then took one tape home and hid it.

As it turned out, the forty-five-minute videotape was a surprising travelogue in the life of a celebrity. The first section showed Lowe and another man named Justin having a threesome with a girl named Jennifer in a Paris hotel room. The next segment showed Lowe taking batting practice with the Atlanta Braves, followed by footage of Lowe rubbing elbows with California politician Tom Hayden at a Braves game. Next up, it showed Lowe mugging while preparing for a TV interview, then shots of an anti–Ku Klux Klan rally, all bookended with more grainy sex scenes, this time featuring Parsons and Siebert as an off-camera Lowe gave them studio directions.

A heavily edited version of the videotape first landed at WAGA-TV in Atlanta (although some said the tape had been circulating in the city's more tawdry nightclubs for a while). Then it broke on CNN. But the tape quickly became more controversial than just a salacious celebrity sex tape. As it was soon revealed, Parsons had been only sixteen years old at the time, which made her a minor in the state of Georgia, although the state's age of consent was fourteen. The case first became public through a civil suit, filed by Parsons's mother, Lena A. Wilson, who was seeking damages. Unsealed court papers showed Wilson accused Lowe of "using his celebrity status as an inducement to get females to engage in sexual intercourse, sodomy and multiple party sexual activity for his immediate sexual gratification, and for the purpose of making pornographic films of these activities." She also alleged Lowe intentionally inflicted emotional distress on her family. Wilson had found the videotape in her daughter's room and turned it over to the district attorney nine months previously. That's when the Fulton County district attorney began investigating whether Lowe had sexually exploited a minor to produce pornography, which was a felony under Georgia law. If found guilty, Lowe faced the possibility of twenty years in prison and a $100,000 fine.

According to the *Washington Post*, Wilson was in the midst of a bitter divorce and when she lost custody, she filed affidavits in Cobb County Superior Court charging that her daughter Jan spoke of "blackmailing" Lowe for $2 million, that her daughter had threatened a neighbour's daughter if she squealed on Jan, that her daughter had slept in the same bed as a "known lesbian" (presumably Siebert), that she had used marijuana and alcohol to excess and that she drove around town in a flashy red 1966 Porsche paid for by her father. Wilson wanted to prove that Jan's father, John Parsons, a retired Air Force major, was failing to exercise sufficient discipline over their children and maintained she was concerned over the safety and security of her daughter. Lowe's legal team requested that the civil suit be dismissed since it was Parsons's father who had custody, not Wilson, and he was not party to the suit. Plus, Wilson and her daughter Jan were estranged at that point.

Meanwhile, Rob Lowe's defence centred on the fact he didn't know Parsons was underage because he had met her in a twenty-one-or-over nightclub. Everyone entering, including Lowe, had to show proof of age and Parsons had gained entry with fake ID, apparently looking much older than her sixteen years. Lowe's lawyers also alleged Wilson had approached his manager looking to extort money weeks before she filed the suit. While Lowe couldn't deny he was in the video, he denied having actual sexual intercourse with Wilson's daughter.

Meanwhile, the circus came to town. Porn king Al Goldstein of *Screw* magazine paid five thousand dollars for a copy of the tape and broadcast portions of it on his New York cable TV program, *Midnight Blue*. Goldstein also sold brief snippets of Lowe at full staff via mail order for $29.95 per clip. Historically speaking, it was one of the first celebrity sex tapes sold commercially (the genre would come to full fruition with the Pamela Anderson/Tommy Lee sex tape in 1998). Lowe has claimed in many interviews since that his was the first celebrity sex tape and jokes that "Sometimes being a trailblazer is overrated." But he wasn't the first. That dubious distinction belongs to sportscaster and actor Jayne Kennedy and her then husband, Leon, who had a private sex tape stolen from their home and leaked without their consent in 1982. It predated not only the internet but also the prevalence of home VCRs, so the Kennedy sex scenes circulated mostly via grainy still photos. (Personal video cameras and home videotape machines were fairly new technology at the time. In the mid-eighties, Betamax was still battling it out with VHS for supremacy. Blockbuster Video stores didn't launch until 1985.)

Soon, the aboveground press also got into the Rob Lowe action, as MTV, *Entertainment Tonight*, *Inside Edition* and various local news programs aired pixelated clips of Lowe, al dente. NBC's Tom Brokaw led the evening news that night with the Rob Lowe sex tape story. The second story was the uprising in Tiananmen Square.

In a freaky twist of fate, Lowe had signed on to star in a new film just as the scandal began percolating. It was a dark thriller titled *Bad Influence* with Lowe playing a satyric sociopath who seduces a meek, average Joe into a life of dangerous debauchery. For a cherry atop this lusty cake, Lowe's character uses a video camera to tape a sexual encounter, and if that weren't enough, there is a scene where Lowe is in bed with two young girls. As movie critic Roger Ebert wrote at the time, the parallels between the movie and the scandalous videotape were so numerous, "I would have almost believed [Lowe] if he claimed to have been doing research."

Lowe was in Cannes promoting the upcoming film when his lawyers reached him with news of the lawsuit. He and his team immediately went into crisis control mode. As the case progressed, Lowe threw himself into the filming of *Bad Influence*. While rehearsing in a big church hall in Hollywood, Lowe was asked to meet and approve his makeup artist. In walked Sheryl Berkoff. They had actually met on a blind date in 1983, when both were just coming off breakups and the timing wasn't right. Berkoff would soon become a much in-demand makeup artist, working with Al Pacino, Harrison Ford and Alec Baldwin. Berkoff and Lowe bonded during the filming and eventually became lovers. When Lowe was asked to promote *Bad Influence* in Australia, he was offered an exotic, luxurious vacation of his choice, with a guest, as compensation afterward. He chose Fiji and Sheryl Berkoff. They had a wonderful time together. Away from the pressures of his career and relentless L.A. partying, Lowe began to feel the potential of a different life. Berkoff was unpretentious, centred and grounded. She cooked, she read, she was a calming presence who was level-headed about his scandal. Just as the vacation ended, they realized they had fallen in love. But once back in Los Angeles, Berkoff left for her next on-location film job and Lowe fell back into his usual pattern of booze, pills and partying. When Berkoff called to check in on Lowe one night and heard the giggle of a girl in the background, that was it for their relationship.

Meanwhile, Lowe's Hollywood Hills home was under siege twenty-four hours a day by camera crews, his intercom was buzzed at 6 a.m. by reporters asking for interviews and photographers snapped pictures of everyone who came and went, including gardeners and fast-food delivery people. Lowe became depressed and started to self-medicate. He felt abandoned by the entertainment industry in those dark days, saying the only supportive note he received was from Jodie Foster. (Although he did get a thumbs-up from Hugh Hefner, who said, "You had to do it. The technology was there.")

Four months before *Bad Influence* was released, Lowe's lawyers paid an undisclosed sum to Jan Parsons and her father. Wilson's lawsuit was tossed out not long after. The Fulton County district attorney chose not to prosecute him for taping a sexual encounter with a partner under eighteen, and in return, Lowe agreed to do twenty hours of public service. He spoke at halfway houses and prisons, some of which were as far away as his hometown of Dayton, Ohio. *Bad Influence* was released in March 1990, and Lowe began a limited press tour. He didn't shy away from answering questions about the scandal, saying, "I've learned the importance of admitting when you've made a mistake, when you've been wrong or made bad judgements. And I learned that you must accept the consequences of your actions. That's part of being the man I want to be." The movie was overshadowed by the scandal, with many believing the film was made to capitalize on Lowe's downfall. It underperformed at the box office. Then the one thing everyone in Hollywood fears most happened.

The phone stopped ringing.

In that silence, Lowe wondered if that was the sound of his promising career ending. Or the slide into direct-to-video purgatory. Then the phone suddenly made a noise one day.

It was Lorne Michaels.

He wanted to know if Lowe would consider hosting *Saturday Night Live*. Lowe knew exactly what that meant. Michaels wanted to poke fun at the scandal. It was a classic *SNL* first-mover call. The show prided itself on being the first to land a host after a heroic moment, a career high or a stupefying fall from grace. Lowe's lawyers didn't want him to do it. His agents didn't want him to do it. It was March 1990 and the sex tape was still being freshly rewound in the zeitgeist.

On his twenty-sixth birthday, March 17, 1990, Rob Lowe defied his management team and took the plunge to host *SNL*. The cold opening of that episode, with Dana Carvey playing George H.W. Bush, is intercut with backstage scenes of a fretful Rob Lowe, nervous about delivering his monologue. Various people, including Lorne Michaels, tell him that nobody cares about the sex tape scandal anymore. Old news. People just want to know about your movies, like *Oxford Blues*. It's a funny set-up for the monologue. When longtime *SNL* announcer Don Pardo bellows in his inimitable way, "Ladies and gentlemen, Rob Looooowe," there is no applause—just a horrible, awkward silence. The audience looks unhappy and annoyed. Of course, it's all planned. As Lowe begins his monologue, someone from the audience yells, "You've got a lot of nerve. I've got a daughter!" The monologue is purposefully awkward and painful. Lowe starts to say he regrets the incident the audience member is referring to, adding that when you go through something like that, you really find the value and loyalty of friends, but he is interrupted again by someone yelling, "We're not your friends!" quickly followed by another "I've got a daughter!" Lowe tries to salvage the situation by announcing that the musical guests are the Pogues—but no one applauds. He begs the audience not to hold it against the band, who don't even know him. Silence. Then Jon Lovitz strolls onstage and tells Lowe to go backstage and change for his first sketch, he'll take it from there. Lowe walks off dejected and Lovitz yells, "The Pogues are here! We'll be right back!" The crowd erupts into applause. It was a funny bit. Later in the show, Lowe did a sketch with Church Lady, who ended up paddling his rear end yelling, "Get out of his buttocks, Satan!" He also did a hilarious "Sprockets" sketch with Mike Myers.

While hosting *SNL* looked like a risky opportunity, it was a seminal moment in Rob Lowe's career. First, he mocked himself openly in the monologue and, by doing so, shortstopped the humiliating punchlines the media was lobbing. Second, he met Lorne Michaels. Third, and most importantly, he hit it off with Myers. This intersection would lead to the Lazarus moment in Lowe's career. It opened the door to a second act and—who knew—the way in was going to be his untapped gift for comedy.

But there was an undertow in Lowe's life that threatened to pull him under just as this surprising turn in his career was materializing. Rob Lowe was struggling with an alcohol and cocaine problem. Not long after the *SNL* appearance, the toxic cocktail of his lifestyle and the pressure of the scandal accelerated the ride to rock bottom. It happened the morning he got an urgent phone message from his mother saying his grandfather had suffered a massive heart attack. She was panicking and needed help. Lowe stared at the answering machine until his mother hung up. He couldn't pick up the phone because he was too drunk. That day, at twenty-nine years of age, he made the decision to call a drug-and-alcohol counsellor. Soon after, in May 1990, he entered rehab in Arizona. It was a tough but fair facility that took its mission seriously. Lowe was there for four weeks. The only person he allowed to visit, besides family, was Sheryl Berkoff. She moved mountains in her schedule to see him for the one single hour he was allotted for visitors every Thursday. Over the four weeks, he earned back her trust and another chance at being together. He has since maintained rehab was critical in his life, saying it gave him life tools that helped him cope. He said he admired people who could make those changes themselves, but he needed the guidance of experts.

After a year of daily recovery meetings and group therapy sessions, Lowe asked Berkoff to marry him. She said yes, and they held a small, secret wedding ceremony just one month later. They performed their vows in front of semi-stunned friends who had thought they were just attending a wedding-themed charity lunch. Just before Lowe stepped out the door to go to the wedding, he got a call from Lorne Michaels to attend a very important studio meeting that very evening, about a new Mike Myers movie called *Wayne's World*. Lowe said he couldn't make it. Lorne insisted it was a *very* important meeting. Lowe said he was on his way to his wedding. Lorne dryly replied, "Then I guess even dessert is out of the question."

Myers cast Lowe as the slightly seedy video producer in *Wayne's World* based solely on his comedic ability in the "Sprockets" sketch (and the notoriety of the sex tape, no doubt). That performance would open the doors to more comedic roles by proving Lowe wasn't just pretty—he was indeed funny. Comedy roles in the *Austin Powers* trilogy and the Lorne Michaels–produced *Tommy Boy* eventually led to a major dramatic part in Aaron Sorkin's *West Wing*. Then came the role of Chris Traeger on *Parks and Recreation* in 2010. Lowe has had a series on the air continuously from 1999 to this day. Much of this work has been based in comedy, which in the end, has arguably given him a career that exceeded all of the other Brat Packers'.

As Rob Lowe told the *Guardian*, what happened after the scandal was the best thing that ever happened to him. "I would do everything the same," he says. "If you go back in time to try to change things, you could end up changing the future, and I like where I am in my life. I love my life, I'm really grateful for the things I have, and if I did something different it wouldn't turn out this way." The scandal got him sober. Sober got him married. Marriage gave him two sons. And none of this career exhumation—due to a second chance rooted in comedy—would have happened if he hadn't taken that chance on *SNL*. It can all be traced directly back to that night.

And that *Saturday Night Live* monologue wouldn't have happened without the fallout of the scandal.

14.

The Who

Who Are You?

Back in 1957, Roger Harry Daltrey was singing "Heartbreak Hotel" at the neighbourhood youth club in East Acton in London, England. He began to realize that singing was a "magical friend maker." People swarmed him after the performance to chat. A few of his friends that night talked to him about starting a band. It was a formative moment for young Roger.

The school friends all shared a love of music and they put together a ragtag collection of instruments, including a set of drums, one electric guitar, a tea-chest bass and a washboard. Daltrey played a handmade guitar he had cobbled together himself at his sheet metal factory day job. A friend named Colin Dawson was on lead vocals. The band had one amp and everyone was plugged into it— including the microphones. It was, for all intents and purposes and penny-pinching, a skiffle group. Skiffle was a popular form of music in the late fifties, combining blues, jazz and folk music played on largely improvised instruments. Part of what made skiffle all the rage was the fact most of its instrumentation could be found in the kitchen.

Over time, Daltrey's band progressed from skiffle to basic covers of current hits. One of their best numbers was a mash-up of Little Richard's "Lucille" with "Tutti Frutti." The band loved the subversive nature of the lyrics. "A-whop-bop-a-lu-bop-a-whop-bam-boom" just sounded like noise to the censors at radio stations, but teenagers knew it was code for sex. While it has been said that the difference between rock 'n' roll and pop music is that pop is all about fun and rock is all about anger, rock is also all about sex, hence the very term "rock 'n' roll."

The band managed to land gigs at local weddings and church hall gatherings. They pooled their money to upgrade their meagre gear whenever they could. After a few months, the band also pooled their thinking to decide on a name: the Detours. Just when they were starting to get an ounce of traction, the bass player up and quit because the gigs weren't paying him enough to afford the payments on the bass. It was a classic early band catch-22: you can't afford the instruments, but you can't earn money without the instruments. That departure put a sizable dent in the rhythm section of the Detours.

Then one day, as Daltrey was walking home from work, he spotted a big guy he recognized from his school days, carrying the biggest guitar Daltrey had ever seen. It was a bass guitar. Well, sort of a bass guitar. Like Daltrey, he had made the massive thing himself. The big guy carrying the big guitar was John Entwistle. Nicknamed "the Ox," Entwistle's size gave him a very particular John Wayne style of ambling. Daltrey says if you put Entwistle in a line of a thousand people, all the same height, all the same weight, all wearing balaclavas, you'd still be able to pick him out instantly because of his gait. John Alec Entwistle was born into a musical family and was formally trained on the French horn, which he played in the Middlesex Youth Orchestra. But the siren call of Duane Eddy's rock 'n' roll records made him ditch the brass for the bass. Daltrey got to talking with Entwistle and discovered he was a trainee tax officer by day, but played in a trad jazz band called the Confederates by night—which meant he wasn't making any money. Daltrey stretched the truth and said the Detours were earning real money. That's all Entwistle needed to hear. By the summer of 1961, the Detours had a new bass player.

Another schoolmate caught Daltrey's attention because, like Entwistle, he stood out. Whereas Daltrey's prominent jawline was a constant source of ribbing and Entwistle had that crazy walk, this tall and skinny guy's most notable feature was a sizable nose. Daltrey said he looked like "a nose on a stick" and was bullied mercilessly because of it. It would have a profound, lifelong effect on him. His name was Pete Townshend. He was more middle class than the blue-collar Daltrey and Entwistle families. His father, Cliff, played alto sax in the Royal Air Force's dance band, the Squadronaires, and his mother, Betty, was a singer with two local orchestras. Their marriage was very volatile, as both had explosive tempers fuelled by alcohol. There were separations and affairs, but life seemed to settle down eventually when the Townshends bought a house in Acton, in west London.

In 1956, young Peter Dennis Blandford Townshend was transfixed by the movie *Rock Around the Clock*. When he went to his very first live concert, it was Bill Haley & His Comets. An aunt encouraged Townshend's musical interest by trying to teach him the piano, but his first real instrument was the banjo. He and Entwistle, who were friends, decided to form the Confederates, with Entwistle on trumpet and Townshend on banjo. Hard to imagine the future windmill strumming guitar-god Townshend rockin' the banjo and Entwistle soloing on trumpet, but there you have it. The Confederates were short-lived, however, after Townshend got into a dust-up with the drummer and left the band. Because he wanted to pursue rock 'n' roll, his grandmother helped by buying him a cheap Spanish guitar, his father taught him a few chords and young Pete spent endless hours teaching himself the instrument.

While the Detours kept landing gigs, Entwistle kept complaining to Daltrey that Reg, their lead guitarist, wasn't very good and he knew just the guy to replace him. Pete Townshend came to audition for the band in January 1962. He was just sixteen but possessed a unique guitar style, a strange mixture of banjo moves and intricate guitar chords. There was no debate: Pete was in and Reg was out. That also meant the only amp in the band was out, as it belonged to Reg. But Townshend had an idea. He suggested they all buy amps on long-term payment plans. So the boys rushed down to the Tottenham Court Road electrical stores and each of them purchased an inexpensive amp. They were beyond excited, until they tried them out. The tinny sound from all the amps together barely filled the front room of the Townshends' home. That problem inspired a solution. Daltrey already understood that image was everything in rock 'n' roll, so he built large plywood boxes to look like amps, covered them in wood-grain peel-and-stick paper and placed them over the tiny amps. The optical effect of the huge amps was jaw-dropping, even if the aural effect was, well, just dropping. After about a year, the band was able to afford better gear and the rehearsals at Betty Townshend's house got louder. She was the band's biggest fan and believed they really had something. She just wanted them to take that something out of her home, so she found them a local promoter. He wasn't enamoured with the band, but Betty was persistent and he reluctantly took the Detours on.

Slowly but surely, the promoter started finding the group gigs on the west London pub circuit. As Daltrey remembers, the deal was simple. If the band was terrible, it was pelted with beer bottles. If the band was less than terrible, it was asked back. By this time, the Detours were actually getting pretty good and were starting to build their own audience. They were playing an average of three nights a week, fairly steadily. In January 1963, lead singer Colin left the band to pursue a life of a bacon salesmanship, so the lead vocals fell to Daltrey.

Shortly thereafter, the band changed its name. They were beginning to get confused with another band called the American Detours, so one night they started kicking around new names. Someone suggested the Group. Then No One—as in "Ladies and gentlemen, No One!"—or the Hair. When the next suggestion was thrown out, someone didn't quite hear it and said, "The who?" That's when they all stopped. They loved it. The Detours were now officially the Who.

In the spring of 1964, the Who landed a new manager, a German doorknob manufacturer who was willing to spend money on the band. He bought them a secondhand van and professional amplifiers and even got them a session in a recording studio. The band's music was changing, employing fewer covers and more original music. The Beatles were the current sensation, so everyone wanted a Fab Four Liverpool sound. Then the Rolling Stones hit the scene with a more bluesy vibe. The Who found themselves on the same circuit as the Beatles and the Stones, but were more influenced by the latter.

Doug Sandom, their thirtysomething elder statesman drummer, decided to take a detour and leave the Who. Or more accurately, his wife decided he needed to leave the Who. That left them without a steady backbeat until one night when a cocky lad named Keith Moon walked up during a gig at a hotel in west London, introduced himself and performed an impromptu audition with the band. Keith John Moon was a surf music fan while in school and played in three different local bands—the Escorts, Mark Twain & the Strangers and the Beachcombers. He was also a wild man. In Daltrey's excellent book, *Thanks a Lot, Mr. Kibblewhite*, he quotes Moon's art teacher describing him as "retarded artistically, idiotic in other respects." But Moon's music teacher said he had "great ability, but must guard against a tendency to show off." That specific tendency was what impressed the band most that night. As Entwistle said once, most drummers play their kit left to right, but Moon played *forward*. His aggressive drumming kicked the band up to a new level. He instantly clicked with Entwistle's bass playing and splashed some new fuel on Townshend's powerful rhythm guitar. It all came together that night in April 1964.

Shortly after Moon the Loon joined the Who, an adman walked into the band's headlights. His name was Pete Meaden and he had been business partners with the Stones' manager, Andrew Loog Oldham. Meaden liked the Who but said they had a big problem, namely, they had no image. Without that, the Who were just another soggy version of the Stones. He expanded on this theory in a very interesting way. He explained that the Beatles were the good guys, a.k.a. the white sheep. The Stones were the bad boys, the black sheep. Meaden's marketing instincts saw the opportunity and framed it perfectly. He said, don't be the white sheep or the black sheep; those images are already taken.

Be the red sheep.

It was something the band never forgot. They just needed to find that hook. Something that would brand them as the red sheep in the flock of fledgling British bands. Something highly unusual they could call their own. Meaden also hated the name the Who and convinced them to change it to the High Numbers. At the time, the cool fashion was stolen bowling shoes. The higher the number on the heel, the bigger the feet, and the bigger the feet, the bigger the codpiece. Meaden was trying to find a cocky hook.

In the summer of 1964, the Who found a new management team. They had a grander vision, got rid of Meaden, offered to pay the band every week, took 40 percent commission and insisted they change their name back to the Who. They also bought them a bigger van because they wanted the band to start lugging lighting around with them for a bigger, more visually impressive stage show. Even though Meaden was now gone, the idea of becoming the red sheep lingered. The band needed to find that hook, that thing that defined them and separated the Who from the hundreds of other British invasion bands that were crawling all over London.

Then Pete Townshend made an embarrassing mistake.

It happened one night in September 1964.

The Who was playing a regular Tuesday night gig at a local west London spot called the Railway Hotel. They were in the middle of their regular set and the crowd was mostly their regular fans, with the exception of some new, cute girls at the front. The only other thing that wasn't regular was the stage. It was new and the floor was a few inches higher than the stage the band had been playing on for weeks. In the middle of a big windmill strum, Pete Townshend lifted his Rickenbacker to gear up for the power chord and mistakenly jammed the instrument right through the ceiling—instantly snapping the neck off his guitar.

The place went quiet.

The girls in the front row rolled their eyes and sniggered. So Townshend made a quick and interesting choice. He decided to cover up his mistake by making it seem as if the hole in the ceiling was intentional. He did that by immediately smashing his guitar to pieces. Right there on the stage. He made it look as if he'd intended to destroy his guitar all along, first by jabbing it into the ceiling, then by slamming it repeatedly against the stage until it was just a mass of splintered wood and shivering guitar strings. This completely unexpected move shocked, then infuriated, Daltrey. In that split second, he knew the band would have to pay for the hole in the ceiling as well as buy a new guitar for Townshend. Townshend called it art; Daltrey called it expensive.

The next Tuesday at the same hotel on the same stage, Keith Moon kicked his drums over at the end of the set. And there it was. From that point on, the audience came to expect—and relish—the moment when the Who destroyed their instruments at the end of the show. It became their signature move. It was the thing that separated them from the hundreds of other bands. It was punk rock fifteen years before punk rock.

Above all, it painted their sheep red.

The press lapped up this spectacle of a young band smashing their instruments. In no time, Townshend wasn't just destroying his guitar, he was sticking the neck of it right up into the amps and through the speakers to make surreal feedback sounds. Entwistle was swinging his bass against the stage like an axe murderer. Moon revelled in the destruction of his massive drum kit, progressing to the installation of cherry bombs for added fire power.

What had started as a mistake became a ritual.

Rolling Stone would later call the original Townshend Rickenbacker incident one of the "50 moments that changed the history of Rock and Roll." Daltrey says the destruction wasn't about the visual but about the sound of destruction, the animalistic noise. The Who was all about sound. Big, rude sound and the energy it created. Townshend would sometimes take ten minutes to destroy his instrument, creating a screaming, sonic experience. Daltrey says even though the critics missed the point at first, the kids got it.

But over time, the powerful optics overrode the art. People came to watch the razing but stopped listening. In his autobiography,

Daltrey says the real reason Townshend destroyed his guitar that first night was because he felt humiliated by the girls laughing at him. Townshend, on the other hand, has since said the reason for breaking guitars was his frustration with his own playing. He couldn't channel the notes in his head through his guitar. He wanted the sound to be epic but couldn't pull it off, so he made the visuals epic instead. In 1967 alone, Pete Townshend would destroy over thirty-five guitars, saying he considered them tools, not instruments, at that time. In other interviews, he has rationalized the violent act by saying it was his reaction to our ever-growing addiction to materialism.

Whatever the reason, the fact remained that the demolition finale was breathtakingly singular. It belonged completely and absolutely to the Who. Within weeks, the lineups to see the band went around the block in every single town they played. According to Townshend, word of the spectacle "built and built and built and built." People wanted to see the rock band that demolished their instruments. If rock 'n' roll is based in anger, this powerful purging at the end of the show was rock at its most pure. It became the art of destruction. And it sold tickets. Not long after, the Who would release its first Townshend-composed single, "I Can't Explain," which was the first in a long line of Top 10 hits. The band still opens concerts with the song today. And even now, when Townshend is admonished by people for destroying beautiful guitars, his response is not exactly ambivalent: "Fuck off. It's how I got you to listen to me."

With that red sheep move of smashing instruments, born of an utter mistake, the band answered the eternal question facing all struggling bands: "Who are you?"

Ellen DeGeneres

When a Door Shuts, a Closet Opens

Back in early 1992, I was a busy commercial director and was hired to produce a big radio campaign for Labatt. The beer category, at that time, was one of the most active in the advertising business, so finding superb actors who weren't already appearing in commercials for competing brands was very difficult. And if you needed great comedic actors, it was almost impossible. So I recommended we cast in Los Angeles. For starters, the talent pool is deep and any actors in beer commercials in the United States wouldn't pose a conflict for beer brands in Canada.

For this particular campaign, I needed about ten actors to play recurring roles across five commercials. One of those roles specifically called for a very funny female in her mid-twenties. I hired an L.A.-based casting company, briefed them on the roles I needed, and a week later received an audition tape of just over 150 actors reading for the various characters. There were a lot of excellent choices on that tape. But one was especially funny. She nailed every line. I rewound the tape over and over again to listen to her audition. Many wonderful actors can come close to nailing a line without a lot of direction at the casting stage. You learn to ignore slightly off-point reads and listen instead for attitude and instincts, knowing you can fine-tune their delivery once you get them in the studio. But this young actor was different. The lines were short, so she didn't have anywhere to hide. The actors either delivered the goods or they didn't. She delivered—big time. She was simply hilarious. When I presented my casting choices to Labatt and their advertising agency, there was some debate on a few roles, but everyone agreed that young actor was absolutely terrific and she was approved right away.

On recording day in L.A., the studio was populated with very experienced actors. I had chosen performers you have seen in sitcoms over the years. The great second bananas of television land were always my favourite performers. They were funny, they were smart and they were pros. They were also comfortable and chatty because they all knew each other. Except for that one young actor. She was unbelievably shy. She clearly didn't know anyone else in the room and I noticed she slowly backed into a corner. She was obviously brand new to the voice-over world. But when it came time to deliver her lines, she stepped up to the microphone and was so funny that even the experienced actors stifled laughs.

That shy girl was Ellen DeGeneres.

She was a star before she was a star. I remember she was discreetly fielding a number of phone calls from her agent between takes and she seemed to be anxiously awaiting news on something big.

Long before that, way, way back in 1981, Ellen froze up during a public speaking event and panicked. So she used humour to get herself through it. She was a surprise hit, which then actually led to offers to do stand-up comedy. She began performing in small venues with moral and financial support from her mother. In those early days, she made a promise to herself: that she would one day appear on the Johnny Carson show and be the first female comic invited over to the couch. One year later, Ellen came close to big-time success. She had performed a "Phone Call to God" routine for a comedian contest sponsored by Showtime. Ellen had written the bit after losing her girlfriend in a fatal car crash. In the routine, she is asking God questions about the unpredictable and seemingly random aspects of life, like, do fleas serve any purpose? With that, she was crowned "Funniest Person in America."

Then came her first big network TV break. Jay Leno had suggested the *Tonight Show* scouts catch Ellen's set at the Improv in Hollywood. They did and booked her to appear on Carson in 1986. She chose to perform her "Phone Call" bit. Carson laughed mightily and then gave the wave most comedians dream of. Ellen became the first female comedian to be waved over to the couch in *Tonight Show* history. She had willed this moment into being.

Her break on Carson led to appearances on other late-night talk shows, spots on stand-up specials and walk-ons in sitcoms like *Open House*, but it hadn't led to any big opportunities. She was still a jobbing comedian, which was probably the reason she was doing voice-over gigs when I worked with her. But all that changed in 1994.

At that time, there was a wave of high-profile comedians landing their own shows, like Roseanne Barr, Tim Allen and Fran Drescher. Ellen, meanwhile, was going to audition for a single line in a new show called *Laurie Hill*. She thought it was crazy she was trying to land a part with a single line when all these other comedians were landing their own sitcoms. So she went to the producers of *Laurie Hill*, Carol Black and Neal Marlens, to ask, "If this show gets cancelled, can you create one for me?" That show did indeed get cancelled and the two producers turned to creating a show for Ellen. But she felt the need to be honest with them before they went any further. She said, "I need to tell you something, because you may not want to create a show for me, but I'm gay. And I know that could hurt the show if it got out." The producers told Ellen they already knew she was gay and asked if Ellen wanted her character to be gay. "No! Absolutely not!" Ellen replied.

The new sitcom, *These Friends of Mine*, premiered on Disney-owned ABC in March 1994. I suspect this was the opportunity she was anxiously on the phone about at our recording session. After the first season, the sitcom was retooled a bit and the name was changed to *Ellen*—mostly to distinguish it from *Friends*, which had launched on NBC a few months later. The premise had Ellen playing the owner of a bookstore/cafe surrounded by the usual crew of friends and sidekicks. Hijinks ensued. The show debuted in the Nielsen top five, but over time it began to decline in the ratings. A number of cast, staff and time-slot changes never seemed to jell. The show slowly slid down the ladder to number thirty, hitting every rung on the way down. Heading into the fourth season, the show had stalled, the storylines were thin and Ellen's character motivation was getting fuzzier. The situation got so desperate, one executive even suggested Ellen could inject some new interest by adopting a puppy on the show.

Around this time, I was in Los Angeles to direct a television advertising campaign. My production company had hired a local crew and cameraman. I had briefed the casting company, scouted locations and even had one exterior set decorated like it was Christmas in Canada, with fake snow piling up on the warm Los Angeles sidewalks. My liaison with the L.A. crew was a smart and resourceful local producer. She picked me up at my hotel to drive me to a casting session and we talked shop as we inched our way down the freeway. She mentioned she had recently done some work on *Ellen*. I mentioned my previous experience with Ellen and how impressed I was with her in that recording session. The producer said that Ellen's staff and crew on the show wasn't that impressed with her these days. I asked why. She said it was because they all wanted her to come out on the show and stop pretending she wasn't gay. There was genuine anger and frustration brewing in Ellen-land. And this producer's tone suggested she felt the same way, too. I looked at her quizzically and asked if she agreed with Ellen's staff. She said absolutely—the show was risking cancellation and Ellen was being selfish. Coming out would be truthful and would give the show a boost. I then asked this producer if she understood what was at stake for Ellen. It wasn't just a storyline decision. Ellen would be risking everything. Her show. Her career. Her future. And if she was hesitating, it was completely understandable.

The producer disagreed.

She said it was common knowledge Ellen was gay, so why not just embrace it and save the show? I said that bit of information wasn't common knowledge to people outside the entertainment industry. Not only would Ellen risk her audience deserting her, but she also risked advertisers backing out of the show. That, in turn, would panic the network. It was a seismic decision that could send a sharp fissure all along Ellen's world in the zeitgeist of 1994. But the producer was adamant that Ellen's trepidation was weakness. I just shook my head.

We changed the subject.

Somewhere along the line, Ellen either felt that pressure, was tired at having to play dodgeball with questions about her sexuality or needed to convince the network her show had a future. She was also in a relationship with actor Anne Heche at the time and Heche urged her to go for it. Ellen's producers loved the idea as a fix for the flailing show. So together with her producers, Ellen decided to tentatively approach ABC with the idea of her character coming out on the show. First, she had a discussion with Dean Valentine, president of Disney Television, and then she met with

Jamie Tarses, head of ABC Entertainment. Valentine told Ellen he was not interested in standing on political soapboxes—first and foremost it had to be great TV. Tarses also pumped the brakes, saying, "It's not a no-brainer." ABC was cautious and wanted to proceed slowly. Permission was given to write a script, pending final approval by the network.

Valentine turned down the first draft of the script because he felt it didn't dig deep enough into the character. Meanwhile, everybody on Ellen's business team begged her not to do it—including her publicist, her agent and her manager. Collectively, they all felt it was a huge mistake. A career-ending mistake. But Ellen pressed on. Her writers finally came back with a workable script and, as an inside joke, titled it "The Puppy Episode."

Word started to spread that Ellen's character on the sitcom, Ellen Morgan, was going to come out of the closet. But there was an odd disconnect. People also wondered whether Ellen herself was going to come out. After all, there were two Ellens. One was a character on a sitcom; the other was a living, breathing human being. Three weeks before "The Puppy Episode" was set to air, on April 14, 1997, *Time* magazine put Ellen on the front cover with the headline "Yep, I'm gay." As the *Time* article stated, the announcement shocked more people than it surprised, presumably for two reasons: first, not everyone in Middle America knew Ellen's secret, and second, this declaration meant there was going to be a sitcom on prime-time television with a gay leading character for the first time in history. Lead characters are the sun that sitcom solar systems revolve around and we as viewers are asked to identify with those lead characters. The reactions came swiftly.

The Gay & Lesbian Alliance Against Defamation was thrilled. The Reverend Jerry Falwell referred to Ellen as "Ellen DeGenerate." The American Family Association issued veiled threats saying they were prepared to boycott *Ellen*'s advertisers. Both JCPenney and Chrysler announced they would be pulling their ads. (Amid the fallout, ABC apparently turned down a commercial from a gay cruise line.) An affiliate in Birmingham, Alabama, refused to air the episode. Dick Wolf, creator of *Law & Order*, said if it were his show, he probably wouldn't have done it, adding, "This is one specific area that a large percentage of the population is still very uncomfortable with." Ellen received death threats.

The episode itself was filmed over two consecutive Fridays at Disney's Burbank lot. During production, the studio received a telephone threat and the set had to be evacuated. Bomb-sniffing dogs were brought in. Amid all these jittery moments, Ellen did two important interviews. The first was on ABC's *20/20* with Diane Sawyer on April 25, 1997, five days before the episode aired. Ellen talked about what it was like to be gay. She said gay people are not just a minority in the country; they are a minority in their own families. Ellen explained how she told ABC it was she who was taking the huge gamble, not the network. The network might be boycotted for a week or so. It could always just produce another sitcom. But Ellen was the commodity risking her audience, her show and her career. She also said she didn't want to be a gay activist but was doing this to shed the shame she'd felt her entire life. She wanted to live openly and honestly. At the end of the taping, she said she felt nothing but joy.

The second interview was with Oprah on the afternoon of April 30, only a few short hours before "The Puppy Episode" would air that evening. On Oprah's show, Ellen talked about her fear of the reaction people would have to her if they knew she was gay. She said she even worried that Oprah herself would stop liking her. Oprah's format allowed for audience questions and several people cited the Bible, saying a homosexual life was to live in sin. Oprah talked about her decision to be in the episode, playing Ellen's therapist. She said she had agreed to do the part immediately. An audience member suggested Oprah was chosen to be in the episode for strategic reasons, namely to sway Middle America. Ellen said the decision to cast Oprah was simply because she just had a lot of respect for her and thought Oprah would be good in the part of a sympathetic therapist. Oprah agreed, pointing out she plays the part of a therapist on her show every day.

The plot of "The Puppy Episode" revolves around the visit of a reporter friend who is in town on a business trip. He's with his producer, a woman named Susan, played by Laura Dern. The male friend makes a pass at Ellen one night. Ellen is uncomfortable, leaves his room, bumps into Susan in the hall and goes to her room instead. They hit it off and Susan admits to Ellen she's gay and suspects Ellen is gay, too. Ellen denies it and accuses Susan of trying to "recruit" her. Later, Ellen's therapist (Oprah) asks if she has ever truly "clicked" with someone. Ellen says yes . . . Susan. Then Ellen gets a message from her male friend saying he is leaving town early, so Ellen rushes to the airport to tell Susan something she has never told anyone before: that Susan was right, Ellen *is* gay. Ellen wonders why she still has so much trouble saying it out loud. The moment when Ellen finally does say it is a classic television moment. She inadvertently leans into a ticket counter microphone and says "I'm gay"—which is broadcast all over the airport. Susan gives her a hug and says, "I'm so proud of you. I remember how hard it was when I told my first airport full of people."

Forty-two million people tuned in that night. Both ABC and Disney said they were pleased with the way the episode was handled. However, ABC president Tarses did say, "Obviously, this is an experiment. We're not sociologists. We don't know how this is going to be received." The network told the press the show wasn't going to become a lesbian dating show. While the groundbreaking episode would go on to win two Primetime Emmy Awards, the negative fallout was interesting. Ellen received more death threats.

People yelled at her from cars. Some violent events happened on the street. Oprah said she had never received so much hate mail in her career. The day after the episode aired, her company had to bring in an additional person to handle the switchboard. People told her to "Go back to Africa." Over nine hundred negative calls poured in. Laura Dern, who isn't gay in real life, did not work for a full year. She was offered no roles.

Over the next season of *Ellen*, her producers clashed with network executives who asked that not every episode have a gay theme and at one point even requested that a special viewer's advisory about the content be aired. Ellen protested, saying that heterosexual content never had to include similar warnings. The tension continued.

On April 24, 1998, ABC cancelled *Ellen*. The show had experienced declining ratings and a new sitcom that had replaced the show during its hiatus had performed better. No one from the network actually called Ellen to tell her the show had been axed. An assistant read the news in the trades. ABC made no other official comment. Even though three episodes had been taped, only an hour-long series finale would be broadcast. Ellen felt the network had simply let the sitcom wither through lack of promotion. Without that network support, the show got less and less attention and slid down the ratings.

Suddenly, Ellen was unemployed. Then her worst fears came true. People who loved her seemed to hate her overnight just because they now knew she was gay. She was the butt of jokes on late-night TV. Magazine articles said it had been a disastrous decision to come out. Ellen lost her career. Then she lost her agent. Then she went into a depression. She moved out of Los Angeles to escape the media noise and moved to Ohio. She was by herself. She was running out of money because she hadn't been paid much for the sitcom and she didn't own a piece of it when it went into syndication. There were some small pockets of support. Even though Madonna and Ellen had never met, Madonna called and told her she was brave and to trust that this would end up being the best thing that ever happened to her.

Ellen would receive no job offers for the next three years.

In 2000, Ellen decided to mount her third solo HBO special, auspiciously titled *The Beginning*. It would be nominated for two Primetime Emmys. But still no job offers arrived. Then, around 2001, a man named Andrew Stanton was experiencing writer's block. He was writing a screenplay for an animated movie called *Finding Nemo*, and he had an idea for a fish character named Dory who had short-term memory loss. But everything he wrote was flat and unfunny. He also wasn't sure how to write the character without offending some of the audience.

He was stuck.

One day, the television was on in the background and a syndicated episode of *Ellen* was on. As it played behind him, he overheard Ellen's character change the subject five times in a single sentence. A light bulb went off—that's Dory! From that moment on, Stanton began chipping his way out of his writer's block by writing the character with Ellen's voice in mind. He eventually tracked Ellen down and begged her to say yes to the role. Stanton had no idea her sitcom had been cancelled or that she had been unemployed for a long time. Ellen jumped at the opportunity.

In hindsight, she would say the role saved her life in many ways. Dory's motto of "Just keep swimming" was one she took to heart. It would take three years for the animation to be completed and the film released. Meanwhile, she decided to re-emerge from her exile by doing some stand-up comedy gigs. She needed to regain her confidence. She needed to test the waters. The immediate assumption was that her material was going to be strictly gay-themed. Although it wasn't, the shows were mostly attended by a gay audience and Ellen realized she was going to have to work hard to win back a straight crowd. But there were signs the zeitgeist had begun changing in the time since Ellen's show had been cancelled. The sitcom *Will & Grace* hit the air in September 1998 and became the highest-rated sitcom for adults eighteen to forty-nine from 2001 to 2005. This was an important milestone, as two of the leading characters were gay. While it was labelled a gay show for straight people, it certainly didn't shy away from very funny gay storylines.

Then in 2001, CBS decided the time was right for Ellen to try another sitcom.

The premise of *The Ellen Show* featured Ellen as a gay dotcom executive whose company has gone bankrupt, so she decides to move back to her quiet hometown and live with her eccentric mother. The townsfolk are accepting of her gay lifestyle and the phys ed teacher is the only other lesbian in town. Hilarity ensues.

CBS never questioned that Ellen would play a gay character, and the show's producer, Carol Leifer, said the network would have fought an attempt to make the character straight. In an interview with the *Advocate* magazine, Ellen said the difference between her first sitcom and this new one was that being gay was now a non-issue. This sitcom was about a woman who just happens to be gay. She told the *New York Times* she was proud of her last sitcom, but she had tried to do something that just didn't work: "I tried to incorporate educational things about what people actually go through when they're coming out and it wasn't funny. Because it's not funny. And that's why it failed. And by 'failed' I mean 'got cancelled.'" The homecoming premise in the new sitcom was a metaphor for starting over. As Ellen said, "I am starting all over.

I lost a huge job, a love, a lot of things and suddenly I'm moving again. It's a very humbling experience."

Things definitely started to look up. That same year, Ellen was asked to host the Primetime Emmys, which were cancelled twice because of 9/11, then finally aired in November. She was praised for her handling of the hosting duties, turning in what the press called a "witty, respectful and wise" performance. Then she hosted *Saturday Night Live*. Then in January 2002, *The Ellen Show* was cancelled. Eighteen episodes had been filmed but only thirteen would ever air. Even though Ellen's second attempt at a sitcom had failed, she was gaining momentum. She appeared on an episode of *Will & Grace*. She occupied the coveted centre square on *Hollywood Squares*. Ellen embarked on a very successful thirty-five-city stand-up tour that was filmed for an HBO special called *Ellen DeGeneres: Here and Now*. Disney/Pixar finally released *Finding Nemo*, which would quickly become the highest-grossing animated film of all time.

Then in the fall of 2003, Ellen wanted to create a syndicated daytime talk show. She still had no representation, so she went to see Jim Carrey's manager and begged him to take her on. "I said: I promise you I can do this—just help me. I need someone with power, I need someone to make phone calls." An influential TV producer named Jim Paratore, who had founded TMZ, backed her. But it was a hard sell to stations; Paratore couldn't believe all the resistance they were getting from station managers. Many were wary of buying a talk show helmed by a gay woman, with one actually saying, "No one's going to watch a lesbian during the day." Paratore told Ellen she had to go on tour, saying, "You're going to show them who you are." So as Ellen went city to city, Paratore persuaded station managers to attend the shows so they could see the kind of audience Ellen attracted. Ellen did meet and greets after every show and eventually won them over.

On September 8, 2003, *The Ellen DeGeneres Show* launched. The format was comedy, interviews, games—and dancing. The show generated positive reviews and the ratings grew steadily over the course of its first year. Remarkably, it earned twelve Emmy nominations, the most ever received by a talk show in its debut season. It would win four, including the Emmy for Outstanding Talk Show. Commenting on the awards in an article on CNN.com, Ellen said, "I have fun every day. It's the best job I've ever had."

Ellen had finally hit her stride. She was also experiencing something very few people in Hollywood have ever experienced— she was a forty-five-year-old woman starting over and finding success. The talk show continued to pick up steam year after year. As of this writing, it has received 166 Daytime Emmy Award nominations and won 63, including four for Outstanding Talk Show and eleven for Outstanding Talk Show Entertainment. It has won seventeen People's Choice Awards. In its seventeenth season, it was the top-rated talk show for the eighth straight year. The Ellen Digital Network has a reach of over 268 million followers or visitors, and 1 billion monthly views across all platforms.

By most measures, it is a juggernaut.

Forbes magazine lists her as one of the most powerful people in the entertainment industry, with an annual income of $75 million. It's a long way from being broke in Ohio. But more than all the awards and rating points, Ellen's success has very personal rewards. She had been living with so much fear for so long. She was afraid people wouldn't laugh at her material anymore if they knew she was gay. She worried she would lose her career. Her secret fuelled a constant feeling of shame. But when she openly announced she was gay, that fear and shame dissolved. She married Portia de Rossi in 2008. Ellen was no longer afraid to say the word "wife" in interviews. As *Newsweek* so aptly put it, just like her character in the airport scene, DeGeneres was now advertising her sexuality over the PA system of national TV. She has stated coming out has been the most freeing experience because people can't hurt her anymore. She doesn't have to worry about reporters discovering her secret.

As soon as she made the decision to speak frankly about her life, she immediately lost weight and her skin cleared up. The funny lady with the sad eyes didn't have to hide anymore. She had fame. She had money. But she was willing to risk it all to feel proud and live her truth. And she did lose it all. She was a pioneer because she didn't have anyone else's career to look at. "Which is why I did it so wrong," she says. "I had to do it my own way and make huge, public mistakes." But as Ellen now says, "It was the best part of my journey. Because it is when I realized how strong I was. It's when I learned the truth will always win. And that's when you grow. Like everyone has a fear, everyone's scared of something. But it's not until you've faced that fear head-on that you realize your power."

In 2009, Ellen became a CoverGirl spokesperson. The following year, she was a judge on *American Idol*. A full-circle moment happened in 2012, when Ellen became a spokesperson for JCPenney, the very company that pulled its advertising from "The Puppy Episode."

On November 22, 2016, a very emotional Ellen DeGeneres received the Presidential Medal of Freedom. President Obama had this to say, in part:

> *It's easy to forget now, when we've come so far, where now, marriage is equal under the law, just how much courage was required for Ellen to come out on the most public of stages almost twenty years ago . . . What an incredible burden that was to bear. To risk your career like that. People don't do that very often. And then to have the hopes of millions on your shoulders . . . And she did pay a price . . . For a long stretch of time. And yet, today, every day,*

in every way, Ellen counters what too often divides us, with the countless things that bind us together. Inspires us to be better, one joke and one dance at a time.

Looking back now, Ellen maintains she wouldn't change a thing. Even though everyone around told her it would be a catastrophic mistake, she still feels she had to lose everything to realize the most important thing.

You have to be true to yourself.

16.

The Incredible Hulk

Fifty Shades of Grey

When Stan Lee was dreaming up a new character for Marvel Comics in 1962, he hit on the idea of creating what he would later call a "loveable monster." As a kid, Lee had loved books and movies. He especially liked high-concept characters like Tarzan, King Kong and the Wolf Man. In particular, he was drawn to the movie *Frankenstein*, starring Boris Karloff. He was especially moved by the fact Frankenstein's monster wasn't trying to hurt anyone. It was his physicality that was monstrous, not his intentions. He was pieced and sewn together and the result terrified people. Just because of the way he looked, he was hunted, feared and hated. The monster didn't know why he was hated, what to do or where to go as he was being pursued by pitchforks and torches. He was a sympathetic monster.

Lee was also enamoured with the story of Dr. Jekyll and Mr. Hyde. He was intrigued by the duality of a character who was both good and terrifying, someone who would switch back and forth with no apparent control. Drawing on both of those inspirations, Lee came up with a character he called the Incredible Hulk. His

Hulk would be a normal person who, for some reason, would turn into a terrifying monster. Lee had a firm philosophy that every character had to be someone the reader, or viewer, could sympathize with, care about and believe in. That heroic character could, hypothetically, exist in real life and, if that character was heroic enough, the reader, or viewer, would want to, hypothetically, be friends with them. If Lee could achieve that, he would have the perfect superhero. If his audience could relate to the heroic side, the Jekyll personality, they would accept the evil Hyde side. Lee just had to figure out how that transformation could happen to his character in a way his audience would buy into. It had to be a device that would make the audience suspend disbelief and imagine it could actually happen.

Lee had heard the phrase "gamma rays" somewhere and was intrigued by it. He had absolutely no idea what gamma rays were, but the term sounded very scientific. So he concocted a storyline where a gamma ray bomb was being secretly tested in a small town. Next, he needed the "normal" side of the Hulk to be heroic, to make people care about him. Clearly influenced by Dr. Jekyll, Lee named the "normal" personality Dr. Bruce Banner, making him a renowned physicist who specialized in gamma radiation. Just as the bomb is about to be detonated, a young boy walks across the field, unaware he is walking directly in the line of fire. Banner sees this and runs to save him, throwing his body over the boy. When the bomb explodes, he absorbs all the radiation, thereby sacrificing himself to save the boy. The result of that radiation alters his body chemistry and causes a strange metamorphosis to occur, turning Banner into the powerful Hulk. Yes, it was a tad silly, but as animator Chuck Jones once said, it doesn't have to be realistic, just believable.

The character Lee created along with his legendary artist partner, Jack Kirby, was interestingly complex. The normal Dr. Banner hated his monster side, and the Hulk hated his normal alter ego. Plus, both personalities were powerless to stop or control the transformation. Originally, Lee had Banner change into the Hulk at sundown, inspired no doubt by the Wolf Man movies of his youth. But this important transformation moment was later changed to be triggered when Banner was stressed by anger. Conversely, when the Hulk got too angry, he would become weak and transform back into Dr. Banner.

When thinking about the monster side of the character, Lee and Kirby imagined him not only huge and muscular, but unusual in one other way. They didn't want to just use a uniform or a costume, à la Spider-Man or Captain America. Neither could think of an excuse for a monster to slip on a costume. So they decided to identify the transformation in another way—they would give him a different skin colour. Not wanting to offend any ethnicity, Lee decided on the colour grey. It was spooky, sombre and in keeping with the melodramatic mood Lee and Kirby wanted to establish. So in the very first issue, they made the Hulk grey.

Then a colourful mistake happened in the printing process.

For some reason, the printer had trouble with that particular grey colour. On one page the Hulk was light grey, on another he was dark grey and on still another he was black. Every single page was a different colour. The problem was the printing process: the density on the press was either light on magenta or heavy on some combination of cyan and yellow. Lee didn't want a character with variable skin colours on top of his already dramatic body and temperament changes. So he called the printer and asked what single colour could be used without problems.

The printer said virtually any colour; it was just grey that was tricky. With that, Lee asked himself one quick question: What colour was not being used in the comic world at the time? The first answer that popped into his mind was green. Lee didn't give it more than a moment's thought.

Green.

Let's go with green.

That initial printing mistake opened up a plethora of creative opportunities for Stan Lee. First, green gave the Hulk a completely unique look in the comic world. Lee was a big fan of advertising and catchphrases, so the colour green allowed him to give the Hulk fun nicknames in the storylines, like the Jolly Green Giant or the Green Goliath or Old Green Skin.

The looming green Hulk became the first popular superhero who was actually a monster. It had never been done before. When the Hulk made the leap to TV in 1977, actor Bill Bixby played Dr. David (changed for some odd reason) Banner and bodybuilder Lou Ferrigno played the Hulk. The series produced one of the most quoted lines of the decade, Banner's inevitable statement, "Don't make me angry. You wouldn't like me when I'm angry." Whenever Banner began turning into the Hulk, viewers would see his shirt strategically tearing as the green muscles burst through. It became one of the most iconic recurring moments of the TV series. Lee has often said it was also one of the favourite moments for female viewers.

The process of bodypainting Ferrigno green took four hours every shoot day and the paint had to be retouched constantly over the course of the filming (to avoid sweating and causing his makeup to run, he would spend much of his time on the set in a refrigerated motor home). One night after an extra-long and gruelling shoot, Ferrigno was frustrated and just wanted to get home. He told the makcup person not to spend yet another hour removing the green body paint—he would wipe it all off himself when he got home. As he drove home on the freeway at 1:30 in the morning, a fellow driver happened to glance over at Ferrigno's car. He saw a Hulking green face staring back at him. His eyes bounced open, his jaw dropped and he promptly collided full force with the car in front of him. Ferrigno was mortified and sped home. As he said in telling the story, can you imagine Ferrigno in full green body paint and costume trying to explain the situation to a police officer at the accident scene?

It's interesting to note that although the green Hulk is one of the most instantly recognizable characters in the Marvel world, the comic wasn't popular at all when it was launched. Stan Lee and Jack Kirby struggled with the storylines in the first issues, with the Hulk bouncing back and forth between a slow-moving character and one who could make quick, superhuman leaps. In issue 4, Banner created a machine that would allow him to transform into the Hulk's body while retaining his physicist brain. Then in issue 6, Banner transformed into the Hulk but retained his human head, requiring him to don a green Hulk mask.

Lee was clearly trying to get a bead on his green creation, but the swerving storylines led Marvel to cancel the comic after that sixth issue. The Hulk wouldn't reappear until Marvel decided to mirror the success of DC Comics' Justice League, a superhero team including Superman, Batman, Wonder Woman, the Flash and the Green Lantern. The Marvel equivalent was called the Avengers and included Iron Man, the Wasp, Thor, Ant-Man and the Hulk as founding members, appearing in *The Avengers* issue 1 in 1963. It wouldn't be until issue 102 in 1968 that the Hulk would regain his own comic book title and become more and more popular as time went on.

All told, the Hulk has spawned hundreds of comic book iterations, motion pictures, a television series, three made-for-TV movies, a syndicated daily newspaper strip, four animated series, novels, animated films, video games and endless collectibles.

Not bad for a comic book character that didn't catch on, started life out grey, then finally found his true colours.

All due to a printing mistake.

17.

Anthony Carter

Turning Up the Heat in Miami

Anthony Carter's chance of making it to the NBA was a long shot. He had grown up in a supportive home with his mother and thirteen other siblings, all crowded into his grandmother's house. Carter was one of forty-seven children chosen to participate in Atlanta's "I Have A Dream" project, which randomly selected classes of third-grade students and provided tutoring, cultural experiences, contacts for role models and, eventually, money for college. But Carter was a truant and his low grades made him ineligible to play sports. So he dropped out of high school after his first year. Between the ages of sixteen and nineteen, he hustled around the city playing pickup games for money. Carter, a point guard, was better than most on the court and settled in for a life of street basketball, sometimes splitting a thousand-dollar winner's pot with his pickup teammates after a game.

During one of those games in 1994, Carter dunked eight times one night. One of the opposing players took note, asked if he could videotape Carter at the next game, then sent that grainy footage to his old basketball coach at Saddleback College in Mission Viejo, California. The coach liked what he saw and offered Carter a two-year financial aid package. One day, Carter stopped in at the YMCA to ask an "I Have A Dream" project coordinator he knew if she could help him fill in a form. He pulled a crumpled piece of paper out of his back pocket and put it on the table. It was his acceptance letter to Saddleback. According to the letter, he was supposed to have been in California two days earlier to report for training. The coordinator called the school and asked the coach if he still wanted Carter. He said, "Yes!" Two days later, the foundation paid for a plane ticket to Los Angeles.

Carter led the state in scoring in the 1995–96 season, including a season-high forty-four points in one game. He also earned enough credits to qualify for a Division 1 scholarship at the University of Hawai'i. By the end of his first year on the island, he was considered good enough to be a late first or mid-second round draft choice for the NBA. He injured his shoulder in practice during his third year in Hawaii, but seemed to recover. Sports agents hovered around the hopeful.

Then came a second fateful injury.

At the 1998 pre-draft camp in Chicago, where players scrimmaged before an audience of scouts, coaches and general managers, Carter reinjured his shoulder just three minutes into the first game. This time, the injury needed surgery. It scared the scouts away. He went undrafted. From that point on, he ping-ponged between playing in the Continental Basketball Association and trying out for various NBA teams. While playing for a Dallas Mavericks summer league, he was spotted by Miami Heat coach Pat Riley, who offered him this deal: Carter would show up to camp and the Heat would pay his living expenses. If he made the roster for the new season, Riley would sign him to a one-year, free-agent deal worth $385,000.

When star Tim Hardaway got injured, Carter started in thirty games. Hardaway then sprained a foot as the season ended, meaning Carter started all three games in the first round of the playoffs. Riley liked his style, especially his fearlessness on the court. He began entrusting the rookie with important shifts. Maybe the most memorable moment of Carter's Miami rookie year was when he sunk the winning basket with two seconds remaining on the clock in game three of the Eastern Conference semifinals against the Knicks.

While he was solid, Carter was never a star. He spent the first four seasons as a reserve player for the Heat, averaging only 4.1 to 6.3 points per game. Then, when Anthony Carter was about to exercise his option to stay with Miami, something happened. It was a mistake that would cost him dearly.

Anthony Carter was now twenty-seven years old. The 2002–3 season had ended and he wanted to exercise a $4.1 million player option to stay with Miami. It was a good deal for Carter. He was coming off a poor season where he only averaged 4.1 points on 35.6 percent shooting in forty-nine games. With that lacklustre performance, he was being paid millions more than that stat was worth. It was just a matter of signing on the dotted line. That's when Carter's agent, Bill Duffy, made a mistake. He failed to notify the Heat by the June 30 deadline that Carter was going to accept the deal. Instead of securing his spot, Carter accidentally became a free agent without a team.

The only offer he got was from the San Antonio Spurs, who offered Carter $750,000, just slightly above the NBA minimum salary. The math was simple. Not locking in his Miami contract had cost Carter $3 million. The press rained criticism on Duffy. He was one of the most respected agents in the game, but this was a rookie mistake. Then Bill Duffy made an unprecedented move. He offered to pay Carter the $3 million out of his own pocket. They agreed to a payback schedule. And through it all, Carter never once thought of firing Duffy.

There was a reason.

When Carter had injured his shoulder in Chicago just before the NBA draft all those years ago, when all the agents stopped chasing him, Duffy had stayed with him. He had faith in Carter and eventually helped him sign with the Heat after he went undrafted. Even though various lawyers contacted Carter to represent him pro bono to sue Duffy, Carter refused. The mistake could have derailed Duffy's business, too. Predatory agents no doubt licked their lips thinking of all the players who would be abandoning Duffy. But because he took responsibility and offered to make Carter whole, his loyalty to his client gained the respect of the league. As Carter told the *New York Times*, "He was there for me from Day One. I just knew I was going to stick with him regardless, and to this day, we have a close friendship."

Carter went on to play in the league for another nine years and was a clutch player for the Denver Nuggets in the 2008–9 Western Conference finals. He is remembered as a hardworking player with total salary earnings over his career estimated to be just under $20 million, less than what most players now earn in a single year.

But the ramifications of that $3 million mistake extended past Carter and Duffy.

When Carter didn't exercise his option in 2003, Pat Riley suddenly found himself with close to $11 million in salary cap room, substantially more than the $7 million he had planned for. That made the Heat a major player on the summer free-agent market, eventually allowing Riley to sign Lamar Odom. The following year, Odom was a key component in a trade with the Lakers that brought Shaquille O'Neal to the Heat. Two years later, Miami won its first NBA championship.

It was Duffy's blunder, in part, that allowed that championship to happen.

Carter and Duffy have an enduring relationship to this day. Carter says that, in the end, it was all a blessing. He got his name into the history books twice—first for the buzzer-beating shot against the Knicks and second, for the famous contract that wasn't.

In a Simba circle-of-life moment, Anthony Carter rejoined Pat Riley and the Miami Heat as a player-development coach in 2016.

They have never discussed the blunder.

Popsicles

Air Conditioning on a Stick

One evening back in 1905, Frank Epperson was sitting on his porch in Oakland, California. He was mixing a fruit-flavoured drink with water, using a stick to stir the concoction in his cup. By mistake, he forgot it there on the porch when he went in for the evening.

As fate would have it, the temperature dropped to a rare record low that night. The next morning, Epperson discovered the drink had frozen to the stick. He ran it under hot water and was able to pull the icy treat out of the cup using the stick as a handle. He looked at it, licked it and found it tasted pretty good. In that instant, he knew he had stumbled on a fun idea. So he made more of the treats for his friends. Playing off the word "icicle," Epperson named it the "Epsicle."

Did I mention Frank Epperson was eleven years old at the time?

Eighteen years later, Epperson was established in the real estate trade. Serving Epsicles to his own kids at home and seeing again how much they loved the product, he decided to try selling them. He introduced the frozen drink-on-a-stick at a fireman's ball and it was a sensation. Next he set up a stand at Neptune Beach, an amusement park in Alameda, California, and Epsicles were a hit there, too. His kids never did like the name "Epsicle" and preferred to call it "Pop's Sicle," so Epperson listened to his future target market and renamed the product the "Popsicle."

Convinced there might be a national market for his product, Epperson collaborated with employees from the Loew's movie company to form the original Popsicle Company in 1923. As the company grew, a new entity called the Popsicle Corporation of America was formed in 1924. It purchased the operating rights from the Loew group and reported sales of 6.5 million Popsicles that year.

The same year, at the age of thirty, Epperson sought a patent for his "Frozen confection of attractive appearance, which can be conveniently consumed without contamination by contact with the hand and without the need for a plate, spoon, fork or other implement." The patent documents discuss texture (syrup results in a crystalline product of hard snowy consistency), stick material (employ a wooden stick of relatively porous though sapless and tasteless wood, preferably bass wood, birch or poplar), freezing method (rapid refrigeration results in a more uniform product) and vessel shape (ordinary test tubes). On August 19, 1924, patent number 1,505,592 was granted, and Epperson immediately sold his patent rights to the Popsicle Corporation, while retaining royalties. The company then launched a huge national advertising campaign in trade journals and other publications promoting Popsicles as a "frozen lolly pop" and a "drink-on-a-stick."

The Joe Lowe Company approached the Popsicle Corporation in 1925 to become its exclusive sales agent. The New York–based company was the largest supplier to the ice cream industry in the country. Knowing the Popsicle Corporation owned a patent, the Joe Lowe Company was convinced it could use its extensive marketing contacts to grow the business and an agreement was reached in August of that year. Enforcing the patent became an ongoing process. Between 1924 and 1929, the Popsicle Corporation brought infringement suits against numerous competitors, claiming they had marketed similar products. With the patent as their shield, they won all the cases or settled out of court.

Like most people when the Depression hit in 1929, Epperson got into financial trouble. He went flat broke and had to liquidate all his assets. Part of that entailed selling his royalty rights back to the Joe Lowe Company—a decision he would regret for the rest of his life. Interestingly, the Great Depression crushed the ten-cent ice cream market, but not the five-cent Popsicle market. As a result, the Popsicle Corporation advertised itself as "Depression Proof" and, remarkably, stated its sales had actually doubled between 1930 and 1931. People who could not afford quarters or dimes could still afford a nickel treat for their families. Over 200 million Popsicles were sold in 1931 alone, with the most popular flavour being cherry. The company then debuted the "twin Popsicle" so two children could share an ice pop for just a nickel, the same price as a single. In April 1939, a mascot called Popsicle Pete debuted on the radio program *Buck Rogers in the 25th Century*.

During the fifties, as American industry got back to manufacturing consumer goods after the war effort, most homes acquired modern refrigerators with freezers and the sales of Popsicles soared. Based on that kitchen innovation, boxes of Popsicles were introduced so families could keep a supply of frozen treats on hand at home.

The addition of the newest and most exciting piece of furniture in modern homes, the television, brought the most powerful marketing machine into living rooms across the nation. Popsicle Pete was cleverly tucked into kids' programs, creating what the marketing industry calls a "pull strategy." Instead of "pushing" marketing to the people with the money (parents), the commercials were put into children's programming so kids would keep asking for the product, creating a "pull" effect on parents. With that, the Popsicle business continued to grow.

While the shape of Popsicles is unique, the flat, wooden stick handles with their round ends are as popular as the treat itself. Even though the twin Popsicle was discontinued in 1986 (but brought back in 2019 thanks to a Twitter push from none other than Justin Bieber and his army of Beliebers), Popsicle sticks are still sold by the box to children and adults for arts and crafts projects. Good old Popsicle Pete continued making appearances in Popsicle marketing until 1995. By the way, the most popular flavour is still cherry.

Good old Frank Epperson died in Fremont, California, in 1983 at the age of eighty-nine. Today the Popsicle Corporation is owned by Unilever and sells over 2 billion Popsicles every year.

All due to the time Epperson mistakenly left a cup of soda on the porch overnight and accidentally invented one of the most beloved treats in the world—at the ripe old age of eleven.

Sam Phillips

Rocket 'n' Roll

S am Phillips was an ambitious record producer with a small
recording studio in Memphis, Tennessee. He was hungry
to find new acts, fresh sounds and songs that didn't sound
like anything else on the charts. In 1950 he met a man named
Leonard Chess, who had a small, struggling record label based
in Chicago. Chess was a smart, hungry street hustler and Phillips
liked him. Chess dropped by Phillips's studio one day, they hit it
off and Chess proposed a deal right there on the spot. They agreed
to a fifty-fifty split of the profits on any recording of Phillips's that
Chess Records released.

One of the acts Phillips was recording at the time was B.B.
King. He knew a terrific piano player named Ike Turner, who
led a band called the Kings of Rhythm. One night, twenty-year-
old Turner and his band joined King onstage at a roadhouse in
Chambers, Mississippi, and tore the place apart. The crowd went
wild. King told Turner that his band was red hot and should be
cutting records. Turner said he had absolutely no idea how to make
that happen. King was recording with a guy named Sam Phillips

who had a recording studio in Memphis, and offered to introduce them. Turner was shocked that it could be that easy.

Sure enough, Phillips called Turner that Monday and asked him how fast he could get his band to Memphis. Turner said they were on the way. The band was giddy at the thought of getting into a recording studio, but as Turner said, they had "no idea—none—what we were gonna do when we got there."

In March 1951, the five-man band piled into a small sedan and stuffed in their saxes, guitar and drum set. The car trunk was secured with a rope to tie the down the guitar amp and big bass drum. With the knot tied, the car's suspension moaned as it set off on a rainy night to Memphis, seventy miles away down Route 61. Somewhere along the line, they were pulled over by the highway patrol and made to pay a fine for what was described as an "overloaded" vehicle.

A little while later, the car suffered a flat tire. In their hurry to dig the spare out of the trunk, one of the band members made a fateful mistake. He dropped the guitar amp onto the pavement, destroying the speaker cone. They were in a hurry to get to Memphis and had absolutely no way to fix the amp or get another one on such short notice.

They had one shot at a recording session. And their sound depended on the guitar.

When they arrived at 706 Union Avenue in Memphis, the band figured they must have written the address down wrong. They had no idea what a recording studio looked like, but it couldn't be this tiny, sorry-looking storefront they found themselves standing in front of. When they went in to ask the receptionist if she knew where the Memphis Recording Service studio was, she said, "You're standing in it."

A neatly dressed Sam Phillips came out to meet the band and ushered them into his tiny recording space. When guitarist Willie Kizart plugged his guitar into his amp, it made a horrible sound and Phillips instantly knew the speaker cone was blown. As the band fretted, Phillips listened to the weird, distorted sound the amp made while Kizart tried to fiddle with the knobs. He told Kizart to stop. He was fascinated by the sound the amp was making. He liked it because it sounded different. Then Phillips ran to the restaurant next door and got some brown paper to wad up inside the amp to steady the vibration a bit. Turner had no idea what to make of Phillips. He seemed intense and determined, but at the same time strange because he seemed most excited about the damaged equipment.

When the band was ready to go, Phillips asked them what original material they had and Turner took his band through a few numbers. Phillips wasn't impressed. He asked if they had anything else. Anything else that was different. Turner said they had one more song, but it wasn't fully finished yet. The title was "Rocket '88'"—named after the hot new Oldsmobile 88 with the Rocket V-8 engine and Hydra-Matic Drive. The band ran through the number a few times and Phillips's assistant, Marion, wrote down the lyrics as they played. Phillips loved the sound of the song as soon as he heard it. He loved the driving combination of horns and piano, and he especially dug the distorted, damaged guitar sound. There was just one thing he didn't like.

Ike Turner's vocal.

So Phillips brashly asked if anyone else in the band could sing. Turner "narrowed his eyes" and reluctantly pointed to baritone sax player Jackie Brenston. It was a good choice, because Brenston had written the song. So Turner counted the band in and they took off with a raucous version of "Rocket '88.'" The band was cookin', the lyrics weren't bad and the vocal was pretty good, but what Phillips loved most was what he referred to as the "rubbing" sound between the saxophone and the distorted guitar. It was a sound he had never heard before. Without a doubt, Sam Phillips knew the damaged amp gave the song its most unique quality. As Peter Guralnick says in his definitive biography, *Sam Phillips: The Man Who Invented Rock 'n' Roll*, Phillips was completely taken with the sound of the broken amp taking the bass part, the horns riffing in unison and Ike's storming piano cutting through the churning mix. Even fifty years later, Phillips couldn't explain the magic of the sound that day. It was just a sound no one had heard before.

"Rocket '88'" would be the first record Sam Phillips licensed to Leonard Chess. When the record was released on Chess Records, the label didn't credit Ike Turner and his Kings of Rhythm. Instead, it said "Jackie Brenston and his Delta Cats"—a name no one in the band had ever heard before. Turner was furious, but Phillips told him he was going to release another track of Ike's and didn't want two songs out at the same time from the same band. The logic made no sense to Turner, but Phillips was insistent and decisive.

By the end of the month, the record had taken off beyond everyone's expectations. By June 9, "Rocket '88'" was Chess's first number-one hit on the Billboard rhythm and blues charts, staying on top for three weeks. It also spent two weeks at the top of the Most Played Juke Box R&B Records chart. It would eventually be inducted into the Blues Hall of Fame, the Grammy Hall of Fame and the Rock and Roll Hall of Fame singles category.

Time for a little context.

"Rocket '88'" was recorded in 1951. It predated Sun Records by one year. It predated Elvis Presley by three years. Sam Phillips is credited as the man who invented rock 'n' roll. Sam Phillips cites "Rocket '88'" as the first rock 'n' roll record ever made and many music historians agree. Little Richard said that song influenced him in such a profound way, he tried to emulate it on "Good Golly, Miss Molly." *Time* magazine said the song was "brash and it was sexy. It took elements of the blues, hammered them with rhythm and attitude and electric guitar and reimagined black music into something new." While other historians say it's impossible to name one song as the first rock 'n' roll record, almost all agree it was the prototype for rock 'n' roll. It was the first record to pull it all together.

Ike Turner himself didn't consider "Rocket '88'" a rock 'n' roll record. He said it was R&B. But he firmly believed "Rocket '88'" was the cause of rock 'n' roll. It was one of the very first Black records played on WHBQ/560, the most influential white radio station in Memphis, hosted by pioneering DJ Dewey Phillips. The song's driving style, unique futzed sound and lyrical content was the Black bridge to white listeners. As Turner points out, when Phillips said, "If I get me a white boy to sound like a black boy, then I got me a gold mine," he was right. "Rocket '88'" was the match that lit that fuse in Sam Phillips. And all we know that led to Phillips signing that young Crown Electric truck driver a few years later.

A lot of history came out of "Rocket '88.'" All fuelled by the mistake of dropping the guitar amp on the pavement that fateful night and the damaged sound it emitted that infatuated Sam Phillips.

Kathleen King

Watching the Cookie Crumble

Kathleen King grew up on a farm in Noyac, Southampton, Long Island. While the Hamptons are the summer playground of the rich and famous, King's family scraped to get by. Her father's modest farm raised chickens and cows on thirty acres. Her mom worked outside the home and brought in a small paycheque. King was the youngest of four kids, and from an early age, they were expected to work the farm. Nobody was coddled; everybody had to pull their weight. The kids did chores, collected eggs, tended the small crop. The family had a roadside farm stand where they sold eggs, beef, vegetables and baked goods. When they needed something expensive like dental work, their father would barter half a steer to the dentist so the kids could get their teeth done. The family philosophy embraced the value of grit—if you fall down, you dust yourself off and get right back up again.

King's older sister and her friend baked cookies, brownies and bread to sell at the stand. But when they turned fourteen, they wanted to work in town at the local ice cream stand to earn a little extra money and meet boys. So at the age of eleven, King's father told her to start baking to earn money so she could buy her own clothes for the next school year. She started with the recipe on the back of the Nestlé Toll House chocolate chips bag. She was young, so her ingredient measuring and mixing abilities were not all that accurate, but somehow, someway, that made for delicious cookies. She preferred a thin, crisp yet chewy cookie and decided on a five-inch diameter, so they would be unique. King would bake her cookies and put them in little plastic bags while keeping one eye on the farm stand out the window. When a customer drove up, she would run out, serve the folks, then run back to take the next batch out of the oven. Word began to spread that the cookies were especially good. People began to make their trek out to the farm stand just for the cookies. Business increased and King started earning more than pocket money. Eventually, her dad said they had to re-evaluate their business arrangement. King had to start buying her own ingredients. But the eggs were free.

During high school summers, King toiled in the kitchen seven days a week, ten hours a day. She even earned enough to buy a secondhand car. The next stop was college, where she pursued her love of food by studying restaurant management. She dreamed of travel and maybe working on a cruise ship one day. She graduated in 1979 and went home again to bake cookies in time for the lucrative Hamptons summer rush. It was then that her mother asked King what her plans were, since this was her last summer making cookies at the farm.

That was news to King.

But standing on your own two feet was another firm family philosophy and it was time for King to make her way in the world. Her mom also mentioned one other thing—there was a fully equipped bakery for rent in town. King went to look at it. Two bakeries had failed there in the past, but it was perfect. Without much more thought, twenty-one-year-old King rented the space.

She had five thousand dollars saved and her brother lent her some more money so she could get set up and buy baking supplies. The decorating budget was nil, so she got creative and painted old barrels from the farm, put plywood down as counters, added fresh flowers and hand-wrote the labels. It wasn't fancy, but it turned out to be just the right ambiance for a store that sold hand-baked cookies. She rented the location in November and opened Kathleen's Cookie in May 1980. Soon, she increased her offerings and began offering carrot cake, blueberry muffins and apple pie. To reflect the expanded menu, she changed the name to Kathleen's Bake Shop. Her father steered customers to the store and King ran a series of print ads. Business was good in the summer of 1980. Then a food writer stopped into the shop.

Florence Fabricant was a food writer for the *New York Times*. Clearly, the gentle waft of freshly baked cookies was starting to reach Manhattan. King had no idea who Fabricant was—until an article came out in the *Times* saying "it's worth putting miles on the odometer." That brought a surge of new customers out to the Hamptons. As that busy summer started to crest, King started thinking about how to keep her bakery going during the cold months. A large chunk of her biggest fans were New Yorkers who often told her they wished they could find King's cookies in the city. So she hatched a plan to wholesale her cookies in New York. With a shopping bag full of cookies and gumption, she started knocking on doors in Manhattan. Many stores turned her away, but King wasn't worried. She was confident in her product and knew she had very little competition in the quality department. Sure enough, many other stores liked what they saw—and tasted. Upscale establishments like Dean & DeLuca, Balducci's and Bloomingdale's took her cookies and started ordering hundreds of bags weekly.

Soon King hired drivers to deliver her cookies to her customers in New York. The increased income allowed her to get labels printed for the first time instead of doing it by hand. She started to tweak the recipe a bit, making the cookies slightly smaller and crisper. As she experimented, she used her staff as a test market. When new products were developed, she watched the reaction of her staff closely. If they took a bite and said, "This is good," but walked away without taking another nibble, King would decide the product wasn't good enough yet. As the business continued to grow, the hours grew longer, too. King's work life was her entire life. She got in her car in the dark at 1:30 a.m. and arrived at work at two to start baking. Then she would open the store at seven, work all day and finally get home around eight at night. It was a nonstop routine of eighteen-hour days, six days a week. She never feared failure because the hard work was paying off, but it was also taking its toll. One night at 2 a.m., King said, she actually thought about driving into a tree so she could go to the hospital and just get some rest. And it wasn't just the early baking hours; it was running the business of the business, on top of the chocolate chips and flour. As she would later say, she gave up her youth for the company.

Soon she was outgrowing her location. That's when her mom, who clearly had a nose for real estate, mentioned there was a building for sale in Southampton. King went to look at it and liked it. Not only was it the right size, she was tired of having a landlord. She met with the owner and discussed the terms. He wanted $350,000 and $50,000 down. He would agree to hold the mortgage at 9.5 percent interest. King had $40,000 saved, so she needed to find another $10,000. That's when serendipity stepped in.

Her father used to help an older woman up the road, tending to her chickens and assisting her from time to time. The woman died and left him $10,000 in her will, and King's father lent her the money. The building was hers. While it was exciting to expand, she also realized she would have to double her revenues in order to pay the mortgage. The new location became extremely popular. Loyal customers came in religiously and children who were raised on her cookies grew up to become customers themselves. Business was good, even in spite of some big competition. David's Cookies and Mrs. Fields were able rivals with a unique offering— they served cookies warm out of the oven. While that feature got a lot of attention, it didn't bother King. As a matter of fact, she saw that as a drawback for those brands. How could they grow if the product had to be hot out of the oven constantly? Cold Mrs. Fields cookies were not nearly as tempting. The businessperson in King saw the opportunity for real growth.

Soon, she was making enough money to buy herself a small house in the village and pay off the mortgage on her parents' farm. She was able to hire more staff and take an occasional day off for the first time in years. That led to weekends off and even a few vacations. At almost forty, Kathleen King had spent twenty years running the bakeshop and building a modest wholesale business. But her priorities were changing. She was now married and divorced. The time to have children had passed her by. She wanted more out of life, more time for travel and learning languages, less responsibility. She decided to sell the company and maybe semi-retire.

Just before she went out to formally look for a buyer, her long-time bookkeeper expressed an interest in buying in. He didn't have the cash to buy her out or buy in, but he devised a plan to pay her over time. He would take over the management of the company, which would leave King free to have a life. She would still be involved, but the burden of management would be lifted from her shoulders. The offer sounded feasible. She liked the bookkeeper. He understood the business, he understood the brand and he had a full appreciation of King's product and business standards. But before he signed the deal, he had one caveat.

He wanted to bring his brother into the business as a third partner.

King wasn't 100 percent comfortable with that request. She didn't know the brother. But they told her the business had enormous potential and they wanted to expand the wholesale division right across the country. King yearned for some freedom, so she ended up accepting the brothers and the terms of their agreement. In 1998, they agreed to pay her about $900,000, no cash down, but instalments over time. All three would share in the profits along the way.

Then Kathleen King made a mistake.

The brothers wanted to be equal partners in the business. King was unsure, but agreed because she wanted to embrace this new chapter in a positive spirit. Her lawyer asked her to reconsider, but King said she had already given her word and wanted to honour it in good faith. So the deal was struck.

At first, the brothers worked at the bakery in Southampton. Then they proposed a plan to open a cookie factory in Richmond, Virginia, to ramp up production for a big national expansion push. The idea sounded reasonable to King, so she handed over the day-to-day business reins and ran the Southampton shop while the brothers ran the Virginia production facility.

The trouble started around December 1999.

The cookies sent back from Virginia weren't the same. The pies were terrible. One time, King actually found an entire uncut apple in a pie. The factory had the recipes, but the staff wasn't trained well and they appeared to be using cheaper ingredients. Some of the packaging changed. King refused to sell low-quality products in her bakeshop and complained to the brothers that the products were generating customer complaints. That created tension. Then she began getting phone calls from suppliers. She discovered her partners weren't paying the vendors who were supplying the factory, nor the local vendors King had known and grown with. She started taking the money the bakeshop generated to pay her valued vendors. According to King, the brothers were furious and accused her of stealing. Bakery workers grew disgruntled, with some saying their payroll cheques had not cleared while they were forced to work longer hours. The tension torqued.

Just before she was to leave on a long-planned cycling trip in January 2000, she got a call from a loyal employee who had moved down to Virginia to work in the factory. He told her the brothers planned on coming up to Southampton when she was away to take over the bakeshop. Then they were going to fire her. King postponed her trip. One morning, she walked up to the shop to find the brothers blocking the entrance. They handed her papers that said she was fired. Then they hired armed security guards and got a restraining order preventing her from entering the store.

The brothers could fire Kathleen King because they controlled two-thirds of the company. Her mistake in giving away control had whipped back to sting her. King was fired from the company she had toiled over and had given up her youth for. She was devastated. It was the lowest point in King's life. She said all she could do was hold her breath, which seemed like the only thing she could control. She told herself things could be worse. At least she woke up in her own home every morning. She became grateful for the simplest things in her life.

After King had absorbed the impact of that decision, she decided to fight for her company. She wanted out of the deal because she also discovered the brothers had saddled the company with $600,000 in debt. She was fired, she had no job, the company had no retained earnings and because she still owned one-third of the company, she was responsible for one-third of the debt. The lawsuits began. When news of the battle went public, it prompted a wildcat employee walkout. Customers picketed the store for six straight months with signs saying, "No Kathleen, No Cookies." The townsfolk rallied around King because she had been a generous part of the business community for over twenty years and she had given back. They gave her words of support and sent her cards of encouragement. While it was difficult not to focus on the darkness of the lawsuits, she tried to focus on the goodwill. With the boycott, business started to decline. The brothers maintained they were unable to meet their instalment payments to King because she and the staff were purposely inducing the boycott, and King countered by saying they had signed the notes personally and were thus obligated to make payments regardless of profit levels.

After eight months of suing and countersuing, with the damage and collateral destruction mounting, both sides eventually agreed to settle. King lost the right to the company name—Kathleen's Bake Shop—her recipes and the Virginia wholesale business. She kept the Southampton store and building, which she owned, and she terminated the brothers' lease. She never saw a penny of the money they had agreed to pay her for the business. On top of it all, she was left with one other thing: $200,000 of debt. She was forty-two years old, emotionally drained and broke. The only way forward was to start all over again.

From scratch.

Remarkably, King decided to do what she knew best. She got back up, dusted herself off and started another bakeshop. She hired back her staff and named the new store Tate's Bake Shop. She chose the name Tate because of her father. He had worked in the potato fields as a kid and somewhere along the line picked up the nickname Tater, which morphed into Tate over the years. It was a genuine local name that symbolized kindness and integrity to King, because those were her father's traits. But now she had to scramble. August was just weeks away and that was the month she could make the most revenue from Hampton sun seekers. Her loyal staff rolled up their sleeves and King remortgaged the building to free up cash to float the business. She called the local sign company to design a new sign and they rushed over ten minutes later. A local plumber did some work but refused to bill her. She needed gardeners, and they showed up the very next day. The support was heartfelt and instant. She decided to open on August 5 and organized an open house the day before. Over seven hundred people showed up in a line that went around the block. The community spirit was overwhelming.

Then she made a smart decision—she hired a business manager. She was in dangerous financial waters now and needed guidance.

There was one other bizarre turn of events. She not only had to bake great cookies again, but bake better cookies than she had ever baked before, because now she had a new competitor: Kathleen's Bake Shop. But King was confident, encouraging people to put the cookies side by side and compare. She even predicted Kathleen's Bake Shop would eventually go out of business. Together with her business manager, she focused on the products with the highest margins. She also had to try and get back all her Long Island and New York clients. Because the lawsuit had been so public, it divided clients into camps. Some stuck with King, some stuck with Kathleen's Bake Shop and some insisted on carrying both products. Some stores that had done business with King for twenty years treated her as if she had no credit, which was heartbreaking. On the other hand, others wanted to help. One gourmet store that was owed $40,000 told her to pay it off when she could. They were going to stand behind her. The generosity of some people was uplifting.

As King began the Herculean task of starting all over again, she decided she would do it differently this time. For starters, she was going to take the emotion out of her business dealings. While it was important to be passionate, she had learned that being too emotionally invested was a trap. Emotion creates drama. Even choosing the name Tate instead of her own name was part of the emotional distancing. Thinking the business was her baby and her baby alone had created a self-imposed limitation on growth. Losing her first company had taught her this brutal lesson. Being stripped of a company that was her heart and soul had been too painful. She wasn't going to bleed for this new company. This time, she was able to release the emotional attachment, and letting go was liberating. Eliminating the emotion from the mix gave her profound clarity. Business decisions became easier to execute and scaling up became more achievable. This time she planned an exit strategy with a clear goal. She was going to build a great company, then sell it and retire at the age of fifty-five.

After a few years, she hit about $2 million in revenue. With the guidance of her business manager, she expanded and rented out an additional five-thousand-square-foot kitchen. She outgrew that in no time and purchased a school building twenty-five miles away in East Moriches, New York. She converted the building into a fifteen-thousand-square-foot commercial kitchen, then outgrew that. More space was added to accommodate the increased production and demand.

Then something interesting happened.

Kathleen's Bake Shop went out of business, just as she had predicted. The brand she had originally built and lost was gone. But King was too busy to mourn that passing. That was ancient history. She was after bigger fish. Over time, Tate's Bake Shop started to build its wholesale business. Her business manager would draw up three plans at the start of every year. Together they would evaluate the pros and cons and King would decide on the one that was the greatest area of opportunity. The one that was the most achievable. They began landing contracts with smaller stores and delivering the products in Tate's Bake Shop trucks. Once that was established, they strategically chose areas of the country where they could establish a foundation in upscale gourmet shops. Then they aimed at the third tier, large stores like Whole Foods and Fresh Market. Sometimes the buyers contacted King; sometimes her business manager arranged the meetings and helped negotiate the deals.

The hard work began to pay off and attract the attention of celebrity influencers. Rachael Ray said it was "the best cookie in America." Gwyneth Paltrow was a fan. *Consumer Reports* voted it Best Cookie in America in 2011. Business was increasing 30 percent year over year. King was selling her baked goods in forty states, her kitchens were turning out 24 million cookies a year, she had fifty-five employees and $6 million in annual revenue.

As she approached fifty-five years old, it was time to execute her exit plan. She sat down with her business manager, determined to do everything right this time. They interviewed several bankers and chose TM Capital in New York to package and set up the company to go to market. King had built a strong brand and there was immediate interest. Over fifty companies responded to the prospectus. That list was narrowed down to twelve and second bids were invited. From there, the list of contenders came down to five. In the end, 80 percent of Tate's Bake Shop was sold to an investment firm called Riverside.

The selling price was $100 million.

King was now wealthy, like the clientele she used to serve in the Hamptons. Four years later, Riverside sold the company to Mondeléz International for $500 million. King tucked 20 percent of *that* sale in the bank. Today, she is a big supporter of local nonprofits, land preservation, mentoring and empowering young women. She has placed a large portion of the sale proceeds into a charitable fund she has created.

Looking back, Kathleen King says the biggest disaster of her life became the greatest gift of her life. She had the benefit of dying and coming back. She says when you learn you can survive, you become fearless. She no longer allowed emotion to crush her. She learned, she lost, and in that loss, she recalibrated her business philosophy and life goals. She could never have built Tate's Bake Shop into a $100 million company without the critical mistake of signing away control of her first company. That experience informed every decision she made from that day forward.

Her epic failure led to her epic success.

Fiberglas Pink

How a Successful Product Dyed

They say Fiberglas Pink home insulation is chosen seven to one over the competition. That's a huge market share, especially considering the product has the distinction of benefiting from two big mistakes in its eighty-nine-year history. The first mistake happened during the Depression years. In 1932, a Corning Glass researcher by the name of Dale Kleist was attempting to join glass blocks together to create transparent, weatherproof walls. While trying to use glass as a sealant, Kleist mistakenly aimed a stream of compressed air at the molten glass. That moment created a spray of tiny, lightweight fibres.

Those fibres were easy to manufacture into light, puffy square batts that had incredible insulating properties. This new product was named fibreglass as a tribute to its unplanned discovery. It was economical to make and remarkably easy to produce in large quantities. A magazine article from 1938 called it a "new marvel of Science," stating a single glass marble, weighing only a quarter of an ounce, could produce an incredible ninety miles of glass fibre. Kleist's mistake would be patented in 1936 and would soon turn into a multimillion—then multibillion—dollar product.

Prior to fibreglass insulation, builders in the nineteenth century insulated buildings by mixing horsehair into the first coating of lime-based plaster. Paper, straw and rags were also used as insulating materials. Many houses were insulated with newspapers. The problem with these materials was that they deteriorated when wet and were highly flammable when dry. When Corning Glass realized it had a new, non-flammable, water-resistant insulation on its hands, it merged with Owens-Illinois, another glass manufacturer, to create a company dedicated to fibreglass insulation.

Owens Corning thrived as the postwar housing boom of the 1950s surged and, in 1954, the company invented a process to make insulation using a centrifuge to spin the fibreglass wool. But the construction boom also brought with it a wave of competitors. The company wanted to distinguish its product in the marketplace somehow. At that time, all insulation was either white or slightly yellow in colour. Owens Corning made a bold decision to dye its insulation red. That led to a second mistake that would define it for all time.

For the first hundred years of modern branding, you could not trademark a colour. But all that changed once and for all thanks to Fiberglas insulation. In 1957, the Owens Corning plant in Newark, Ohio, added red dye to the insulation. But a mistake was made. The red dye wasn't sufficiently concentrated for the amount of insulation going through the plant. As a result, the Fiberglas wool came out pink. The company was understandably concerned, as their clientele was decidedly male, and pink was decidedly un-male. But a lot of pink insulation had been manufactured and builders needed product, so the pink product was shipped out with an apology, saying the next batch would be red, as originally intended. When the colour was eventually corrected and shipped, Owens Corning got a surprising response: installers began asking for the pink insulation instead. Stunned, the company wasn't sure what to do. But the pink requests kept coming. That's when Owens Corning realized they had stumbled into a marketing master stroke. Pink was an unexpected and completely unique way to distinguish their insulation in a drab industry. By the seventies, the company had adopted the slogan "Put your house in the Pink."

Then in 1985, Owens Corning applied to trademark the colour pink. The courts had never permitted that before, but Owens Corning presented a compelling case. It proved its insulation was clearly identified as pink and had been since 1957. The company explained it had spent over $50 million marketing it as Pink.

In order for the courts to grant a colour trademark, a company must prove its colour has acquired a secondary meaning. The robin's egg blue Tiffany boxes are a great case in point. First seen on the cover of its catalogue in 1837, that particular shade of blue now immediately signals Tiffany as a brand to a large percentage of the population. Louboutin shoes are another example. Their distinctive red soles are immediately recognized as Louboutin and as a result, the company was granted a trademark. The key to trademarking a colour has to do with that secondary meaning, as well as the specific application of a particular Pantone shade. No company can trademark the colour red. But Louboutin can trademark Pantone 18-1663 TP Chinese Red for its soles. Tiffany trademarked Pantone colour 1837 Blue, named after the year of its first catalogue, for its signature robin's egg blue jewellery boxes and store bags. And it was Owens Corning that made this all possible. The company made legal history in 1987 when it was granted the very first trademark for a single colour. The insulation brand and the colour pink had become inseparable in the minds of consumers. Hence, the courts agreed Pantone 210 pink was a protectable trademark for insulation.

Then came a pink mascot.

Back in 1963, animators Fritz Freleng and David DePatie created the Pink Panther character for the opening credit sequence of the movie *The Pink Panther*, directed by Blake Edwards and starring Peter Sellers as the hilarious, bumbling Inspector Clouseau. Most people have probably forgotten what linked Inspector Clouseau with the Pink Panther. In the 1963 film, Clouseau is investigating a glamorous jewel thief who plans to steal an enormous, extremely valuable pink diamond. This diamond is named the Pink Panther because it contains a flaw at its centre that, when held to the light, resembles a leaping panther. Director Edwards wanted a funny animated sequence to open the film, so DePatie and Freleng personified the jewel as a panther and presented over a hundred sketches to Edwards, who eventually chose the panther we all know and love. The movie was a hit and so was the cartoon. So popular was the animation, United Artists commissioned a series of theatrical cartoons beginning one year later. The first, titled *The Pink Phink*, won the 1964 Academy Award for Best Animated Short Film. By 1969, the 125 animated shorts became a pop culture phenomenon when NBC broadcast the cartoons on Saturday mornings, accompanied by Henry Mancini's incredible Pink Panther saxophone theme from the original feature films.

While working on an advertising campaign for Fiberglas Pink insulation, Roger Butler, a copywriter at ad agency Ogilvy & Mather, suggested Owens Corning adopt the Pink Panther as a mascot. It made perfect marketing sense. The cartoon panther was beloved, it was pink and it was ownable. So in 1980, Owens Corning struck a deal with Metro-Goldwyn-Mayer to feature the Pink Panther as its official mascot. It has become one of the longest-running marketing associations. For over forty years, the Pink Panther has adorned every batt of Pink insulation and has become a famous spokes-character for the brand without ever uttering a single word. With most insulation products being more or less the same quality these days, it is a testament to the Pink Panther branding that Fiberglas Pink enjoys the lion's share of the insulation market.

When I worked for Campbell-Ewald, the advertising agency for Fiberglas Canada in the eighties, the brand claimed over 70 percent of the Canadian insulation market due in large part to the funny commercials our ad agency produced. For some reason that escapes me now, the Canadian company did not employ the Pink Panther branding. It may have been that the original deal with MGM did not include Canada. In any event, the ad agency was able to leverage the unique pink colour in another memorable way. The first commercial showed a couple boasting about the money they saved insulating with Pink by buying 262 bee-yootiful pink flamingos, which covered every available inch of their tiny front yard. So popular was the commercial that pink plastic flamingos sold out across the country. Subsequent commercials leveraged similar humorous situations. It was one of the biggest lessons I ever had in the power of a colour.

Insulation is a hidden purchase. People buy it once or twice in their lives, stick it between their walls and never see it again. I'll never forget the challenge our Fiberglas client, Grant McDiarmaid, put to us. He said: "I sell the most boring product in the world, make me famous." And by leveraging nothing other than that counterintuitive colour, we did. Pink gave us a marketing edge and the resulting campaign became one of the most famous in Canada during the eighties. We created pink print ads, pink-themed radio ads and a series of award-winning, beloved TV commercials. I remember being in a cab driving to downtown Vancouver in the late eighties. The cabbie and I were chatting when he asked me what I did for a living. I told him I wrote commercials. He asked which ones. I thought for a moment, quickly assessing which ones he might have seen out here in Vancouver, and when I mentioned the Fiberglas Pink commercials, he spun around in his seat and jammed on the brakes. He stared at me for a few seconds with a giant grin and told me that not only were they his favourite commercials, but he and his wife had just been to a Halloween party dressed as the couple from the latest ad.

It's a remarkable story. An innovative product, created in error, goes on to capture the largest market share in a very competitive category—all due to another embarrassing, then lucrative, mistake.

The colour pink.

Mario Puzo

An Offer Everyone Can Refuse

Every family has a chooch.

That family member who never seems to have their act together, who never really gets something resembling a career off the ground or makes what can reasonably be called "a living." A chooch is the person the rest of the family has long ago understood needs continual help or, at the very least, sporadic fiscal handouts.

According to Mario Puzo, he was the chooch in his family.

He had written two novels. The first was published in 1955, titled *The Dark Arena*. It received decent reviews. Royalties netted Puzo a total of $3,500. His second book, *The Fortunate Pilgrim*, was written in 1965 and got excellent reviews. That one netted him close to $3,000. He considered himself a serious writer. He wanted to carve out an author's life, writing novels that moved people, novels that reviewers would respect, novels that would fund not just a living but a luxurious lifestyle.

That wasn't happening.

Mario Puzo was born the third of seven children on October

15, 1920, and was raised in the tenements of Hell's Kitchen in New York. His parents were illiterate Italian immigrants. His father, Antonio, later diagnosed with mental illness, worked on the railroad and abandoned the family when Mario was twelve. His mother, Maria Le Conti, was strict and managed to keep him clear of the gangs that roamed what Puzo would call a "Neapolitan ghetto." She wanted him to become a railroad clerk, but young Mario preferred roaming the library. At the age of sixteen, he announced he wanted to be a writer. His family quietly assumed he was delusional. But Puzo found encouragement early in high school when his teachers told him his writing was good enough to be published. In the Second World War, he served as a U.S. Army corporal, and after the war, he attended City College of New York on the G.I. Bill. He found freelance work writing pulpy fiction for a men's adventure magazine published by the owner of Marvel Comics. Stan Lee had an office down the hall.

But at forty-five, Puzo still dreamed of being a serious author. He knew that unless his third book was a hit, there wouldn't be a fourth. He asked his publisher for an advance to write that third book, but they declined. He couldn't believe it. His two books had attracted good reviews. Sure, there had been a ten-year gap between the books, but serious authors need serious thinking time. He approached his publisher again and pitched an idea about an organized crime family. The title of the book was *Mafia*. His publisher said it sounded like another loser. They insisted Puzo write a hundred pages before they would even consider an advance. He agreed to ten pages.

His publisher said thanks, but no thanks. Not interested.

Months went by. Eight other publishers turned *Mafia* down. The economic pressure was mounting on Puzo. He was forced to do some freelance magazine writing and editing to pay the bills. His heart wasn't in it, but he needed a gig.

He was also borrowing a lot of money. He had a wife, five kids and a mortgage. He was always in need of a quick loan to tide him over till the next month. This is where the chooch part kicked in. He borrowed often, from one of his brothers in particular. This brother always answered Puzo's frantic calls for a few hundred bucks to pay his mortgage or to buy his kids shoes. Puzo also had an expensive habit. He loved to gamble. Those debts kept mounting until it got to the point where he owed the equivalent of $150,000 (all equivalents are in 2021 dollars). He kept borrowing from family, relatives, financial companies, banks and bookies. He was in constant search for the next bridge financing to keep the wolves from the door.

Then he made the mistake of borrowing from sharks.

Loan sharks aren't as understanding as, say, a brother. Their repayment schedules were rather firm. Then there was the matter of the compounding vig. Puzo desperately needed a book advance so he could calm the shady lenders down for a while. The thing about an advance was that you didn't have to deliver the entire manuscript and it was a nice grab of fast cash. Emphasis on the "fast" part.

One day in 1965, a writer friend dropped by the magazine's offices to say hello to Puzo. They went out to lunch. Puzo told him about his ten-page outline and regaled him with amusing Mafia stories. His friend liked what he heard and arranged a meeting between Puzo and his publisher, G.P. Putnam's Sons. When they met, Puzo spent an hour talking about his book outline and told the editors his amusing Mafia stories. They agreed to an advance of five-thousand-dollars. That was great news. Thirty-eight hundred dollars of that five-grand advance was up-front; the rest was contingent on handing in the finished manuscript. Except Puzo didn't want to write *The Godfather*. It was a cheap, commercial idea he was only doing for quick money. He still considered himself a serious author. But he could feel the breath of impatient money-lenders on his collar, so he took the partial advance.

And didn't work on the book.

Meanwhile, paying the loan sharks in piecemeal chunks meant Puzo still required ongoing cash. He needed a flow, not a fund. So he wrote three adventure stories a month for the same magazine. He wrote a children's book that got rave reviews in the *New Yorker*. He wrote stories for the *New York Times* Sunday magazine. They didn't pay much, but gave him a thin lifeline he could stretch like an elastic band until the next gig appeared. Still, chipping away at the debt only resulted in more debt, as those gambling chips just seemed to form another mountain. Over the next three years, Puzo wrote more than he had written in his entire life, all to keep the wolves and sharks from the door. Then there was that thing hanging over his head.

That novel he'd promised to write.

He set a self-imposed deadline of July 1968. Puzo had promised to take his wife and family to Europe that year, because his wife hadn't seen her family there in over twenty years. Puzo had no money, just nearly maxed-out credit cards. He needed the final $1,200 of the advance. So he raced to the end of the manuscript. As Puzo later admitted, he wrote *The Godfather* completely from research. He knew no real gangsters personally, other than the aforementioned loan sharks, who were freelance lowlifes. They didn't control anything but small loans with big interest. Puzo knew the gambling world, but from the outside, not the inside. He did the best he could with *The Godfather* and handed a very rough manuscript to his new publisher just before he was scheduled to leave for Europe. He told Putnam not to show it to anybody yet. It needed a big polish.

The Puzos had a good time in Europe. American Express offices in London, Cannes, Nice and Wiesbaden happily cashed five-hundred-dollar cheques against his credit cards. He gambled in the poshest casinos on the French Riviera—and lost. When he got back home, there was a stack of credit card bills from American Express waiting for him. He owed the credit card company an additional $60,000. He didn't tell his wife, but he feared his only option was to sell their house.

He arranged a lunch with his agent, hoping she had another magazine assignment waiting for him. Instead, she told him that his publisher, Bill Targ, had just turned down $375,000 for the paper-back rights to *The Godfather* (that's $2.8 million in today's dollars). Puzo just stared at her. Then he dove for the phone, called Targ and asked him what the hell was going on. He casually told Puzo they were holding out for $410,000 because $400,000 was the previous record and they wanted to break it. Targ asked him if he needed to talk to the guy negotiating the paperback rights. Puzo said no, he had complete faith in anyone who could confidently turn down $375,000. A few hours later, word came that Fawcett had purchased the paperback rights for $410,000 ($3.1 million), setting a new rec-ord—and the hardcover hadn't even been released yet.

Puzo was reeling. He made his way to the magazine office to quit his job and hoisted a few drinks to celebrate with his fellow magazine friends. He had given his brother 10 percent of *The Godfather* because he had supported Puzo for most of his life. Puzo's share of the paperback rights was 50 percent or $205,000 ($1.5 million), shared with his publisher. That meant his brother's share was about $20,000 ($150,000). He called his brother. The one who always answered the phone when Puzo made panic calls for money. He wasn't home. When Puzo finally got home that night, he found his wife dozing in front of the TV. He kissed her on the cheek and said they didn't have to worry about money anymore because he had just sold his paperback rights for $410,000. She just smiled and slipped back to sleep. So Puzo went to bed and in the morning his wife asked what he had been trying to tell her the night before. He told her. Their life was about to change.

Puzo got his publisher to cut him a cheque for $100,000 ($748,400) and paid off all his debts. He paid his agents, financial companies, banks, his brother and presumably the people who had instigated this entire write-a-quick-commercial-book-for-money business—the loan sharks. Three months later, he called his publisher for more money. They were stunned. Puzo just shrugged his shoulders, saying, "A hundred grand doesn't last forever." Although he still spent like there was no tomorrow, for maybe the first time, Mario Puzo was out of hock.

It was a strange and unnatural feeling.

Now there was talk of a motion picture.

That's when Puzo's second big mistake was revealed.

Earlier, when he had about 114 pages of *The Godfather* written, the William Morris Agency had shopped it around Hollywood. Paramount was mildly interested. The studio, which was owned by conglomerate Gulf & Western, desperately needed a hit. At the time, Paramount ranked a dismal ninth among film studios. As a vanity investment, it wasn't contributing much to the G&W coffers and would probably be worth more sliced and diced and the real estate sold off. In 1970, Gulf & Western made five times more money selling cigars than movies. On the strength of those 114 pages and an outline of where the story was headed, Paramount offered a paltry

$12,500 option payment ($93,500) to Puzo, against $80,000 ($643,100) *if* the film eventually went into production. William Morris advised Puzo against taking the offer. The agents strongly recommended he wait to see how the book did when it was published because the prelaunch buzz was good. If it was a big hit, they could negotiate a much more lucrative deal. But Puzo was in urgent need of cash, as he always was. Legendary Paramount movie chief Robert Evans said the author came to see him in March 1968, desperate for Evans to purchase a film option on the as-yet-unpublished book. Evans asked him if he was in trouble. "I owe eleven Gs bad. They've been waiting too long for it," Evans recalls Puzo saying. "If I don't come up with it, I'll have a broken arm." Evans was a fellow gambler so he understood their mutual addiction. He considered the money a chit. One gambler helping another gambler "out of a heavy muscle jam." While Evans wasn't that enamoured with the book idea, his development executive, Peter Bart, wanted to make a deal. They offered $12,500. Puzo later said $12,500 looked like Fort Knox to him because he was in such dire straits.

William Morris again said, do not take the offer. They told him to wait.

He took the offer.

Paramount had, for all intents and purposes, just purchased the property for $80,000. To put that in some perspective, Jacqueline Susann's *The Love Machine* had just been optioned for $1 million, and the film rights to Philip Roth's *Portnoy's Complaint* went for $400,000. *Variety* magazine called the amount Paramount paid for *The Godfather* "a bargain basement literary buy."

Paramount then brought Puzo to the west coast, put him up in a hotel and gave him an office to finish banging out the book. Puzo had his usual ongoing money issues, so the studio had to keep feeding him small advances to keep him calm and focused, $5,000 here, $7,500 there.

The first prelaunch ads for the book began to appear in March 1969, proclaiming, "To Know Him Is to Love Him. To 'No' Him Is to Die." The ads showcased a long list of rave reviews and featured the memorable book cover design with the title lettering dangling from puppet strings. The *New York Times* review said, "Mr. Puzo's novel is a voyeur's dream, a skillful fantasy of violent personal power without consequences." The *Saturday Review of Literature* called it a "big, blunt battering ram of a novel . . . a staggering triumph."

When *The Godfather* finally hit the shelves on March 10, 1969, it shot past *The Love Machine* to the number-one spot and stayed on the *New York Times* bestseller list for sixty-seven weeks. It very quickly earned Puzo $1 million ($7.4 million). The book was translated into twenty languages and went to number one in England, France, Germany and other countries. According to Fawcett, it was the fastest-selling paperback up until that time, moving 5 million copies in 1970 and 7 million more by January 1971. It was the single most profitable book published by Putnam's and the single most profitable paperback ever put out by Fawcett. It has sold somewhere north of 25 million copies and is still in print.

He still should have waited.

But that's how Paramount got *The Godfather* so cheap. Puzo later said he didn't fault Paramount for getting the film for next to nothing. The studio had offered him an option and Puzo hungrily took it. Producer Albert Ruddy then surprised Puzo by hiring him to write the screenplay. Puzo was only in this for the book money, and now Ruddy was offering him $100,000 (plus expenses and 2.5 percent of the profits) to write the movie. That was more than Paramount had originally paid for the rights to the entire project. Puzo had never written a screenplay before. But it was cash money.

The Godfather opened on March 19, 1972, in 316 theatres. It quickly turned into a money-making machine. By mid-April, the film was grossing more than $1 million a day—a first in the history of motion pictures. Paramount recouped all its expenses within two weeks of the film's release and it was straight profit after that. The stock price of Gulf & Western jumped from $38 per share to $44. By the late summer, *The Godfather* was dominating popular culture. The *Los Angeles Times* joked that lineups to see *The Godfather* "could conceivably cross three zip codes." Apparently, even mobsters were lining up to see the film. Interestingly, the word "mafia" is never once mentioned in the book or the movie.

The picture was a sensation around the world, including Italy. By the end of 1972, only two other films had amassed similar earnings: *Gone with the Wind* (1939) and *The Sound of Music* (1965). Even the word "godfather" took on a different meaning from that point on. Puzo was surprised the Vito Corleone phrase "I'll make him an offer he can't refuse" took off the way it did. Even with all the success and the instant millionaire status, Puzo still maintained it was his least favourite novel and that he wished like hell he had written a better book. He knew he had lucked out by creating a central character that is now seen as mythic, but admitted he wrote "below his gifts" on the entire project.

But without his mistake of borrowing money from a loan shark, *The Godfather* would not be on 25 million book shelves. And without his mistake of quickly accepting an insulting $12,500 option, Paramount would never have cobbled together the team— an inexperienced director, a cast of mostly unheard-of actors and a star who was seen as box-office poison—who, collectively, created the Oscar-winning Best Picture masterpiece. We certainly would have never had what many consider the best sequel of all time, *The Godfather: Part II* (another Best Picture winner). Or *The Godfather: Part III* (but still).

In the end, the book everyone was happy to refuse turned out to be one of the most famous cultural blockbusters, which nobody could refuse.

The Old Farmer's Almanac

White Day in July

B ack in 1792, a man named Robert B. Thomas decided to publish an annual reference book. He called it the *Farmer's Almanac* because he thought his publication would be particularly helpful to those on farms. His goal for the *Almanac* was to be "Useful with a pleasant degree of humour." The content would cover topics like planting charts, recipes, gardening, sports, astronomy, tide tables and, especially, weather forecasts. The first issue was published when George Washington was president, and the upstart *Almanac* was an immediate success. By the second year, circulation had jumped from three thousand to nine thousand. You could pick up a copy for just nine cents.

Over the years, the *Almanac*'s ability to predict the weather was uncannily accurate. Thomas used a complex series of natural cycles to devise a secret weather forecasting formula, based on a theory that Galileo developed in the seventeenth century. The idea was that sunspots, on cycles of eleven years on average, influenced the climate and weather on earth. Predicting the weather was a matter of life and death for farmers at that time and the

Almanac seemed correct almost 80 percent of the time. Thomas oversaw the publication until 1846, and over those fifty years, he established the *Farmer's Almanac* as America's leading periodical. It outsold and outlasted all its many competitors. Thomas died at the age of eighty, apparently while reading page proofs for the 1847 edition.

When the new editor, John H. Jenks, took over, he not only added the word "Old" to the title but changed the cover to include a four-seasons drawing by artist Hammatt Billings, engraved by Henry Nichols. In 1861, a new editor took over and provided his readers with a heavy emphasis on farming. Over the next seventy years, a number of editors would take the wheel and the *Almanac*'s content began to slant less toward agriculture and more to nature and life in general. Remarkably, the *Old Farmer's Almanac* managed to survive both the First World War and the Depression.

Starting in the 1970s, it hired a NASA weather specialist to create a formula that combined solar science, climatology and meteorology. Only a few people have ever seen the *Old Farmer's Almanac* weather formula. It is kept locked in a black tin box at the head office in Dublin, New Hampshire.

But that accuracy was severely tested back in late 1815.

According to a 2016 CBC interview with the *Almanac*'s editor, Jack Burnett, a printer's helper who was putting together the 1816 issue noticed the forecast for July was missing. The helper was dispatched to Thomas's farm to retrieve the missing information. As it turned out, Thomas was extremely ill that day and told the kid to just "put something in there to hold the space." So as a joke, the kid put "snow and sleet" in the July forecast. For some reason, the temporary placeholder joke slipped everyone's mind, the issue was published and distribution began as usual. When Thomas finally noticed the weather forecast for July called for snow, he raced to destroy all the copies, but some had already been sent out. He reprinted the issue with more conventional summer forecasts, but the word was out and the "snow in July" mistake made Thomas a laughingstock among farmers.

Then something strange happened.

That year, a massive volcano erupted in the Dutch East Indies, now Indonesia. The dust from that eruption circled the globe for the next six months, lowering worldwide temperatures. Then guess what happened.

It snowed in July.

That "summer of no summer" solidified the *Farmer's Almanac* as the go-to publication for weather forecasting for all time. It is now the oldest continuously published periodical in North America and has never missed a single year of publication. The closest it came was in 1942, when the *Old Farmer's Almanac* almost stopped publication. American forces captured a German spy at Long Island, presumably dropped off by a German U-boat. The spy had a copy of the *Old Farmer's Almanac* in his pocket. At that point, the War Department wondered if it was dangerous for the *Almanac* to continue publishing, lest its pinpoint accurate weather forecasting be used against them by the enemy. But the editor of the *Almanac* managed to convince the War Department to keep the publication going by changing the title of the "Weather Forecasts" to "Weather Indications."

That small change calmed the War Department down and saved the *Almanac*.

To this day, the cover still shows the four seasons, it still retains the hole in the top left corner so readers can hang it from a string and millions still consider it the best predicter of weather, bar none.

That mistake back in 1815 just might be the best thing that ever happened to the *Old Farmer's Almanac*.

Atul Gawande

Planes, Pains and Operating Tables

There are thirteen thousand different ways the body can fail. The World Health Organization classifies thirteen thousand different diseases, syndromes and injuries that can befall any one of us. Many of those maladies require surgery to repair, remove, reattach or save a life. The average American undergoes seven surgeries in a lifetime and surgeons perform over 50 million operations annually. It's a stunning number to contemplate. Here's another stunning number: in 2009, 150,000 deaths in the United States happened immediately after surgery.

That number was three times the number of fatalities that happened due to road accidents.

Half of those post-surgical deaths or resulting major complications were completely avoidable. And *that* stunning number intrigued one surgeon named Atul Gawande. He practises general and endocrine surgery at Brigham and Women's Hospital in Boston. Gawande is also a professor at Harvard Medical School, among many other impressive achievements. He wondered if there was a way to minimize or at least dramatically reduce the number of operating room errors, and thus save hundreds of thousands of lives.

Gawande noted that, in the twenty-first century, we have accumulated stupendous know-how in almost every known profession and industry. Yet he thought it was remarkable that, for example, between the years 2004 and 2007, lawsuits against attorneys for legal mistakes increased 36 percent. We experience software flaws, foreign intelligence failures, exploding space shuttles, teetering banking systems and a pandemic that halted the world. How can these problems happen in spite of all our knowledge? And more importantly, is there some procedure that could tame mistakes and errors? So Gawande looked to other fields for clues.

Back in 1935, the U.S. Army Air Corps held a competition for airplane manufacturers to design and build the next generation of long-range bombers. While the government tender was to be fair and square for all involved, the runaway winner was, for all intents and purposes, predetermined. Boeing's technology was aeronautical miles ahead of rivals Martin and Douglas. Boeing's aluminum-alloy Model 299 could carry five times as many bombs as the army requested, could fly faster than previous bombers and could go twice as far. The army planned to order sixty-five of the aircraft.

Army brass gathered to watch the first test flight of the Model 299. It was an impressive sight, with a 103-foot wingspan and four gleaming engines instead of the usual two. The mighty plane sped down the runway, climbed to three hundred feet, stalled, then crashed in a fiery ball of flames. Two of the five crew died, including the pilot, Major Ployer P. Hill, the Air Corps' chief of flight testing.

Surprisingly, the investigation stated nothing had gone wrong with the plane mechanically. The crash was due to pilot error. But how could the chief of test flights make a mistake—or series of mistakes—that would lead to the crash of such a sophisticated aircraft? As the investigation revealed, the Model 299 required Major Hill to monitor the four engines—which each required its own oil-fuel mix—as well as attend to the retractable landing gear and the wing flaps, adjust the electric trim tabs in order to maintain stability at different airspeeds and regulate the constant-speed propellers with hydraulic controls, among other requirements. While doing all this, Major Hill forgot to release a new locking mechanism on the elevator and rudder controls. It was that simple and that complex. One newspaper article called the Model 299 "too much airplane for one man to fly." The Air Corps decided to award the contract to Douglas instead.

Boeing almost went bankrupt.

But a group of pilots at Boeing believed the plane was indeed flyable. So they got together to think the problem through. When they returned from their deliberations, they didn't request any mechanical changes. They didn't require pilots to undergo extended training. Instead, they came up with a simple and ingenious solution.

They created a pilot's checklist.

The list was made short enough to fit on an index card. It covered all the mundane step-by-step checks for takeoff, flight, landing and taxiing. As Gawande says, the checklist covered all the dumb stuff. With that checklist, pilots flew the Model 299 over 1.8 million miles without one single accident. To take the stink of failure off the plane, the name was changed to the B-17. The army ultimately ordered thirteen thousand B-17s, and that aircraft gave the Air Corps a decisive advantage over the Nazis in the Second World War.

For years, since at least the 1960s, nurses have used a vital signs checklist in hospitals. Patient charts were designed to list all the things nurses had to attend to for a patient over a typical shift: dispense medications, dress wounds and check pulse, blood pressure, respiration and pain levels, rated one to ten. Nurses depended on this checklist—even though they didn't call the charts "checklists."

Doctors saw those lists as "nurse stuff."

But tending to patients is a complex task. In the late nineties, a study was done in which engineers observed patient care in intensive care units for twenty-four-hour stretches. They deduced the average patient required 178 individual actions per day, every one of which posed risks. Remarkably, doctors and nurses made an error in only 1 percent of these actions, but that still amounted to two errors per day for every patient. Multiply that by every hospital in the United States—then the world—and there are millions of hardworking medical people who are as apt to harm as they are to heal.

In 2001, a critical care specialist at Johns Hopkins Hospital named Peter Pronovost decided to try designing a doctor's checklist. He chose to focus on one particular procedure common in the ICU—putting in a central line (a tube placed in a large vein to give medication). On a single sheet of paper, he outlined the steps to take in order to avoid infections when inserting a central line. They are (1) wash your hands with soap, (2) clean the patient's skin with chlorhexidine antiseptic, (3) put sterile drapes over the entire patient, (4) don a mask, hat, sterile gown and gloves, and (5) put a sterile dressing over the insertion site once the line is in. All of this was routine stuff. A no-brainer, as Gawande calls it. Then Pronovost asked the nurses to observe the doctors for a month and record how often they carried out each step.

In more than a third of all patients, at least one step was omitted.

Nurses were then given permission to insist doctors follow each of the steps. Doctors didn't like the new rules and nurses weren't sure their nudging was welcome, but the nurses were backed up by the hospital administration. One year later, Pronovost and his colleagues gathered to assess the experiment. The results were so dramatic, they weren't sure they should believe them. The ten-day line-infection rate went from 11 percent to zero. So they followed the checklist for fifteen more months to be sure. It was calculated that, at this single hospital, the checklist had prevented forty-three infections and eight deaths and had saved $2 million in costs.

It was hard to argue with the checklist's success, yet uptake was slow to come. Pronovost was surprised at how many experienced doctors failed to grasp the importance of certain precautions. Many doctors were offended at the very suggestion of checklists. Some hospitals without the staff and resources of Johns Hopkins were skeptical of how well the checklist would work in their very different environments. And time-stressed doctors really didn't need one more sheet of paper in their lives. So Pronovost was invited to test his checklist idea more broadly, at hospitals in Michigan. One of those hospitals experienced 75 percent more central line infections than any other hospital in the nation. Implementing the new procedure was a huge undertaking and Pronovost would have to ascertain whether the checklists produced any real change. There was pushback and reluctance at first. But slowly the hospital staff and the executives found a way to implement Pronovost's idea.

In just three months, the rate of bloodstream infections from IV lines in Michigan hospitals dropped 66 percent. Most hospitals, including the one with the highest infection rate, cut their quarterly infection rate to zero. As a matter of fact, Michigan's infection rates fell so low that its average ICU outperformed 90 percent of ICUs nationwide. Over eighteen months, it was estimated the hospitals saved more than fifteen hundred lives and nearly $200 million in costs.

All due to a little checklist.

But that little checklist performed an essential function. It was a "mental net" to catch stupid mistakes. In other words, it was a way to focus on the elevator and rudder controls, freeing medical staff to deal with the complicated, unpredictable elements of their jobs. As Gawande says in his superb book *The Checklist Manifesto*, the checklists were compiled from collective experience.

Man is fallible, but men are not.

That is one of the benefits of being part of the WHO, or World Health Organization. Members gain access to the health system reports and data from the organization's 194 member countries. By 2004, surgeons around the world were performing over 230 million major operations annually—one for every twenty-five human beings on the planet. Yet even with that level of assembled knowledge, over 7 million people a year were left disabled and at least 1 million died as a result of surgery. This mortality rate was virtually equivalent to that of malaria, tuberculosis and other major health concerns. Atul Gawande wondered if a checklist could be created for surgeons around the world.

Could the collective worldwide mistakes be felled by a simple checklist?

A director of surgical administration at a hospital in Columbus, Ohio, decided to create a checklist for the operating room in 2005. Many of the appendicitis patients were suffering from high rates of infections. Antibiotics had to be administered exactly one hour before surgery to prevent that. Give the antibiotic too soon and it would wear off before surgery; give it too late and it would not activate in time. The timing was complicated by delays in the operating waiting area. The director wasn't just a pediatric cardiac surgeon; he was also a pilot. So he designed a pre-incision "Cleared for Takeoff" checklist. He put it on a whiteboard in the operating rooms. The steps were the epitome of simple. There was a checkbox for a nurse to verbally confirm they had the correct patient on the table. There was a checkbox to confirm they had the correct side of the patient prepped for surgery. There was another checkbox to confirm that the antibiotics were timed correctly.

That was it.

But getting people to adhere to the simple checklist was difficult. So the surgical director added one more interesting element: He designed a little six-inch metal tent stencilled with the phrase "Cleared for Takeoff" and had nurses set it over the scalpel when preparing the instruments before an operation. It not only served as a reminder to observe the checklist, but the surgeon could not pick up the scalpel until the nurse confirmed the boxes were checked and removed the tent.

After three months, the surgical director measured the effect of the checklist. Eighty-nine percent of appendicitis patients got the antibiotic at the right time. After ten months, 100 percent did. An astounding result.

Meanwhile, the chair of surgery at the University of Toronto started a feasibility study by implementing a twenty-one-step surgical checklist. That list covered the usual pre-surgery elements, including verbally confirming with one another that antibiotics had been given, that blood was available if required, that critical scans and test results were on hand, that any special equipment was ready, etc. But the checklist also included something called a "team briefing." The team was to stop before proceeding and discuss how long the procedure was expected to take, how much blood loss everyone should be prepared for and whether the patient had any risks or concerns. As it turned out, a group of Southern California hospitals had begun using a thirty-item checklist, too.

The interesting aspect of a checklist was that it spread the responsibility around the operating room. That was a significant departure from standard procedure. As Gawande puts it, surgery had been traditionally regarded as an individual performance. Gawande points out that there is a reason most of the world uses the phrase "operating theatre." It was the surgeon's stage.

Like a virtuoso pianist.

And ego was a major part of that recital.

The checklists transformed surgery into teamwork. But that didn't sit well with top surgeons. Over 64 percent of surgeons rated their operations as already having high rates of teamwork. Just 39 percent of anesthesiologists, 28 percent of nurses and 10 percent of anesthesia residents agreed. Plus, one in four surgeons did not believe junior team members should have a voice in the operating room. But the checklist insisted the operating team talk to one another before starting. It was a smart strategy, because it fostered the feeling of teamwork. One of the first checklist stipulations asked everyone to introduce themselves. Like "Hi, I'm Atul Gawande, the attending surgeon." And "I'm Betty McDonald, the circulating nurse." And so on. Surgeons rolled their collective eyes, but a magical thing happened. Teams worked better together when they knew each other's names. This might seem blindingly obvious, but when studies were done asking surgical team members coming out of the operating room if they knew the names of the other team members, half the time they did not. Hospitals are big facilities with large staffs and rotating shifts. Not everyone knows everyone. But when people did know each other's names, communication ratings jumped significantly.

So Gawande and his team started to tweak and refine a surgical checklist for a pilot study. For example, before starting an operation, someone has to get everyone's attention to start checking the boxes. Usually, that task fell to the surgeon in the room. But members of the surgical team protested and pointed out that in airplanes, the "pilot not flying" is in charge of starting the checklist. The actual pilot can be distracted by flight tasks and might skip a step. So Gawande's team determined the circulating nurse should call the room to order. Next, his team decided on a DO-CONFIRM rather than a READ-DO format. That way everyone in the room could hear the checklist read out loud. The list also had to be just the right length. Too short and important steps could be missed. Add too much and the list would become too long and risk becoming too tedious. Other hospitals were consulted. Knowledge was collected. Points were strenuously debated. It was a difficult tug-of-war between detail and brevity.

Then in 2008, pilot hospitals in eight cities around the world began implementing team Gawande's two-minute, nineteen-step surgery checklist. It was embraced in some operating rooms and protested in others. "This checklist is a waste of time!" Gawande was often told. Gawande and his team sat back for three months and waited for the results. He was uneasy. There were many variables among the eight hospitals in various countries. But slowly they began to hear some encouraging things. In London, during a knee replacement by an orthopedic surgeon who was one of the checklist's most vocal critics, it was discovered while checking the boxes—and before the point of no return—that the knee prosthesis on hand was the wrong size. The surgeon became an instant checklist evangelist. In India, teams realized that delays in the operating waiting rooms resulted in the antibiotics wearing off too soon and were able to change their procedures to remedy the problem. In Seattle, a surgical team found that the checklist helped them respond better when they ran into unexpected trouble during a procedure, like bleeding or technical difficulties. They simply began working better as a team.

Finally, the results were tabulated. The rate of major complications for surgical patients in all eight hospitals fell by 36 percent. Deaths fell by 47 percent. Infections fell by almost 50 percent. The number of patients who had to return to the operating room fell by 25 percent. These results far surpassed the Gawande team's most optimistic expectations. They double-checked. They scrutinized the results at the poorer hospitals, expecting aberrations. But none existed.

The trial was a consistent success.

The fascinating thing about checklists is that they dramatically improved the outcomes without any increase in skill or expenditure. Although some expected checklists to lead to rigidity, the opposite was true. Checklists freed people by getting the dumb stuff out of the way. In a step-by-step list for pilots suffering engine failure in a single-engine Cessna, the checklist offers six key steps for restarting the engine. But the first step is the most interesting. It is FLY THE PLANE. Pilots can become so overwhelmed by dealing with the mechanical problem that they forget to fly the plane. When the checklist reminds them to keep flying, it frees them to deal with the problem while giving them a real shot at getting home safely. The same principle was true in operating rooms. Today, a full 90 percent of hospitals in North America use a checklist and over 70 percent do worldwide. An astoundingly positive outcome was born of wanting to reduce mistakes—not just in one city, but worldwide.

Back when the original eight pilot hospitals were asked to fill in an anonymous survey after three months of using the checklist, 78 percent said the checklist had prevented errors. But there were still 20 percent who didn't like the checklist, found it took too long to implement and didn't think it eliminated mistakes.

So Atul Gawande asked them one more question. "If you were having an operation, would you want the checklist to be used?"

A full 93 percent said yes.

Embrace the Obstacle

When I look back on all these stories, it's fascinating to spot the connective tissue linking so many disparate circumstances. In almost every situation, someone made a mistake that seemed small at the time. In some instances, the mistake wasn't even noticed by the person whose life it was about to reshape. But when the ripples of the mistake eventually turned into a tsunami of consequences, they all realized the same thing.

They were stuck with it.

Brian Williams couldn't pretend he hadn't told that story for years. Ellen DeGeneres couldn't put the genie back in the bottle. Bill Maher couldn't alter his politically incorrect DNA. Mario Puzo couldn't seem to get out of the rut of always needing quick money—then needing quick money to pay off the quick money. Yet in each of the cases, from Kathleen King to Steve Madden to the Dixie Chicks, a mistake fuelled extraordinary growth and creativity.

If I've learned anything in my career, it's to embrace the obstacle. The answer to life's most vexing moments is always sitting at the heart of the mistake, waiting patiently to be discovered. When you peel the problem like a banana, an opportunity slowly comes into focus. That opportunity may feel, in the moment, like a desperate gamble or a Hail Mary pass, but it's often much more meaningful than that. Billy Joel ended up writing his opus. Steve Jobs had to spend his forty days in the desert before he could build one of the world's great companies. Steven Spielberg sat in his hotel room with no working script and a giant malfunctioning fish, then filleted that problem down to its core and discovered he could actually make one of the best movies of all time—because of the mistake.

Rob Lowe risked being turned into a piñata on *Saturday Night Live*, only to find comedic career redemption. Swanson embraced its turkey catastrophe and ended up in the National Museum of American History. Bombardier ran with the typo "Ski-Doo" and created an unforgettable brand name.

Some turned a mistake into an opportunity right on the spot. Pete Townshend changed his band's destiny from "who?" to the Who when he seized the moment. Sam Phillips heard a new sound in a broken amp and invented a little thing called rock 'n' roll. Other mistakes had to be thrown in people's paths. Seth MacFarlane was so hungover he made a mistake that ensured his future. And Atul Gawande ended up saving lives when he accepted the inevitable truth of humanity: people will always make mistakes.

That is the nugget here. When an epic mistake feels like it might be career-ending or debilitating or humiliating, when you feel like you may have lost your credibility, your livelihood or even your sanity, it might be destiny preparing you for what you've asked for all along.

Just remember to ask one question: What is the hidden gift?

I would be mistaken if I didn't add these tidbits to this book:

When Serge Savard finally hung up his skates, the Montreal Canadiens made another mistake by forgetting to file his retirement papers. Consequently, he was a free agent without knowing it and was scooped up by John Ferguson of the Winnipeg Jets. That means the Canadiens made huge errors on both ends of Savard's career.

Jean-Guy Talbot calls Scotty Bowman on his birthday every year. They are both in their late eighties and have never discussed the incident.

When Billy Joel was asked by Stephen Colbert to name his top five Billy Joel songs, "Piano Man" wasn't even on his list.

Owens Corning's Dale Kleist was inducted into the National Inventors Hall of Fame in 2006.

Bill Duffy finally finished paying Anthony Carter the $3 million in 2020. Carter says he has never brought up the filing error with Duffy, not even to joke about it.

Bill Maher wanted his HBO show to be named *The Truth Hurts* but HBO vetoed the title. Guess it hurt too much. He does not like the name *Real Time*.

The Hulk reverted back to the original grey colour many years later in issue 324 (1986).

Spielberg actually laughed out loud when John Williams first played him the now famous two-note *Jaws* motif. He didn't think Williams was serious.

John Williams was conducting the orchestra at the Academy Awards the night his *Jaws* score won the Oscar. He had to leap out of the orchestra pit to accept the award and then jump back down into it.

Pete Townshend smashed his first instrument at age thirteen. He was playing a new guitar in his room when his grandmother came in and told him to knock off the racket. In a rage, young Pete smashed his guitar against his amp.

The Chicks, political personae non gratae, did an Obama fundraiser and performed the national anthem during the final night of the 2020 Democratic National Convention.

"Rocket '88'" was the first song mourners heard when they attended Sam Phillips's public memorial service.

The COVID-19 pandemic contained a silver lining for snowmobile sales because it created "stranded snowbirds." Eight billion dollars in cruise ship spending had to go somewhere.

Acknowledgements

Brad Wilson—My editor on this book, who suggested the topic to me. Soft-spoken, wise and possesses that rare trait—he listens intently. The sign of a great editor. Thanks, Brad.

Allison Pinches—My remarkable researcher on this book as well as our CBC radio show and our Apostrophe Podcast Company. Resourceful and dedicated, she not only delivered all the research as requested, but dug deep into the granite of this idea to find other perfect stories for this book. She is the best.

Dave Dryden—NHL goaltender who created the first goalie mask with a cage. Dave is the chair of Sleeping Children Around the World, a charity that provides sleeping kits and mosquito nets to 1.4 million children around the world. Dave connected me to his younger brother, Ken.

Ken Dryden—Hall of Fame goaltender. Named one of the hundred greatest players in NHL history. Five Vezina Trophies and six Stanley Cup rings. Ken was incredibly gracious and generous, connecting me to both Scotty Bowman and Serge Savard. I drew heavily from Ken's amazing book *Scotty*, where I first noticed the mistake Scotty and Cliff made with Serge Savard.

Scotty Bowman—Hall of Fame NHL coach and executive. Fourteen Stanley Cup rings, nine as head coach, five as front office executive. Winningest coach in NHL history. Winningest in his absolute willingness to explain to me how the Serge Savard mistake was made and what its domino effects were.

Serge Savard—Hall of Famer. Eight Stanley Cups. Montreal Canadiens player extraordinaire and former general manager of the Canadiens. Named one of the hundred greatest players in NHL history. Serge told me the mistake story from his side of the rink. As a Toronto Maple Leafs fan, I used to boo Savard every game, because he was so damn good.

Bryan Black—I first met Bryan when he was the marketing director of his family's business, Black's Photography. He hired me to write commercials featuring Martin Short. When Black's was later sold, we lost contact for a few years. One day, his name popped into my mind and I wondered how he was doing. Three days later, I passed the Hockey Hall of Fame and thought to myself, that would be a fun place to advertise. The next day, I received a call from Bryan Black out of the blue. He told me he was the new director of marketing for the Hockey Hall of Fame and he wanted me to write some commercials for them. The universe works in wonderful ways. For this book, Bryan connected me to Kristy Fletcher.

Kristy Fletcher—Kristy was kind enough to connect me with her father, Cliff Fletcher.

ACKNOWLEDGEMENTS

Cliff Fletcher—NHL Hall of Famer. Executive and general manager of several teams, including the Stanley Cup–winning Calgary Flames. Cliff took me through the beats of the Serge Savard mistake, with a crystal-clear memory of something that happened over fifty-five years ago.

Marc Lacroix—Brand Director, Ski-Doo and Sea-Doo at BRP Inc. Marc has an in-depth knowledge of the company's history and provided me with all the background information I needed.

Bev Slopen—My literary agent for the past thirteen years. Thanks for everything, Bev.

Debbie O'Reilly—My wonderful wife and business partner. With me every step of the way on everything. Confidante, wise counsel and fierce protector. It's always better when we're together.

Shea, Callie Rae and Sidney O'Reilly—Our extraordinary daughters, who amaze us every single day. Smart, funny and with good hearts. Love you to pieces.

Sources

Chapter 1: *Jaws*

5: *"When Spielberg put himself up"*
John Squires, "Steven Spielberg Reflects on 'Duel' Nearly 50 Years Later," *Bloody Disgusting*, March 29, 2018, https://bloody-disgusting .com/movie/3491073/steven-spielberg-reflects-duel-nearly-50-years -later-qualified-direct-jaws. It's remarkable how similar the story lines are between *Duel* and *Jaws*.

6: *"Alves began with sketches"*
"Jaws Movie," *JawsRide*, https://www.jawsride.net/jaws-movie.html. A remarkable feat, really. Spielberg wanted authenticity, which made the task formidable.

6: *"Each one had a steel skeleton"*
"Remembering Bruce, the Malfunctioning Animatronic Shark That Made 'Jaws' a Horror Classic," *Bold Entrance*, July 15, 2020, https:// boldentrance.com/remembering-bruce-the-malfunctioning-animatronic -shark-that-made-jaws-a-horror-classic. Little did we know there were a number of sharks in the movie.

8: *"Spielberg, faced with a seemingly unsurmountable problem"*
Bill Demain, "How Malfunctioning Sharks Transformed the Movie Business," *Mental Floss*, June 20, 2015, https://www.mentalfloss.com /article/31105/how-steven-spielbergs-malfunctioning-sharks-transformed -movie-business. This was the moment that saved the movie and made Spielberg's career.

8: *"with hints of Stravinsky's* The Rite of Spring"
Until Emmy Award–winning composer Trevor Morris explained this to me, I'd never realized this, but it's fascinating.

9: *"According to the sound technician on the film"*
"Remembering Bruce." Chilling to think that horror was real in the moment.

9: *"it only had four minutes of actual screen time"*
Steve Tilley, "'Jaws' Turns 50: Five Reasons It Wouldn't Work Today," *Toronto Sun*, May 31, 2015, https://torontosun.com/2015/05/31/jaws-turns -40-five-reasons-it-wouldnt-work-today; Zack Walkter, "40 Jaw-Dropping Facts You Probably Never Knew about 'Jaws,'" *Do You Remember?,* https: //doyouremember.com/62828/40-things-probably-never-knew-jaws. Astounding to think your mind tells you differently.

10: *"It delivered a domestic gross"*
"Jaws (1975)," IMDb, https://www.imdb.com/title/tt0073195. Historic numbers for its time.

Chapter 2: Scotty Bowman
11: *"With just thirty seconds left"*
Ken Dryden, *Scotty: A Hockey Life Like No Other* (McClelland & Stewart, 2019). I am indebted to Ken Dryden and his fabulous book for so much of the background to this story.

12: *"Most of the flats"*
Ibid. Suffocating living quarters pushed kids outside to discover their destinies.

13: *"One of those scouts spotted Scotty"*
Ibid. Hockey pants, gloves and a standing-room Forum pass. Heaven.

14: *"Meanwhile, Scotty landed a job"*
Ibid. Latex couldn't prime over Scotty's love for hockey.

16: *"Religion, politics and sports"*
Philippe Cantin, *Serge Savard: Forever Canadien* (KO Editions, 2020). That shrine was duplicated in kitchens all over Quebec.

Chapter 3: Ski-Doo®

22: *"At the age of thirteen"*
"Joseph-Armand Bombardier," Musée de l'ingéniosité J. Armand Bombardier, https://museebombardier.com/en/joseph-armand-bombardier. Yet again, the spark shows up early.

23: *"At the age of seventeen"*
Ibid. A crossroads for young Bombardier: the priesthood or car mechanic. He chose well.

25: *"His two-year-old son"*
Joe Skorupa, "Ski-Doo: 50 Years on Snow," *Popular Mechanics*, January 1992. A heartbreaking story and the instigating moment for Bombardier's future success.

25: *"An unfinished snowmobile sat in his garage"*
Nicholas Van Praet, "From a Wood Garage to the Canadian Backcountry," *Globe and Mail*, April 4, 2017, https://www.theglobeandmail.com/news national/canada-150/great-canadian-innovations-how-the-snowmobile -opened-much-of-canadasnorth/article34590806. An almost unbearable image in the context of his son's death.

26: *"One of his most powerful marketing ideas"*
"Joseph-Armand Bombardier." You can't beat smart marketing.

27: *"By 1947, Bombardier's revenues"*
Ibid. What a difference five years makes.

27: *"The company's increasing demand"*
Ibid. As Henry Ford did with cars, Bombardier created divisions to supply materials for his production line.

28: *"A prototype for a sporty"*
Ibid. That trip was a test market of sorts.

28: *"The machines came with one seat"*
Ibid. The mistake is made.

29: *"Instead of the word 'Ski-Dog,' it was misspelled"*
Ibid. "Ski-Dog" was also a good name, but it probably wouldn't have stuck like "Ski-Doo." What a difference a letter makes.

29: *"In that first year, 225 Ski-Doo snowmobiles were sold"*
Jerry Bassett, "Rants and Raves, Ten Sleds That Shaped the Sport," *Off-road.com*, July 1, 2007, http://www.off-road.com/snowmobile/voice /rants-and-raves-ten-sleds-that-shaped-the-sport-16531.html. The sign of a great idea is when sales don't just go up—they soar.

29: *"Today, some 600,000 snowmobiles"*
Van Praet, "From a Wood Garage." One snowmobile for every sixty Canadians is quite the legacy.

Chapter 4: Brian Williams
32: *"Reynolds said Williams had talked to him"*
Travis J. Tritten, "NBC's Brian Williams Recants Iraq Story after Soldiers Protest," *Stars and Stripes*, February 4, 2015, https://www.stripes .com/news/us/nbc-s-brian-williams-recants-iraq-story-after-soldiers -protest-1.327792. *Stars and Stripes* is an independent newspaper for the U.S. military. As you can imagine, it was particularly interested in the Brian Williams story.

36: *"Brokaw had recruited Williams from WCBS-TV"*
Scott Higham and Amy Brittain, "Storytelling Ability Connected Brian Williams with Viewers but Also Led to His Downfall," *Washington Post*, February 14, 2015, https://www.washingtonpost.com/lifestyle/style /storytelling-ability-connected-williams-with-his-viewers-but-also-led -to-his-downfall/2015/02/14/def95228-b3a4-11e4-854b-a38d13486ba1 _story.html. This *WaPo* article is interesting because it suggests that Williams's storytelling ability was both what attracted Tom Brokaw to recruit him and what led him astray.

37: *"Cronkite considered himself"*
"NBC News Anchor Brian Williams Next Cronkite Award Recipient," Walter Cronkite School of Journalism and Mass Communication, Arizona State University, April 5, 2009, https://cronkite.asu.edu/news -and-events/news/nbc-news-anchor-brian-williams-next-cronkite-award -recipient. Walter Cronkite was known as the "most trusted man in

America," and Lyndon Johnson once famously said that if the White House lost Cronkite's trust, then they had lost America. Credibility is the overriding prerequisite of a national anchorperson.

38: *"According to* New York *magazine"*
Gabriel Sherman, "(Actually) True War Stories at NBC News," *New York*, March 9, 2015, http://nymag.com/intelligencer/2015/03/nbc-news -brian-williams-deborah-turness.html. This article is illuminating because it reveals Williams's desire to host a talk show.

39: *"The CEO summoned Williams"*
Emily Steel and Ravi Somaiya, "Brian Williams Suspended from NBC for 6 Months without Pay," *New York Times*, February 10, 2015, https://www.nytimes.com/2015/02/11/business/media/brian-williams -suspended-by-nbc-news-for-six-months.html. When you're a national network suspending your top talent, the news is delivered by the CEO. Person to person.

39: *"Deborah Turness then issued a memo"*
"Email to NBC News Staff about Brian Williams Suspension," *New York Times,* February 10, 2015, https://www.nytimes.com/2015/02/11 /business/media/email-to-nbc-news-staff-about-brian-williams -suspension.html. Always interesting to see how a high-level reprimand is handled internally by a large company. This statement already hinted at Williams's return.

40: *"Williams was ranked the 23rd-most-trusted person"*
Emily Steel and Ravi Somaiya, "Brian Williams Loses Lofty Spot on a Trustworthiness Scale," *New York Times*, February 9, 2015, https://www .nytimes.com/2015/02/10/business/media/under-fire-brian-williams -loses-lofty-spot-on-a-trustworthiness-scale.html. A breathtaking plunge.

40: *"The cost of a single thirty-second commercial"*
Ibid. It's easy to forget that anchorpeople generate enormous profit for networks. They are not just news readers; they are revenue generators.

40: *"According to an anonymous insider"*
Bryan Burrough, "The Inside Story of the Civil War for the Soul of NBC News," *Vanity Fair*, April 7, 2015, https://www.vanityfair.com/

news/2015/04/nbc-news-brian-williams-scandal-comcast. This was also a revealing and ironic point, that Williams didn't like remote news assignments.

41: *"Pilot Don Helus was in the chopper"*
"Exclusive: Pilots from Brian Williams Story Speak Out," CNN, February 8, 2015, http://cnnpressroom.blogs.cnn.com/2015/02/08/exclusive -pilots-from-brian-williams-story-speak-out. The fact that MSNBC had been notified earlier, and chose to ignore Williams's errors, would rob the network of its ability to get out ahead of the problem.

42: *"Although it was the home team interviewing"*
"Brian Williams Talks to Matt Lauer in First Interview since Suspension," *Today,* June 19, 2015, https://www.today.com/video/brian-williams-talks -to-matt-lauer-in-first-interview-since-suspension-468065347576. This interview is hard to watch for two reasons: Brian Williams is clearly in agony, and Matt Lauer would take an even bigger turn in the barrel one day.

45: *"As* Vanity Fair *writer Emily Jane Fox"*
Emily Jane Fox, "Brian Williams Opens Up about His Unexpected Re-invention: 'Second Acts Are Possible, with a Little Spiffing Up,'" *Vanity Fair*, October 24, 2017, https://www.vanityfair.com/news/2017/10 /brian-williams-11th-hour. This shift in the news cycle would ultimately give Brian Williams his second chance.

46: *"That gave MSNBC its best ratings"*
Mark Joyella, "Brian Williams: MSNBC's Quiet, Confident Success Story," *Forbes*, December 28, 2017, https://www.forbes.com/sites /markjoyella/2017/12/28/brian-williams-msnbcs-quiet-confident -success-story/#42007e546c62. Not only did the ratings for Williams's new show prove it to be a winner, they also proved that Williams could regain his credibility.

48: *"How Brian Williams Made 11 p.m. the Hottest Hour in Cable News"*
Mark Joyella, *Forbes*, December 28, 2019, https://www.forbes.com/sites /markjoyella/2019/12/24/how-brian-williams-made-11-pm-the-hottest -hour-in-cable-news. Williams gets his dream—he is hosting a hot talk show.

Chapter 5: Billy Joel

49: *"Joel said he and his friends all went 'nuts.'"*
Ray Waddell, "Q&A: Turning 60, Billy Joel Is 'Happy and Contented,'"
Reuters, May 8, 2009, https://www.reuters.com/article/us-billyjoel
-idUSTRE5475S120090508. As with so many musicians, Billy's vision of
the future was changed when he watched the Beatles that night.

50: *"Abraham was a horticulturist"*
Crystal Galyean, "Levittown: The Imperfect Rise of the American
Suburbs," *U.S. History Scene*, https://ushistoryscene.com/article/levittown.
Levittown was a pioneering idea. But it could be argued that this cookie-
cutter existence led to generations of angst.

51: *"As Billy later said, although his father did send a cheque"*
Timothy White, "Billy Joel Is Angry," *Rolling Stone*, September 4, 1980,
https://www.rollingstone.com/music/music-news/billy-joel-is-angry
-236693. There is an anger that drives much of Joel's music, and the
source might be traced here.

51: *"Hey Billy, where's your tutu?"*
Chrissy Iley, "'I Stopped Writing Songs. It Took Its Toll. My Personal
Life Went to Hell': Billy Joel Talks about His Three Divorces and the
Woman Who Saved Him," *Mail Online*, June 25, 2016, https://www
.dailymail.co.uk/home/event/article-3656403/Billy-Joel-stopped
-writing-songs-took-toll-personal-life-went-hell-Billy-Joel-talks-three
-divorces.html. Again, there is a simmering anger in Joel's personality,
which led him to boxing.

51: *"There was never any question after that night"*
Waddell, "Q&A." That night, his future was locked in.

52: *"He became a rock critic"*
Larry Getlen, "How Billy Joel Became 'The Piano Man,'" *New York
Post*, January 29, 2014, https://nypost.com/2014/01/26/how-billy-joel
-became-the-piano-man. Joel's many interim jobs were temporary
because music was still pulling at his heart.

53: *"Mazur had a brother"*
Hank Bordowitz, *Billy Joel: The Life and Times of an Angry Young Man,*

rev. ed. (Backbeat Books, 2011). Every little connection counts when trying to reach that first rung on the ladder.

53: *"selling a hundred records over the table and a thousand under the table"*
Ibid. Artie Ripp was old school and his relationship with Joel would become contentious, but Ripp was a believer.

54: *"Somewhere on Long Island"*
Ibid. Ripp's secret sauce was bravado.

57: *"It was easier to be broke in L.A. than in New York"*
Ibid. Living is easier in the summertime.

Chapter 6: Steve Madden
62: *"The drive to succeed was instilled early"*
"Steve Madden," *How I Built This with Guy Raz,* NPR podcast, July 16, 2018, https://www.npr.org/2018/07/13/628961210/steve-madden-steve-madden. Show me the boy and I will show you the man.

63: *"His chunky-heeled boots and platform shoes"*
Laura M. Holson, "Steve Madden Is Back," *New York Times*, February 13, 2013, https://www.nytimes.com/2013/02/14/fashion/steve-madden-is-back.html. Madden's unique product was the right shoe at the right time.

65: *"Here's how the SEC enforcement attorney"*
Ronald L. Rubin, "How the 'Wolf of Wall Street' Really Did It," *Wall Street Journal*, January 3, 2014, https://www.wsj.com/articles/SB10001424-05270230345300457929045070792030 2. This description is complicated but digestible. The movie version stepped outside the narrative to take viewers through the beats—crucial to understanding the twists of this scheme.

69: *"But he considers this time a pivotal moment"*
Ella Chochrek, "Steve Madden Says Getting Out of Prison Took His Career 'to Another Level,'" *Footwear News*, December 3, 2019, https://footwearnews.com/2019/business/awards/fnaa-2019-steve-madden-interview-prison-career-1202883083. A remarkable admission: that his prison stay fuelled his subsequent success.

70: *"When the company faced a problem"*
Holson, "Steve Madden Is Back." Nothing like prison time to recalibrate your life view.

70: *"He employed the inmates he did time with"*
Brianna Allen, "Ex-Con Shoe Designer Steve Madden Makes It a Point to Employ His Jailmates," BET, December 11, 2017, https://www.bet .com/style/fashion/2017/12/08/see-what-steve-madden-is-really-all -about.html. Part of Madden's post-prison transformation involved giving back.

70: *"When he ran into Martha Stewart"*
Jane Wells, "Steve Madden's Tips on How to Come Back and Make It," CNBC, April 25, 2016, https://www.cnbc.com/2016/04/25/steve-maddens -tips-on-how-to-come-back-and-make-it.html. The concept of second chances is an aspect of the American Dream.

70: *"During an interview with Guy Raz"*
"Steve Madden," *How I Built This*. One of the most important insights that we see repeated over and over again in this book. To be afraid of mistakes makes you gun shy, and gun shy means risk averse.

Chapter 7: Swanson's TV Dinners

72: *"When Carl Swanson arrived"*
David Harris, "Swanson Saga: End of a Dream," *New York Times*, September 9, 1979, https://www.nytimes.com/1979/09/09/archives/swanson -saga-end-of-a-dream-they-were-the-pride-of-omaha-but-today .html. A remarkable success story born of having an idea and $456.

74: *"That innovation is credited to the One-Eyed Eskimo brand"*
Science Reference Section, "Who 'Invented' the TV Dinner?," Everyday Mysteries, U.S. Library of Congress, November 19, 2019, https://www .loc.gov/everyday-mysteries/item/who-invented-the-tv-dinner. So many innovations are lost to the pages of time, yet they pave the way for other products.

74: *"Then Swanson made its second big mistake"*
Owen Edwards, "How 260 Tons of Thanksgiving Leftovers Gave Birth to an Industry," *Smithsonian Magazine*, December 2004, https://www

.smithsonianmag.com/history/tray-bon-96872641/ Who could blame them? This was a weird idea hatched in a perilous moment for the company.

75: *"Today, one of the original aluminum trays"*
Erika Wolf, "11 Ready-to-Digest Tidbits about TV Dinners," *Mental Floss*, September 10, 2018, https://www.mentalfloss.com/article/58808/11 -ready-digest-tidbits-about-tv-dinner. What is an oak tree but an acorn that held its ground.

Chapter 8: Bill Maher

78: *"an intense, serious, adult-like kid"*
Bill Maher, interview by David Sheff, *Playboy*, August 1997. Many successful celebrities were the loners in high school; it may just be the fuel for success. Calling Dr. Freud.

79: *"He had dreamed of being a talk show host"*
Ibid. When you have a dream in your heart, you are never alone.

80: "Variety *magazine called the show"*
James Wolcott, "Maher's Attacks," *Vanity Fair*, September 1, 1997, https://www.vanityfair.com/news/1997/09/wolcott-199709. Even though *Politically Incorrect* was getting blockbuster ratings, it could still be brought down by a single sentence.

81: *"The White House addressed the issue"*
Pamela McClintock, "White House Keeps Heat on ABC's Maher," *Variety*, September 30, 2001, https://variety.com/2001/tv/features/white -house-keeps-heat-on-abc-s-maher-1117853351. Maher's downfall resulted in part from the attention his remark got from the White House.

82: *"As a former* Politically Incorrect *producer observed"*
Jim Rutenberg, "Bill Maher Still Secure in ABC Slot, at Least Now," *New York Times*, October 8, 2001, https://www.nytimes.com/2001/10 /08/business/bill-maher-still-secure-in-abc-slot-at-least-now.html. This underlines the reality of network programming: it is largely dependent on the whims of affiliates.

82: *"Political commentator Barbara Olson"*
"Barbara Olson," IMDb, https://www.imdb.com/name/nm1050857/bio. That empty chair foreshadowed what was to come for Maher.

83: *"Maher appeared on* The Larry King Show"
Larry King Show, CNN, May 24, 2002. Maher didn't hold back in this interview with King.

83: *"In a* Playboy *interview, Maher said"*
Interview with Sheff. An early indication of cancel culture.

85: *"There's a contradiction between what's good"*
Ibid. A very interesting insight. When big things go bad for the country, it's often comedy gold. But it's still bad for the country.

85: *"Maher told* Vanity Fair"
Laura Bradley, "Bill Maher Is Sure He Has the Funniest Show in Late Night," *Vanity Fair*, July 5, 2018, https://www.vanityfair.com/hollywood /2018/07/bill-maher-comedy-special-hbo-real-time-liberal. This is Maher's secret sauce. He speaks his mind regardless of the consequences and does it forcefully. It must be an incredibly freeing state of mind—with all the inherent minefields.

86: *"He admits he did have extensive talks with MSNBC"*
J. Max Robins, "Bill Maher: Still Politically Incorrect and Conservative about His Brand," *Forbes*, February 20, 2014, https://www.forbes.com/sites /maxrobins/2014/02/20/bill-maher-politically-incorrect-conservative -about-his-brand/#61abf8776680. Advertisers really were the clear and present danger to Maher. He could speak his mind and enrage his audience, reviewers could lob seething critiques and Maher could let it all bounce off his confidence. But if advertisers left, he was in trouble.

Chapter 9: The Dixie Chicks
87: *"A week later, Martie suddenly worried"*
Noel King and Victoria Whitely Berry, "The Chicks Look Back and Laugh," *Morning Edition*, NPR, July 17, 2020, https://www.npr .org/2020/07/17/892100683/the-chicks-look-back-and-laugh. A funny moment with long-term implications.

92: *"On March 10, nine days before the invasion"*
Shut Up and Sing, documentary directed by Barbara Kopple and Cecilia Peck, 2006. Little did the group know that their world was about to change in the next hour.

94: *"The quote wasn't deemed worthy"*
Jordan Runtagh, "When John Lennon's 'More Popular Than Jesus' Controversy Turned Ugly," *Rolling Stone*, July 29, 2016, https://www .rollingstone.com/feature/when-john-lennons-more-popular-than -jesus-controversy-turned-ugly-106430. Amazing, considering the even tual fallout.

96: *"the band had been overseas for several weeks"*
Patricia L. Dooley, *Freedom of Speech: Reflections in Art and Popular Culture* (Greenwood, 2017). Natalie's first statement was from the heart. The next one would sound very different.

97: *"continuing to play the Dixie Chicks was simply 'financial suicide'"*
Shut Up and Sing. As with Bill Maher, Brian Williams and Ellen DeGeneres, it always comes down to loss of advertising revenue.

97: *"President Bush was still riding a spike"*
"Presidential Approval Ratings—George W. Bush," Gallup, https://news .gallup.com/poll/116500/presidential-approval-ratings-george-bush .aspx. This popularity was a big reason why the Dixie Chicks took so much fire over Natalie's statement.

97: *"that approval rating over Iraq"*
Marcus Mabry, "How Low Can He Go?," *Newsweek*, June 21, 2007, https://web.archive.org/web/20070625170703/http://www.msnbc.msn .com/id/19352087/site/newsweek. Even when Bush's approval ratings tanked, the Chicks were still being punished.

97: *"The Dixie Chicks are free to speak"*
"President Comments on Dixie Chicks," CMT, April 25, 2003, http:// www.cmt.com/news/1471528/president-comments-on-dixie-chicks. Freedom might actually be a three-way street: two sides and the truth.

98: *"when the Dixie Chicks fell from grace, the collateral damage"*
Alice Vincent, "Pariahs or Patriots? How the Dixie Chicks Became the Most Hated Band in America," *Telegraph* (U.K.), June 25, 2020, https:// www.telegraph.co.uk/music/artists/pariahs-patriots-dixie-chicks-became -hated-band-america. Every collision has collateral damage, but this is a remarkable stat.

98: *"if you want to make ratings in country radio"*
Trigger Coroneos, "Country Radio Consultant: 'If You Want to Make Ratings in Country Radio, Take Females Out' (aka SaladGate)," *Saving Country Music*, May 27, 2015, https://www.savingcountrymusic.com /country-radio-consultant-if-you-want-to-make-ratings-in-country-radio -take-females-out-aka-saladgate. Misogyny is alive and well in country music.

99: *"there were more requests for tickets than for refunds"*
Jon Pareles, "The Dixie Chicks: America Catches Up with Them," *New York Times*, May 21, 2006, https://www.nytimes.com/2006/05/21/arts /music/21pare.html. While record sales stalled, crowds still came out to the live performances.

100: *"As a spokesperson for the organization explained"*
Dallas Morning News, "Dust-Up May Be Helping Chicks," *Denver Post*, May 31, 2006, https://www.denverpost.com/2006/05/31/dust-up-may-be -helping-chicks. Such was the fallout that a charity even refused donations from the Chicks.

103: *"It's the best thing that ever happened to me"*
https://watchdocumentaries.com/dixie-chicks-shut-up-and-sing/1:23:25

103: *"It was a huge way for us to grow"*
https://www.npr.org/templates/story/story.php?storyId=5424238/5:20

103: *"We have no regrets and I would never take this statement back"*
https://www.npr.org/templates/story/story.php?storyId=5424238/1:45

104: *"They were witches who could not be burned"*
Amanda Hess, "The Chicks Are Done Caring What People Think," *New York Times*, July 8, 2020, https://www.nytimes.com/2020/07/08/arts /music/dixie-chicks-gaslighter.html. Love this line.

Chapter 10: Seth MacFarlane

105: *"Can I get fries with that?"*
Claire Hoffman, "No. 1 Offender," *New Yorker*, June 11, 2012, https:// www.newyorker.com/magazine/2012/06/18/no-1-offender. Give me the boy and I'll show you the man.

105: *"Seth's middle name, Woodbury, was her homage to Kent's town drunk"*
Josh Dean, "Seth MacFarlane's $2 Billion Family Guy Empire," *Fast Company*, November 1, 2008, https://www.fastcompany.com/1042476 /seth-macfarlanes-2-billion-family-guy-empire. Apple, meet tree.

106: *"where he won the top art prize in his senior year"*
Ibid. Again, sparks can be detected early.

107: *"22 million people watched"*
Brett Gold, "How Family Guy Got Canceled Twice and Still Made Seth MacFarlane a Star," *Motley Fool*, February 1, 2014, https://www.fool .com/investing/general/2014/02/01/how-family-guy-got-canceled-twice -and-still-made-s.aspx. It pays to hitchhike.

107: *"The headmaster of the high school"*
Joal Ryan, "Fox Animator Busted by Headmaster," *E!*, June 30, 1999, https://www.eonline.com/news/38380/fox-animator-busted-by-headmaster. MacFarlane's absolute willingness to offend is his secret sauce.

108: *"The Parents Television Council"*
Hoffman, "No. 1 Offender." See above.

108: *"trying eleven different time slots"*
Dean, "Seth MacFarlane's $2 Billion." TV viewers, like radio listeners, are creatures of habit. Upset that habit and you lose them.

108: *"Canada's Teletoon network"*
"Family Guy Wiki," Fandom, https://familyguy.fandom.com/wiki/Family _Guy. Canada comes to the rescue.

108: *"the show was syndicated to the Cartoon Network"*
Gold, "How Family Guy Got Canceled." This very interesting trade-off would pay off handsomely.

109: *"Gary Newman was the head"*
Lacey Rose, "Five Fox Execs Explain Why They Canceled—Then Revived—'Family Guy,'" *Hollywood Reporter*, November 9, 2012, https:// www.hollywoodreporter.com/news/family-guy-five-fox-execs-387753. Everybody needs at least one champion.

110: *"It is often the highest-ranked scripted show"*
Dean, "Seth MacFarlane's $2 Billion." Thar's gold in them there hills.

110: *"Fast Company puts it closer to $2 billion"*
Ibid. Lots of gold.

111: *"On September 10, 2001"*
"CNN Interview with Seth MacFarlane on his 9/11 experience," YouTube, April 4, 2015, https://www.youtube.com/watch?v=uWnkE-US6sNI. His success came close to killing him.

Chapter 11: Steve Jobs

114: *"The Jobs home was in Mountain View"*
Walter Isaacson, *Steve Jobs* (Simon & Schuster, 2011). Many books have been written on Jobs, but this is the best. Before Jobs died, he asked Isaacson to write his biography, but Isaacson thought Jobs was too young to warrant a biography yet. Upon his death, Isaacson took it on. I owe a great deal to Isaacson's book for this chapter.

117: *"Woz was employed at Hewlett-Packard"*
Ibid. This is a huge moment in the history of the personal computer. Witnessed by Wozniak, all alone one night.

120: *"Scott was one of the few people"*
Ibid. Jobs hated giving up control. Every step of the way.

122: *"But Markkula insisted"*
Ibid. See above.

123: *"When Sculley finally did walk"*
John Sculley, *Odyssey: Pepsi to Apple* (HarperCollins, 1987). This is an interesting moment. It was a subtle but early signal that Sculley and Jobs came from different galaxies.

124: *"Do you want to spend the rest of your life selling sugared water?"*
Ibid. The best lesson in the art of elevator pitches that I've ever come across.

125: *"Jobs would tell Sculley that he was the only one"*
Isaacson, *Steve Jobs*. It took a long time for Sculley to see past his admiration for Jobs.

126: *"ads with a jolt"*
Karen Stabiner, *Inventing Desire: Inside Chiat/Day* (Simon & Schuster, 1993). I worked for Jay Chiat. This was definitely his mantra.

126: *"an odd disdain for any objective"*
Ibid. This was—and is—a strange characteristic in many uber-successful businessmen.

128: *"slayers of IBM"*
Verne Harnish and the editors of *Fortune, The Greatest Business Decisions of All Time* (Fortune Books, 2012). I often say that "1984" positioned Apple for all time. The reverberations of that commercial still shimmy years after Jobs's death.

129: *"the agency had put the ad through research"*
Fred Goldberg, *The Insanity of Advertising: Memoirs of a Mad Man* (Council Oak Books, 2013). A great Jobs insight.

129: *"Jay Chiat had told his media department"*
Ibid. Quite a bold move, even within the crazy world of advertising. But very Chiat.

130: *"200,000 people flocked to stores"*
Bernice Kanner, *The Super Bowl of Advertising: How Commercials Won the Game* (Bloomberg Press, 2004). A vindication of Jobs's belief in that commercial.

131: *"The machine was gorgeous"*
Sculley, *Odyssey*. Sculley had to wrest true control away from Jobs to attempt to right the ship.

132: *"Jobs also created an unhealthy competition"*
Ibid. At this point, Jobs was now in a destructive mode within Apple.

133: *"I don't believe you're going to do that"*
Ibid. The Sculley/Jobs relationship was now hemorrhaging.

135: *"The NeXT workstation was designed"*
Isaacson, *Steve Jobs*. NeXT was doomed, but it taught Jobs lessons about running a company and NeXT would be his key back into Apple.

136: *"Apple actually had its most prosperous"*
Owen W. Linzmayer, *Apple Confidential 2.0: The Definitive History of the World's Most Colorful Company*, 2nd ed. (No Starch Press, 2004). Sculley is often remembered as a failure at Apple, yet these stats are impressive.

139: *"But the real reason Jobs hesitated to take the steering wheel"*
Isaacson, *Steve Jobs*. A very telling insight into Jobs's shrewd reluctance to grab Apple.

139: *"Jobs asked the audience a question"*
Ibid. A very funny moment that contained a big turning point for the company.

141: *"Jobs created the only lifestyle brand in the tech industry"*
Ibid. So very true. Compliments of Sculley's influence.

141: *"As author Kevin Ashton insightfully says"*
Kevin Ashton, *How to Fly a Horse: The Secret History of Creation, Invention and Discovery* (Doubleday, 2015). Many fans (and non-fans) of Jobs fail to grasp this astounding insight. Jobs could look past huge success to see problems.

142: *"Apple board member Arthur Rock"*
Isaacson, *Steve Jobs*. Epic failure leads to epic silver lining.

142: *"Jobs himself later said"*
"Steve Jobs: Apple Founder's Moving Speech on Why Being Fired from Tech Giant Was the Best Thing to Happen," *Independent* (U.K.), February 24, 2016, https://www.independent.co.uk/news/people/steve -jobs-apple-founder-s-moving-speech-why-being-fired-tech-giant-was -best-thing-happen-a6893196.html.

Chapter 12: Kellogg's Corn Flakes
144: *"He was a quick study"*
Scott Bruce and Bill Crawford, *Cerealizing America: The Unsweetened*

Story of American Breakfast Cereal (Faber & Faber, 1985). So many bright sparks can be seen early.

144: *"who read the latest scientific journals"*
Ibid. John Henry was clearly different even at this stage of his life.

Chapter 13: Rob Lowe

147: *"With his cute mug"*
Mike Sager, "New Again: Rob Lowe," *Interview*, September 7, 2016, https://www.interviewmagazine.com/culture/new-again-rob-lowe. The spark emerges.

148: *"It didn't matter to me that it was sunny"*
Elizabeth Day, "The Trouble with Being Rob Lowe," *Guardian*, September 27, 2009, https://www.theguardian.com/culture/2009/sep/27 /rob-lowe-interview-latest-film. Jarring as it was, being that close to the movie-making industry would pay off. And soon.

148: *"It was filled with brand-new BMWs"*
"Rob Lowe on His Early Years As an Actor, His Friendships with the Sheens and Tom Cruise, and the Movie That Launched His Career, *The Outsiders*," *Vanity Fair*, March 29, 2011, https://www.vanityfair.com /news/2011/03/rob-lowes-early-years-press. Lowe's first glimpse of what the spoils of Hollywood can offer.

148: *"After school, he would take the two-hour bus"*
Mike Sager, "New Again." Chutzpah, high school variety.

150: *"As the movie ended and the lights went up"*
Rob Lowe, *Stories I Only Tell My Friends: An Autobiography* (Henry Holt, 2011). Lowe realized *The Outsiders* had suddenly made him a Hollywood insider.

152: *"The night before the convention"*
Raechal Leone Shewfelt, "Remember When Rob Lowe Landed Himself in a Sex Tape Scandal at the DNC?," Yahoo! News, July 25, 2016, https:// ca.news.yahoo.com/remember-rob-lowe-landed-himself-000000044 .html. Luckie Street would turn out to be anything but.

152: *"At the club, Lowe was sequestered"*
Art Harris, "Rob Lowe's Atlanta Smash," *Washington Post*, May 27, 1989, https://www.washingtonpost.com/archive/lifestyle/1989/05/27/rob-lowes -atlanta-smash/7900aba0-e1a8-4768-923c-9b118de89b0c. Breaching the velvet rope.

154: *"using his celebrity status as an inducement"*
"Documents Unsealed in Rob Lowe Sex Scandal," Associated Press, May 24, 1989, https://apnews.com/6e413dbd2794c0123efb9d96de24f3ed. Most forget the severity of the charge Lowe faced at the time.

155: *"Lowe's lawyers also alleged Wilson had approached his manager"*
Ibid. The Wilson family was at war internally.

155: *"Sometimes being a trailblazer is overrated"*
Lowe, *Stories I Only Tell My Friends*. Lowe often jokes about this, but he was lucky that it all happened pre-internet.

157: *"Wilson's lawsuit was tossed out not long after"*
Ibid. Wilson, who had initiated the suit, ended up with nothing.

157: *"I've learned the importance of admitting"*
Michelle Green, "Rob Lowe's Tale of the Tape," *People*, March 19, 1990, https://people.com/archive/cover-story-rob-lowes-tale-of-the-tape-vol-33 -no-11. Lowe would often repeat this, and it would contribute to his career resurrection.

159: *"The only person he allowed"*
Ibid. Berkoff chose to give Lowe a second chance. A fortunate decision that would affect the rest of their lives.

160: *"They performed their vows"*
Lowe, *Stories I Only Tell My Friends*. The pressure exerted by Hollywood can hunt you even on your wedding day.

161: *"If you go back in time"*
Day, "The Trouble with Being Rob Lowe." A very insightful comment. The bad moments in life can be important waystations if you can careen off them.

Chapter 14: The Who

162: *"Back in 1957, Roger Harry Daltrey"*
Roger Daltrey, *Thanks a Lot, Mr. Kibblewhite: My Story* (Henry Holt, 2018). A very entertaining book by the band's lead singer, who has an interesting vantage point when it comes to Pete Townshend.

163: *"the subversive nature of the lyrics"*
Ibid. An insight still lost on many.

165: *"While the Detours kept landing gigs"*
Ibid. Always so interesting when the universe reaches out to fiddle with destiny.

166: *"Doug Sandom, their thirtysomething elder statesman drummer"*
Ibid. The universe decides the band needs a different rhythm section.

169: *"Rolling Stone would later call the original"*
"50 Moments That Changed Rock and Roll: Townshend Smashes It Up," *Rolling Stone*, June 24, 2004, https://www.rollingstone.com/music/music-news/50-moments-that-changed-rock-and-roll-townshend-smashes-it-up-188384. So very true. All born of a mistake.

170: *"the reason for breaking guitars was his frustration"*
Jann S. Wenner, "Pete Townshend Talks Mods, Recording, and Smashing Guitars," *Rolling Stone*, September 14, 1968, https://www.rollingstone.com/music/music-news/pete-townshend-talks-mods-recording-and-smashing-guitars-79369. Townshend's explanation for continuing the destruction of perfectly good guitars.

170: *"In other interviews, he has rationalized"*
Rick Marin, "The Ax Murders," *New York Times*, October 31, 1993, https://www.nytimes.com/1993/10/31/style/the-ax-murders.html. Townshend's other explanation.

170: *"Fuck off. It's how I got you to listen to me"*
Luke Saunders, "The Who's Pete Townshend Admits He Regrets His 'Rock and Roll' Behaviour," *Happy*, November 5, 2019, https://happymag.tv/the-whos-pete-townshend-admits-he-regrets-his-rock-and-roll-behaviour. So there.

Chapter 15: Ellen DeGeneres

173: *"So she went to the producers of Laurie Hill"*
Lynette Rice, "Ellen DeGeneres: We Quiz Her," *Entertainment Weekly*, April 4, 2008, https://ew.com/article/2008/04/04/ellen-degeneres-we-quiz -her. Proving again that it pays to have chutzpah.

173: *"But she felt the need to be honest"*
Jesse Green, "Come Out. Come Down. Come Back. Being Ellen," *New York Times*, August 19, 2001, https://www.nytimes.com/2001/08/19 /magazine/come-out-come-down-come-back-being-ellen.html. Of course, it would eventually become important as the ratings slid.

175: *"Heche urged her to go for it"*
Ibid. Anne Heche would have her own troubles down the road.

176: *"Valentine told Ellen he was not interested"*
Frank Rich, "The 'Ellen' Striptease," *New York Times*, April 10, 1997, https://www.nytimes.com/1997/04/10/opinion/the-ellen-striptease.html. This is the Rubicon between a meaningful human crisis and television ratings.

176: *"It's not a no-brainer"*
Bruce Handy, "Television: Roll Over, Ward Cleaver," *Time*, April 14, 1997, http://content.time.com/time/subscriber/article/0,33009,986188,00 .html Again, the brakes were pumped because advertisers are like deer— extremely skittish and easily spooked.

176: *"Valentine turned down the first draft"*
Rick Marin and Sue Miller, "'Ellen Steps Out': How We Covered Ellen DeGeneres's Coming Out in 1997," *Newsweek*, April 30, 2017, https:// www.newsweek.com/ellen-steps-out-how-we-covered-ellen-degeneres -coming-out-1997-589769. Valentine was still evaluating the situation through the prism of ratings.

176: *"As the* Time *article stated"*
Lily Rothman, "Read the 'Yep, I'm Gay' Ellen DeGeneres Interview From 20 Years Ago," *Time*, April 13, 2017, https://time.com/4728994 /ellen-degeneres-1997-coming-out-cover. The *Time* magazine cover probably sent more shock waves through America than the upcoming

sitcom episode did. Or at the very least, it was the first bowling ball rumbling down the alley.

177: *"ABC apparently turned down a commercial from a gay cruise line"*
Rich, "The 'Ellen' Striptease." Even though ABC was suffering from advertiser fallout, the network turned down lucrative gay-themed advertising. Which revealed the ultimate depth of the truth: not only did advertisers not want to be associated with a sitcom with a leading gay character, but networks also didn't want to be associated with gay advertisers.

177: *"Dick Wolf, creator of* Law & Order*"*
Handy, "Television: Roll Over, Ward Cleaver." Mr. Law & Order, who tackled very uncomfortable subject matter, still wouldn't have touched this subject matter.

178: *"Obviously, this is an experiment"*
Handy, "Television: Roll Over, Ward Cleaver." A bit of damage control going on in that statement.

180: *"she would say the role saved her life"*
Green, "Come Out. Come Down." A life preserver thrown to Ellen in the form of a fish.

181: *"Ellen would play a gay character"*
Ibid. A big change of attitude at CBS compared to ABC.

181: *"In an interview with the* Advocate *magazine"*
Judy Wieder, "Ellen Again," *Advocate*, September 25, 2001. Probably not true in hindsight.

181: *"And by 'failed' I mean 'got cancelled'"*
Green, "Come Out. Come Down." Ellen's last few words in this quote are important. Not "failed" but "cancelled."

181: *"I am starting all over"*
Ibid. Ellen had risked everything, just as she originally feared.

182: *"witty, respectful and wise"*
"Ellen DeGeneres Biography," *Encyclopedia of World Biography*, https://

www.notablebiographies.com/news/Ca-Ge/DeGeneres-Ellen.html. Signs that Hollywood was warming to her again.

182: *"I said: I promise you I can do this"*
Gaby Wood, "Ellen DeGeneres: 'Finding Nemo—and Dory—Saved My Life,'" *Telegraph* (U.K.), July 29, 2016, https://www.telegraph.co.uk /films/2016/07/22/ellen-degeneres-donald-trump-is-a-bully-and-i-dont -like-bullies. Astonishing that liberal Hollywood abandoned her, although Kathy Griffin would experience the same thing years later.

182: *"No one's going to watch a lesbian during the day"*
"Ellen DeGeneres: Relatable (2018)—Transcript," Scraps from the Loft, December 22, 2018, https://scrapsfromtheloft.com/2018/12/22/ellen -degeneres-relatable-transcript. Again, not so much that no one would watch, but that no advertisers would fund it.

182: *"You're going to show them who you are"*
Wood, "Ellen DeGeneres: 'Finding Nemo.'" A very interesting strategy. Paratore wanted affiliates to see—firsthand—the reaction to Ellen's live shows, city by city. That took a lot of hard work, and Ellen was prepared to do it.

183: *"I have fun every day"*
"Ellen DeGeneres Biography." The silver lining appears.

183: *"1 billion monthly views across all platforms"*
Denise Petski, "Ellen DeGeneres Inks Three-Year Deal for 'The Ellen DeGeneres Show,'" *Deadline*, May 21, 2019, https://deadline.com /2019/05/ellen-degeneres-three-year-deal-the-ellen-degeneres-show -1202620307. Extraordinary success considering she had lost her career and moved to Ohio to hide at one point.

183: *"an annual income of $75 million"*
Wood, "Ellen DeGeneres: 'Finding Nemo.'" Again, an astounding position to arrive at after losing it all.

183: *"As Newsweek so aptly put it"*
Rick Marin and Sue Miller, "'Ellen Steps Out.'" But it took an astonishing amount of pain to get to that point.

184: *"As soon as she made the decision"*
Handy, "Television: Roll Over, Ward Cleaver." Heartbreak, fear and humiliation are never just contained internally.

184: *"I had to do it my own way"*
Green, "Come Out. Come Down." Sometimes the only way out is through.

184: *"It was the best part of my journey"*
"Ellen DeGeneres: Relatable." The solution is always found throbbing at the heart of the problem.

184: *"It's easy to forget now"*
"Ellen DeGeneres Receives Presidential Medal of Freedom," YouTube, November 22, 2016, https://www.youtube.com/watch?v=3hEMRkY4pDs. Obama was right. When you see a powerful, wealthy Ellen, it's easy to forget the thousand miles of broken glass she had to crawl through to arrive.

Chapter 16: The Incredible Hulk

186: *"enamoured with the story of Dr. Jekyll and Mr. Hyde"*
"Origins of Iron Man, Hulk, Cap," YouTube, October 2, 2007, https://www.youtube.com/watch?v=aLYJP_duPxk. This is a very good interview with Stan Lee.

187: *"Lee had heard the phrase 'gamma rays'"*
"Stan Lee interview 2/3," March 8, 2010, https://www.youtube.com/watch?v=ETPYe6LEOIo&t=320s. Not realistic, just believable—the cornerstone of the world of comics.

188: *"the problem was the printing process"*
"But for a Printing Error, the Incredible Hulk Would Be Grey," Holland Litho Printing Service, https://www.hollandlitho.com/how_a_printing_error_gave_us_a_green_incredible_hulk.html. I suspect the printing was made even more difficult because the paper used in comic books was low grade.

189: *"the first popular superhero who was actually a monster"*
"Origins of Iron Man, Hulk, Cap." The Hulk was a very unusual comic book anti-hero for its time.

189: *"One night after an extra-long and gruelling shoot"*
"The HULK (Lou Ferrigno)—Cocktails with Stan—Ep 4 Season 2," YouTube, September 14, 2012, https://www.youtube.com/watch?v=WfyTD7iafL8. Hilarious.

Chapter 17: Anthony Carter

192: *"Carter was one of forty-seven children"*
Mike Wise, "Pro Basketball: Carter Has a New Playground; Miami's Guard Goes From Asphalt to Hardwood," *New York Times*, May 5, 2000, https://www.nytimes.com/2000/05/05/sports/pro-basketball-carter -has-new-playground-miami-s-guard-goes-asphalt-hardwood.html. Without this project, Carter may never have had a shot at an NBA career.

194: *"Carter's agent, Bill Duffy, made a mistake"*
Sopan Deb, "An Agent's Mistake Cost an N.B.A. Player $3 Million. He Paid Him Back," *New York Times*, December 14, 2020, https://www .nytimes.com/2020/12/14/sports/basketball/anthony-carter-bill-duffy -miami-heat.html. This must have been a humiliating moment for Duffy.

196: *"They have never discussed the blunder"*
Ibid. A testament to their relationship.

Chapter 18: Popsicles

198: *"Eighteen years later, Epperson was established"*
Associated Press, "Frank Epperson, 89, Inventor of Popsicle, Dies in California," *New York Times*, October 27, 1983, https://www.nytimes .com/1983/10/27/obituaries/frank-epperson-89-inventor-of-popsicle -dies-in-california.html. Amazing that Epperson still held on to that idea eighteen years later.

198: *"Convinced there might be a national market"*
Jefferson M. Moak, "The Frozen Sucker War: Good Humor v. Popsicle," *Prologue* (U.S. National Archives), Spring 2005, https://www.archives .gov/publications/prologue/2005/spring/popsicle-1.html. As Malcolm Gladwell wrote, and I can personally attest to this notion, entrepreneurs truly believe they are on to a sure thing ("The Sure Thing," *New Yorker*, January 10, 2010).

Chapter 19: Sam Phillips

201: *"King told turner that his band was red hot"*
Will Russell, "Is This the First Rock and Roll Record?," Medium, May 25, 2020, https://medium.com/@willrussell_46069/is-this-the-first-rock-and-roll-record-bc24bbd6fa67. The serendipity of that moment will nudge rock 'n' roll into existence.

202: *"The band was giddy at the thought"*
Peter Guralnick, *Sam Phillips: The Man Who Invented Rock 'n' Roll* (Little, Brown, 2015). This is a wonderful book, highly recommended. Sam Phillips was a quirky renegade with an unerring musical compass.

203: *"named after the hot new Oldsmobile 88"*
Kit O'Toole, "'Rocket 88': One of the Pioneering Songs of Rock," CultureSonar, August 8, 2019, https://www.culturesonar.com/rocket-88-one-of-the-pioneering-songs-of-rock. I never knew that. Cars and rock 'n' roll—handmaidens of pop culture.

203: *"narrowed his eyes"*
Guralnick, *Sam Phillips*. A lovely bit of writing. Turner knew in that moment he was going to lose the frontman spot.

205: *"Little Richard said that song influenced him"*
"Good Golly Miss Molly by Little Richard," Songfacts, https://www.songfacts.com/facts/little-richard/good-golly-miss-molly. So interesting to carbon-date "Good Golly, Miss Molly" back to Brenston's song.

205: *"Ike Turner himself didn't consider"*
Holger Petersen, *Talking Music: Blues Radio and Roots Music* (Insomniac Press, 2011). Many still consider this song the origin of the species.

Chapter 20: Kathleen King

206: *"Kathleen King grew up on a farm"*
"Tate's Bake Shop: Kathleen King," *How I Built This with Guy Raz*, NPR podcast, https://www.npr.org/2019/12/13/787897696/tates-bake-shop-kathleen-king. I owe much of this story to this wonderful podcast.

212: *"the brothers were furious and accused her of stealing"*
Kieran Crowely, "L.I. Bakery's Partnership Turns Sour," *New York Post*,

March 6, 2000, https://nypost.com/2000/03/06/l-i-bakerys-partnership-turns
-sour. Founders are sticklers for quality. Equity partners are often sticklers
for stretching quality for profit.

212: *"Bakery workers grew disgruntled"*
Bernard Stamler, "Claiming Victory in Cookie War," *New York Times*,
August 6, 2000, https://www.nytimes.com/2000/08/06/nyregion/claiming
-victory-in-cookie-war.html. King chose paying her valued vendors over
profits and ignited a rift with her partners that wouldn't heal.

212: *"they hired armed security guards"*
Alex Witchel, "One Tough Cookie," *New York Times*, August 1, 2013,
https://www.nytimes.com/2013/08/02/nyregion/how-kathleen-king
-built-her-chocolate-chip-empire.html. When business partners go to
war, the trauma can be staggering.

213: *"When news of the battle went public"*
Ed Lowe, "A Tough Cookie and Her Sweet Friends," *Newsday*,
September 16, 2000, https://www.newsday.com/long-island/a-tough
-cookie-and-her-sweet-friends-1.403604. The goodwill King had accumulated over the years kicked in when her own customers and staff rallied
around her.

214: *"She even predicted Kathleen's Bake Shop would eventually"*
Stamler, "Claiming Victory." King's granular understanding of the
cookie business.

216: *"selling her baked goods in forty states"*
Collen DeBaise, "Building a Chocolate Chip Empire," *Wall Street Journal*,
August 27, 2009, https://www.wsj.com/articles/SB125138613436663821.
The phoenix rises.

216: *"she is a big supporter"*
Hillary Hoffower, "The Founder of a $500 Million Baked-Goods
Empire Says the Failure of Her First Cookie Company Taught Her a
Crucial Lesson about Hard Work and Success," *Business Insider*, July 8,
2018, https://www.businessinsider.com/tates-bake-shop-founder-lessons
-success-failure-2018-7. King gives back.

Chapter 21: Fiberglas Pink

218: *"In 1932, a Corning Glass researcher"*
Josh Ross, "Why Is the Pink Panther Owens Corning's Official Mascot?,"
Silver Leaf Contracting, June 13, 2019, https://www.silverleafroofs.com
/why-is-the-pink-panther-owens-cornings-official-mascot. As with so
many innovations, the breakthrough comes from searching for something else.

218: *"A magazine article from 1938"*
Jane E. Boyd, "In the Pink," Distillations, Science History Institute,
December 22, 2014, https://www.sciencehistory.org/distillations/in-the
-pink. Even today, that is a remarkable statement.

219: *"Prior to fibreglass insulation"*
Ibid. Fibreglass was a huge leap forward in technology.

221: *"animators Fritz Freleng and David DePatie"*
Xavier Morales, "Trademarked Colors: Owens Corning Pink,"
SecureYourTrademark.com, November 21, 2020, https://secureyour
trademark.com/blog/owens-corning-pink. The Pink Panther is so
closely established with Peter Sellers yet few people remember the actual
link.

221: *"While working on an advertising campaign"*
"Owens Corning Marks 40 Years With MGM's Pink Panther," press
release, Owens Corning, August 17, 2020, https://newsroom.owenscorn-
ing.com/all-news-releases/news-details/2020/Owens-Corning-Marks
-40-Years-With-MGMs-Pink-Panther/default.aspx. This personifica-
tion of the brand has lasted for forty-plus years and counting.

Chapter 22: Mario Puzo

224: *"he was the chooch in his family"*
Mario Puzo, *The Making of* The Godfather: *An Original Essay* (Grand
Central, 2013). Puzo's words, not mine.

225: *"she wanted him to become a railroad clerk"*
Harlan Lebo, *The Godfather Legacy* (Simon & Schuster, 1997). Artistic
pursuits were just not seen as a viable option by the previous generation.

225: *"Eight other publishers turned* Mafia *down"*
Jenny M. Jones, *The Annotated Godfather: The Complete Screenplay* (Black Dog & Leventhal, 2007). Hard to believe, in hindsight, that there was zero interest in one of the most popular novels of the twentieth century.

226: *"arranged a meeting between Puzo and his publisher"*
Puzo, *Making of* The Godfather. The serendipity of a friend's favour.

227: *"he wrote three adventure stories a month"*
Ibid. Puzo's gambling habit fuelled his need for writing jobs.

228: *"American Express offices"*
Ibid. An interesting moment in Puzo's life. He is about to lose his house and is about to earn a fortune.

228: *"He owed the credit card company an additional $60,000"*
Ibid. Sixty grand was a ton of money in the late sixties.

228: *"He arranged a lunch with his agent"*
Ibid. Can you imagine Puzo's eyes bugging out when he heard the amounts being thrown around, just as he contemplated having to sell his house?

229: *"In 1970, Gulf & Western made five times more money"*
Lebo, *Godfather Legacy*. At that time of mega-mergers, many corporations made smaller vanity purchases. Something to amuse the CEOs.

229: *"Paramount offered a paltry $12,500 option payment"*
Puzo, *Making of* The Godfather. Small potatoes in Hollywood terms, but a lifeline for Puzo.

230: *"Evans asked him if he was in trouble"*
Robert Evans, *The Kid Stays in the Picture* (Hyperion, 1994). Evans sensed urgency in Puzo's pitch.

230: *"I owe eleven Gs bad"*
Mark Seal, "The *Godfather* Wars," *Vanity Fair*, February 4, 2009, https://www.vanityfair.com/news/2009/03/godfather200903. Evans, a fellow gambler, rolls the dice.

230: *"Evans was a fellow gambler"*
Evans, *The Kid Stays in the Picture*. Empathy seasoned with a little disdain.

230: *"Paramount had, for all intents and purposes"*
Lebo, *Godfather Legacy*. Maybe one of the most profitable studio deals in movie history.

231: *"that's how Paramount got* The Godfather *so cheap"*
Puzo, *Making of* The Godfather. Puzo knew he grabbed the loot early but didn't hold it against Paramount.

Chapter 23: The Old Farmer's Almanac
233: *"based on a theory that Galileo developed"*
Adrienne Lafrance, "How *The Old Farmer's Almanac* Previewed the Information Age," *Atlantic*, November 13, 2015, https://www.theatlantic.com/technology/archive/2015/11/how-the-old-farmers-almanac-previewed-the-information-age/415836. Thomas's secret sauce.

234: *"a 2016 CBC interview with the* Almanac's *editor"*
Dave Dormer, "How the Old Farmer's Almanac Came to Be the Definitive Weather Source," CBC News, September 23, 2016, https://www.cbc.ca/news/canada/calgary/old-farmer-s-almanac-anniversary-1.3777114. Those kooky interns.

235: *"the go-to publication for weather forecasting for all time"*
Andrea Stone Dublin, "No Story Is Too Strange for *The Old Farmer's Almanac* Lovers," *St. Cloud (Minn.) Times*, July 16, 1985. A silvery, snowy lining.

Chapter 24: Atul Gawande
237: *"thirteen thousand different ways the body can fail"*
Atul Gawande, *The Checklist Manifesto: How to Get Things Right* (Metropolitan, 2009). Thirteen thousand? Sounds low to me.

238: *"for example, between the years 2004 and 2007"*
Ibid. Terrifying to think of the number of mistakes still made worldwide, even in this revolutionary and precise digital era.

238: *"Back in 1935, the U.S. Army Air Corps"*
Atul Gawande, "The Checklist," *New Yorker*, December 2, 2007, https://www.newyorker.com/magazine/2007/12/10/the-checklist. Fascinating story that led to one of the most important elements in aviation—the checklist.

240: *"But tending to patients is a complex task"*
Ibid. Stunning revelation when the dominos fall.

240: *"Nurses were then given permission to insist"*
Gawande, *Checklist Manifesto*. Amazing not just in terms of lives saved but dollars saved as well. It always pays to find the root cause.

241: *"In just three months, the rate"*
Ibid. Again, astounding results.

242: *"A director of surgical administration"*
Ibid. The perfect combination, a flying doctor.

243: *"After three months, the surgical director"*
Ibid. Hard to argue with 100 percent results.

244: *"Gawande and his team started to tweak"*
Ibid. Very interesting that a verbal confirmation was key here.

245: *"Finally, the results were tabulated"*
Ibid. Even Gawande's team couldn't believe the remarkable results.

246: *"A full 93 percent said yes"*
Ibid. My favourite moment in Gawande's entire book.